REVISED AND EXPANDED

MORMONISM

101

Examining the Religion of the Latter-day Saints

Bill McKeever and **Eric Johnson**

BakerBooks

a division of Baker Publishing Group
Grand Rapids, Michigan

© 2000, 2015 by Bill McKeever and Eric Johnson

Published by Baker Books
a division of Baker Book House Company
P.O. Box 6287, Grand Rapids, MI 49516-6287
www.bakerbooks.com

Printed in the United States of America

Library of Congress Cataloging-in-Publication Data
McKeever, Bill.
    *Mormonism 101 : examining the religion of the Latter-Day Saints / Bill McKeever and
Eric Johnson. — Revised and expanded edition.
        pages cm
    Includes bibliographical references and index.
    ISBN 978-0-8010-1692-9 (pbk.)
    1. Church of Jesus Christ of Latter-day Saints—Doctrines. I. Johnson, Eric, 1962–
II. Title.
BX8635.3.M35 2015
289.3—dc23   2014040106

Unless otherwise indicated, Scripture quotations are taken from the King James Version of the Bible.

Scripture quotations marked ESV are from The Holy Bible, English Standard
Version® (ESV®), copyright © 2001 by Crossway, a publishing ministry of
Good News Publishers. Used by permission. All rights reserved. ESV Text
Edition: 2007

In keeping with biblical principles of
creation stewardship, Baker Publishing Group advocates the responsible
use of our natural resources. As a
member of the Green Press Initiative, our company uses recycled
paper when possible. The text paper
of this book is composed in part of
post-consumer waste.

15   16   17   18   19   20   21   7   6   5   4   3   2   1

green
press
INITIATIVE

"Bill McKeever and Eric Johnson know Mormonism better than anyone I know, and this volume is the best available for a fair and accurate assessment of the theological claims of Mormonism. Best of all, however, is that McKeever and Johnson not only know Mormonism with their minds, but they love Mormons with their hearts and desperately want them to come to know truly their Lord and Savior Jesus Christ."

—**Mark L. Strauss, PhD**, professor of New Testament,
Bethel Seminary San Diego

"The new revised and expanded version of *Mormonism 101* by Bill McKeever and Eric Johnson will be a great help to Christians who are witnessing to Mormons. It is well documented and clearly shows the difference between Mormonism and Christianity in a factual way without belittling or demeaning Mormon people. It discusses issues that are important to both Mormons and Christians and clarifies Christian doctrines that have been distorted by Mormonism. Mormons who read this book will better understand why biblical Christians don't accept Mormonism as part of orthodox Christianity. I strongly recommend *Mormonism 101* to both Christians and Mormons who really want to understand each other."

—**Marvin W. Cowan**, missionary, Missions Door

"*Mormonism 101* is a rare gift that keeps on giving. The need for such a book grows daily, as many prominent voices seek to deceive the unsuspecting into believing that the differences between Mormonism and biblical Christianity are insignificant and few. Now Bill McKeever and Eric Johnson have amplified and updated their fine work, delivering a sophisticated book in plain language that both Mormons and the non-Mormons who love them will find relevant, respectful, closely reasoned, and meticulously documented."

—**Paul Carden**, executive director, The Centers for Apologetics Research (CFAR)

"Each year the Mormons (the Church of Jesus Christ of Latter-day Saints) send out thousands of young missionaries to gain converts from other faiths. This book will help prepare Christians with answers to their claims. Respected authors Bill McKeever and Eric Johnson have compiled a well-documented yet readable overview of the LDS religion, including discussion of the Mormon concepts of multiple gods, extra scriptures, secret rituals, and the means to attain eternal life. Each chapter ends with a set of questions for further study. This book would be a great addition to anyone's library."

—**Sandra Tanner**, Utah Lighthouse Ministry

"*Mormonism 101* is an immensely helpful book. Bill and Eric have done an enormous amount of research, and they make key beliefs accessible and understandable. While the book provides a critique of LDS beliefs, the authors are fair and generous in their approach. I recommend it to Mormons and non-Mormons who want to think critically about this influential religion."

—**Sean McDowell, PhD**, author, speaker, and professor

"*Mormonism 101* is a tremendously useful tool for Christians and those seeking to know the truth. As a pastor in Utah I am excited for this resource because it accurately explains the beliefs and practices of Mormonism in an age when some are blurring the doctrinal lines between Mormonism and real Christianity."

—**Cory Anderson**, pastor, Shadow Mountain Church, West Jordan, Utah

"*Mormonism 101* is a vital resource for anyone wanting to understand 21st century Mormonism. McKeever and Johnson have devoted their lives to this field of study with over 60 combined years of expertise. They emphasize with clarity the basic beliefs of the Latter-day Saints, using updated quotes from official LDS sources as support for each point. Anyone, whatever their level of understanding, will find much to stimulate their thinking in this book. It is an important resource on modern-day Mormonism and should be in every home library."

—**Daniel (Chip) Thompson**, founder and director, Tri-Grace Ministries; author, *Witness to Mormons in Love*

"With all of the information about Mormonism on the internet and new responses to problems within Mormonism being released by the Mormon Church, this book is a must-read for all seeking to understand the Mormon faith more completely. This book contains an objective overview of Mormon history and their beliefs. Well written, easy to read."

—**Jim Bjornstad**, professor of philosophy (retired), Cedarville University

"McKeever and Johnson fulfill their mission admirably: they explain in clear language what the LDS religion teaches and how it differs from biblical Christianity. Introductory but not superficial, simple but not simplistic, *Mormonism 101* provides a fair-minded survey of Mormon doctrine, scripture, history, and religious practice. The authors live in the heart of LDS culture and their extensive experience of talking with Mormons shows through in every chapter. Well-documented and now including such helpful features as short definitions of Mormon jargon and an appendix on common logical fallacies, *Mormonism 101* is a valuable resource for those seeking to understand why the LDS Church is not just another Christian denomination."

—**Robert M. Bowman Jr., PhD**, executive director, Institute for Religious Research; author, *What Mormons Believe*

"McKeever and Johnson have done the modern evangelical church a great service in updating *Mormonism 101*. With the present obfuscation of theological clarity in evangelicalism and the efforts of Latter-day Saints to mainstream Mormon doctrine, I welcome this well-versed, primary source–driven book. We need to get out of the weeds and into the clear on evangelical/Mormon distinctions. There is no better book available to help truth-seeking people do just that than *Mormonism 101*!"

—**Dr. Bryan Hurlbutt**, lead pastor, Lifeline Community, West Jordan, Utah; author, *Tasty Jesus*

"*Mormonism 101* was already a great book, but Bill McKeever and Eric Johnson have made it even better. Their books and ministry helped me find the true gospel of Christ."

—**Dave Neeley**, former Mormon missionary

"Bill and Eric have nailed it again! Mormon apologetics is an ever-moving target, causing Christian responses to fall quickly out of date. The appearance of this newly revised and expanded edition of McKeever and Johnson's solid classic *Mormonism 101* is both welcome and necessary for the adequate ongoing equipping of the Church. Its respectful tone, care for accuracy, and biblical approach makes it one of the best apologetic books available on the subject."

—**Ronald Huggins**, former professor of New Testament and Greek, Midwestern Baptist Theological Seminary; former professor of Historical and Theological Studies, Salt Lake Theological Seminary

To our children:

Kristen, Kendra, and Jamin McKeever,

and Carissa, Janelle, and Hannah Johnson.

Psalm 127:3 says, "Behold, children are a heritage from the LORD, the fruit of the womb a reward" (ESV). May you always realize the love your dads have for you, but especially the abundant love and mercy of your Father in heaven who gave His Son so that we might experience everlasting life.

Contents

Preface

On October 7, 2012, Apostle Robert D. Hales gave a general conference talk titled "Being a More Christian Christian." After providing general definitions of terms such as the "atonement," "grace of God," and "scriptures," Hales explained, "With these doctrines as the foundation of our faith, can there be any doubt or disputation that we, as members of The Church of Jesus Christ of Latter-day Saints, are Christian?"[1] A year and a half later, on April 25, 2014, radio/TV political commentator Glenn Beck—a Latter-day Saint—told a Christian college audience, "I share your faith. I am from a different denomination, and a denomination quite honestly that I'm sure can make many people at Liberty feel uncomfortable. I am a Mormon, but I share your faith in the atonement of the Savior Jesus Christ."[2]

Are these faithful Latter-day Saints correct? Should Mormonism be viewed as just another Christian denomination? Can it really be said that Mormons and Christians have a "shared faith"? Whenever we go to churches to share our information with Christian congregations, we are typically told by some afterward how they did not know so many differences existed between Mormonism and biblical Christianity. Because it can be so confusing to ascertain the differences between Mormonism and biblical Christianity, we decided to first publish *Mormonism 101* with Baker Books in 2000. Over the years, a number of Christians have told us how this resource helped them to better understand the theology of Mormonism. Others have even shared how the original edition helped them eventually leave the LDS Church and become Christians. Allow us to provide some background information and give you, the reader, a chance to understand our motives and purposes in revising this book.

Testing Everything

Together, the authors have spent a combined total of more than seven decades studying the religion of the Latter-day Saints. Jesus Himself said that the truth will set a person free; in fact, we are commanded to believe in God with our heart, soul, *mind*, and strength (Mark 12:30). In a romantic relationship, it's natural to want to know as much as possible about the other person before committing to marriage. A person in "love" may be driven by pure emotion and thus overlook warning signs about their friend who lies about past history, has bill collectors at the front door, and won't allow anyone to look at personal email messages. How many times have we heard those going through divorces say, "If I had only known about . . . before I got married"?

In the same way, the Bible has made it clear how there are many false prophets in the world who dress up as wolves in sheep's clothing. Those who are emotionally in love may look past the sharp teeth and dog-like tail poking out from the back of the facade. In matters of eternal consequence, taking someone's word for something as important as spiritual truth can be the most dangerous thing anyone can do. (See Matt. 7:15; 1 John 4:1.) Just as there are a myriad of pyramid schemes put together by shysters intending to separate the gullible from their money, there are also many false prophets promoting illegitimate ways to reach God and gain His approval. Truth seekers have been commanded to be like the Bereans who were considered to be most "noble" in Acts 17:11 because they double-checked the Scriptures to see if Paul, a legitimate apostle of God, was correct.

Instead of merely taking at face value the word of our nice neighbors or the sharply dressed and polite missionaries at the front door, we should "test everything" (1 Thess. 5:21 ESV). Thus, our objective in *Mormonism 101* remains the same as when we first wrote it: to take the authoritative claims of the Mormon leadership and see how they compare with the teaching of the Bible. We will write in as straightforward a fashion as we can while doing our best not to delve into areas that go beyond an overview format.[3] All in all, we believe a close examination is the only way to determine whether or not Mormonism is just another form of Christianity.

Just What Is Authoritative?

Although we will provide more detail in chapter 18, it is important at this point to quickly explain our philosophy when it comes to understanding LDS doctrine. According to the LDS leadership, any doctrinal teaching that disagrees with the general authorities should not be considered authoritative. Errors in understanding Mormon doctrine include relying on the words of individual members or following the latest trends coming out of LDS Church–owned Brigham Young University. Although we will quote a number of people who are not or have never been a part of the church's top leadership, we will generally cite official sources that, we are told, can be trusted as being authoritative. As one church magazine explains, LDS doctrine can be found in very specific places:

> **Teach the doctrine.** Approved curriculum materials from the Church, such as scriptures, general conference talks, and manuals, contain doctrine—eternal truths from God.[4]

11

The first area of authority is the church's unique set of scriptures: the Bible (specifically the King James Version),[5] the Book of Mormon, the Doctrine and Covenants, and the Pearl of Great Price. Together these written books are called the Standard Works. While we personally do not believe the latter three books qualify as scripture, Mormons generally do, and so we will quote often from these sources.

It must be understood that Mormonism is a hierarchal religion, based on the authority that founder Joseph Smith claims to have received from God when he "restored" Christian principles after a 1,700-year apostasy. In Mormonism, this authority comes through the LDS priesthood. There are two divisions of the priesthood: the Aaronic and Melchizedek priesthoods, both of which are held only by males. The Aaronic priesthood is known as the "lesser" priesthood and is made up of deacons (12 years old), teachers (14 years old), priests (16 years old), and bishops (the leader of local bodies of LDS believers). Meanwhile, the Melchizedek priesthood is named after the priest mentioned in Genesis 14 and D&C 107. The offices in this branch are elders, high priests, patriarchs, seventies, and apostles. The senior apostle is also called the president or prophet.

For reference, here are the names of the sixteen presidents/prophets of the church (current at the time of this writing) as well as the years they served as the church's top leader:[6]

1. Joseph Smith (1830–1844)
2. Brigham Young (1847–1877)
3. John Taylor (1880–1887)
4. Wilford Woodruff (1887–1898)
5. Lorenzo Snow (1898–1901)
6. Joseph F. Smith (1901–1918)
7. Heber J. Grant (1918–1945)
8. George Albert Smith (1945–1951)
9. David O. McKay (1951–1970)
10. Joseph Fielding Smith (1970–1972)
11. Harold B. Lee (1972–1973)
12. Spencer W. Kimball (1973–1985)
13. Ezra Taft Benson (1985–1994)
14. Howard W. Hunter (1994–1995)
15. Gordon B. Hinckley (1995–2008)
16. Thomas S. Monson (2008–)

The president has two counselors; together these three men are called the First Presidency. The First Presidency, the twelve apostles, and a group of men known as the Seventies are called general authorities. When these leaders speak—whether through official declarations, church handbooks, or at the biannual general conferences—members are told to carefully consider their teachings as authoritative and trustworthy. In the October 2012 *Ensign* magazine, the administrative manual *Handbook 2: Administering the Church* is quoted as saying:

> Teachers and leaders use the scriptures, the teachings of latter-day prophets, and approved curriculum materials to teach and testify of the doctrines of the gospel. Approved curriculum materials for each class or quorum are listed in the current Instructions for Curriculum. As needed, teachers and leaders supplement curriculum materials with Church magazines, particularly the general conference issues of the *Ensign*.[7]

Just because a past leader has spoken authoritatively on a topic does not necessarily mean that particular teaching is taught today. For example, President Brigham Young taught that Adam was God and the "only God with whom we have to do" in an 1852 general conference message;[8] this "Adam-God" teaching was later abandoned after Young's death in 1877. Mormonism is a dynamic religion that has undergone a number of theological changes over the years. At the same time, the leadership gives no wiggle room when it comes to blatantly disagreeing with a position contrary to *current* LDS teaching. If there is a public dispute on doctrine, the dissenting members—not the leaders—are the ones who are corrected or even disciplined, which could include disfellowshipping or excommunication. Thus, when the current LDS leadership speaks, it is not considered to be just their mere "opinions" but rather imperatives that the membership is mandated to follow, regardless of how this may contradict the personal convictions or revelations of any member.

When *Mormonism 101* was originally published, some Latter-day Saints complained that we were creating our own version of Mormon doctrine by taking LDS teachings out of context. The claim is that we were setting up the informal logical fallacy known as a "straw man argument," just as what was described in this LDS Church resource:

> A common tactic used by those who are trying to destroy faith is called a "straw man" argument. This is done by setting up a false image—a straw man—of the

truth and then attacking the false image in order to convince others the true image is false. A simple example of this is a child accusing parents who won't let him play until he gets his work done of not wanting him to have any fun. This is faulty reasoning, but it is often used to deceive others. Sometimes others claim that Latter-day Saints believe something that we don't believe. They claim that the false belief is false and then show that it is false. It has nothing to do with what we really believe but is an attempt to make us seem to be in error.[9]

No matter how we put it, some proponents of Mormonism will continue to make this accusation about our reporting and analysis. As we have said, we are not as interested in what an individual Latter-day Saint believes as much as what the church leadership is teaching. Thus, we have replaced a number of older quotes from the original edition of our book with more up-to-date resources; whenever possible, we will try to provide material from leaders and sources emanating from LDS Church headquarters in Salt Lake City. We have scoured the dozens of current LDS Church writings and have read a great number of conference talks, using these in a liberal fashion as support for what we say Mormonism is teaching.

In fact, some readers may feel that we "over quote" the leaders and manuals, but we will do this on purpose at times, just to make it clear that what we are saying really *is* current LDS doctrine and not just our personal misunderstanding of Mormonism. Not everyone will agree with our conclusions, but we want the reader to know that our goal is to be accurate in our description of LDS doctrine. Mormons are free to believe whatever they would like, even if those beliefs disagree with the teachings of current LDS leadership in their speeches and writings.

Every reader approaches the table with rose-colored glasses, or presuppositions, just as we have our own. When we present the Christian position, you should know that we are Christians (Protestant-based) who hold to conservative biblical beliefs. Our doctrines may differ from those coming from Roman Catholic, Eastern Orthodox, or mainstream Protestant backgrounds. All in all, we do our best to hold to the Bible as our authoritative guide, believing that true worship of God is of the utmost importance.

Is This Book "Anti-Mormon"?

In answering the question "Why does Mormonism arouse such animosity among so many?" Joseph Fielding McConkie writes: "If Mormonism were not true, it could be ignored. The fact that Satan and his cohorts cannot leave it alone is an evidence of its truthfulness."[10] For those who will want to disregard what we have to say and even label this book as "anti-Mormon"—a term we dislike because "Mormon" is a common nickname for a Latter-day Saint—please understand that we love the Mormon people. This is the reason why we even moved our families from California to Utah. It is true that we are against Mormon*ism* because we believe this religious system robs people of the ability to truly have a relationship with the God of this universe, but please don't doubt our sincerity and concern for civil dialogue and mutual respect for Latter-day Saints.

In fact, we agree with President Brigham Young when he said,

> Be willing to receive the truth, let it come from whom it may; no difference, not a particle. Just as soon receive the Gospel from Joseph Smith as from Peter, who lived in the days of Jesus. Receive it from one man as soon as another. If God has called an individual and sent him to preach the Gospel that is enough for me to know; it is no matter who it is, all I want is to know the truth.[11]

And we are in line with President John Taylor when he taught,

> If any person in the religious world, or the political world, or the scientific world, will present to me a principle that is true, I am prepared to receive it, no matter where it comes from.[12]

All in all, we will do our best to be respectful with our approach. Know that we don't hold any animosity toward Latter-day Saints, many of whom we call family, friends, and neighbors. Be assured that we are moved with the same compassion felt by the LDS missionaries and lay members who attempt to defend what they believe to be true. While the facts as presented in this book may be ignored by certain readers who would question our motives, we echo the apostle Paul when he addressed the church of Galatia: "Am I therefore become your enemy, because I tell you the truth?" (Gal. 4:16). This book is the result of our concern for those who belong to the LDS faith as well as for those Christians who want to better engage Latter-day Saints in healthy dialogue.

We have revised the format of this book and included several new features. At the beginning of each chapter, we provide common LDS vocabulary words and their basic meanings in what we call "Mormonese."

Discussion questions are provided at the end of each chapter, which can be helpful in a group format.[13] And to put a close to the chapter, we include a "Final Thought" paragraph. The chapters do not need to be read in chronological order; we have written this book so that each chapter stands on its own. Our goal is to lay out the differences for the layperson in a "101" introductory way, regardless of the reader's previous knowledge of the Mormon religion.

For further information about Mormonism, we direct you to our website, www.mrm.org. This site contains many articles, videos, and podcasts that can help you better understand the differences between Mormonism and Christianity. We invite your comments and questions.

For more information about the differences between Mormonism and Christianity or to receive our free newsletter, *Mormonism Researched*, please write us!

Mormonism Research Ministry
Dept. 101
P.O. Box 1746
Draper, UT 84092-1746
Email: contact@mrm.org
www.mrm.org

To God be the glory!

Other books by the authors:

(McKeever and Johnson). *Answering Mormons' Questions: Ready Responses for Inquiring Latter-day Saints*. Grand Rapids: Kregel Publications, 2013.

(McKeever). *In Their Own Words: A Collection of Mormon Quotations*. Kearney, Nebraska: Morris Publishing, 2010.

Latter-day Saint Abbreviations

D&C   Doctrine and Covenants

BOM   Book of Mormon

LDS   The Church of Jesus Christ of Latter-day Saints (the LDS Church)

PoGP   Pearl of Great Price

Notes

1. *Ensign* (November 2012): 90. *Ensign* is a monthly magazine published by the LDS Church since 1971 (Salt Lake City: The Church of Jesus Christ of Latter-day Saints).

2. Beck spoke at the final convocation of the school year at Liberty University in Lynchburg, VA. See Eric Johnson, "What Glenn Beck didn't explain at last month's convocation talk at Liberty University," Mormonism Research Ministry, http://www.mrm.org/glenn-beck-liberty.

3. One critic of our original book claimed that we were trying to *hide* information in the endnotes. Please know, however, that not putting the information in at all would be a more correct description of *hiding* information. Additional points and a slightly deeper analysis will be placed in the endnotes to maintain an introductory level throughout the main text. More help can be found in another book we wrote titled *Answering Mormons' Questions* (Grand Rapids: Kregel, 2013), which discusses specific issues talked about in this book. We will refer to *Answering Mormons' Questions* often because its chapters expound further on many topics covered here.

4. *Ensign* (July 2014): 10. Boldface in original.

5. While the King James Version is officially used by Latter-day Saints, we will often quote the English Standard Version for easier readability. We will indicate these occasions by listing ESV at the end of the citation. Please know that a Bible translation is nothing more than taking the words from the original biblical languages (Hebrew, Aramaic, and Koine Greek) and putting them into comparable words (in English). If you are a Latter-day Saint, please don't let our quotations from a modern translation stop you from utilizing the King James Version—or even Joseph Smith's Inspired Version for that matter.

6. When the current president dies, the apostle with the most seniority becomes the new president.

7. *Ensign* (October 2012): 11. This is section 5.5.4 in the church handbook.

8. Brigham Young, *Journal of Discourses*, ed. George D. Watt (Liverpool, England: F. D. Richards, 1854–86), 1:51.

9. *Book of Mormon Student Manual: Religion 121–122* (Salt Lake City: The Church of Jesus Christ of Latter-day Saints, 2009), 216. For a list of fifteen common logical fallacies, see the Appendix.

10. Joseph Fielding McConkie, *Answers: Straightforward Answers to Tough Gospel Questions* (Salt Lake City: Deseret Book Co., 1998), 54–56.

11. *Teachings of Presidents of the Church: Brigham Young* (Salt Lake City: The Church of Jesus Christ of Latter-day Saints, 1997), 16. This was the first LDS Church manual of a series featuring different LDS presidents over the next two decades. In 2015, the church covered the teachings of Ezra Taft Benson. During these two decades, members studied two chapters of that year's book each month, meeting twice a month on Sundays for group studies. We will feature these volumes throughout our book, as the Latter-day Saint ought to be very familiar with the manuals.

12. *Teachings of Presidents of the Church: John Taylor* (Salt Lake City: The Church of Jesus Christ of Latter-day Saints, 2001), 215.

13. A leader's guide to *Mormonism 101* is available at www.mrm.org/mormonism-101 -study-guide.

Introduction

A Short History

The story of Mormonism begins on December 23, 1805, when Joseph Smith was born to a farming couple in Sharon, Vermont. Like many other families searching for a better life, the Smiths moved west, settling down thirty miles east of Rochester, New York, in a town called Palmyra. The story of Mormonism really takes shape in Palmyra. Today Smith's faithful followers revere him as a latter-day prophet, chosen by the Almighty God to "restore" true Christianity after a seventeen-century absence from the earth. To many non-Mormons, he is a manipulator who deceived his followers and introduced teachings that hardly reflect the Christian faith.

Though there have been several versions of what Joseph Smith experienced in those early years, most Mormons are familiar with an account written by Smith in 1838. It tells of a fourteen-year-old Smith who wanted to know which of all the churches was true. He said that a passage from the New Testament book of James led him to a grove of trees near his family's farm where he was visited by two personages, God the Father and Jesus Christ. The young Smith claimed these personages told him that all of the Christian churches were wrong, their creeds were an abomination, and their leaders were all corrupt.

As expected, this message of a complete apostasy of the Christian faith did not sit well with the local clergy. Many Christians immediately cast a suspicious eye on the young man who claimed to have had an audience with God and lived to tell about it. Bear in mind that the United States was at that time experiencing the effects of the Second Great Awakening. Revivals were commonplace. For Smith to claim that God did not approve of what many Christians thought was a great work of the Holy Spirit was unthinkable and even blasphemous. Undaunted, Smith continued to insist that his vision was true.

In 1823, while Smith prayed in his bedroom, he claimed that he received another heavenly visit, this time by an angel who introduced himself as Moroni. During his earthly life, Moroni was a great warrior who lived among an ancient people called Nephites. He was a descendant of a Jewish family who escaped the capture of Jerusalem by sailing across the ocean to the Western Hemisphere about six hundred years before the birth of Christ. It was allegedly this same Moroni who, prior to his death, buried a set of gold plates on which was inscribed a record of the ancient American people. Smith was chosen to retrieve that record, but it was several years before he was given permission by the angel to do so. Before leaving, Moroni also warned Smith that he should show the plates to only a select few. Eventually a total of eleven men were chosen to "see" the gold plates, although some later confessed that they saw them only with the eye of faith.

The angel is said to have appeared to Smith on several other occasions until the time finally came to retrieve the Nephite record. On September 22, 1827, Joseph Smith, now almost twenty-two years old, was entrusted with the gold plates and commenced the translation of the "Reformed Egyptian" characters into English.

In April 1829 Smith was joined by Oliver Cowdery, a third cousin of Joseph's mother, Lucy Mack Smith. Cowdery, a schoolteacher by profession, became Smith's principal scribe. Both Cowdery and Smith claimed to have been visited by John the Baptist while praying in the woods near the Susquehanna River in May of 1829. It was here that both men were ordained and received the Aaronic priesthood, known in Mormonism as the lesser priesthood. At a later point in time the two men were ordained to the Melchizedek priesthood, or greater priesthood, by the biblical apostles Peter, James, and John. The exact date of this event is a matter of controversy.

On April 6, 1830, Joseph Smith founded the "Church of Christ" (not affiliated with the Church of Christ denomination) with five of his close followers. By the end of the year, this number grew to almost three hundred members. Smith's prophetical inclinations compelled him to move his church to several locations. In August of 1831, a small group of Latter-day

Saints moved into an area twelve miles west of Independence, Missouri. Smith prophesied that it was in this area where the New Jerusalem would be built. On August 3 Smith laid a cornerstone for a temple, and even though he predicted that this location would become a gathering place where the Saints would wait for the millennial reign of Jesus Christ, his prophecy would never be fulfilled. The great influx of Mormon settlers into the area, coupled with Smith's predictions that "Zion" would be established and the time of the "Gentiles" would soon come to an end, led to many hard feelings between the Mormons and the non-LDS Missourians.[1] The all-important gathering of the Saints was short-lived. Within three years the Saints were forced to leave Independence, and the temple never became a reality.

The Saints moved north and settled for a while in an area called Far West, Missouri. Smith again predicted that a temple would be built, but eventually the Saints were forced to leave this place as well. Hostilities between the Mormons and their Missouri counterparts erupted in such violence that both sides came to an impasse. In October 1838 Mormons attacked a group of Missouri militiamen who were holding three LDS men prisoner. This led to the slaughter of seventeen Latter-day Saints at Haun's Mill one week later. Joseph Smith was arrested and charged with treason. He spent several months in the dungeon of the Liberty Jail until he was allowed to escape in April of 1839.

In the meantime, the Saints had moved to a swampy area on the banks of the Mississippi River known as Commerce, Illinois. Enduring sickness and disease, they were successful in turning the once uninhabitable land into a city that attracted followers from all areas. Commerce later became the city of Nauvoo; within a short period of time, it rivaled Chicago in size. But even here, trouble did not elude Smith and his followers.

The rapid influx of Latter-day Saints to Nauvoo once again made the church both an economic and political threat in the eyes of the local residents. Joseph Smith was elected mayor, and several of his close associates eventually came to hold a number of political offices as well. Compounding the problem was the increasing number of dissidents who had grown to distrust the Mormon prophet. Many of these men were once close advisors to Smith, and some were successful businessmen in Nauvoo. Accusations between Smith and his detractors fueled the tension. Eventually some of the dissidents printed a newspaper called the *Nauvoo Expositor*. As its name implied, the purpose of the paper was to expose Joseph Smith as a false prophet who had exceeded his authority as mayor and was involved with secretly practicing "spiritual wifery," also called plural marriage or polygamy.

The Nauvoo city council quickly reacted by declaring the *Expositor* a nuisance. Under the orders of Joseph Smith, the city marshal destroyed the offending publication and the printing press as well. Of course, this only infuriated Smith's enemies all the more. Negative sentiment increased immediately in Nauvoo and its neighboring communities. Amid threats of violence against himself and his followers, Smith placed Nauvoo under martial law on June 18, 1844. In doing so, he mobilized the Nauvoo Legion, an army of several thousand men who had sworn to protect Smith to the death.

When news reached Illinois governor Thomas Ford, he intervened and suggested that Smith order his army to back down. He then ordered Smith to turn himself in to the authorities in nearby Carthage in the hope of settling the many differences that had escalated over the past several days. On June 25 Smith traveled to Carthage. However, he was once again arrested and incarcerated in the "debtor's cell" at Carthage Jail. With him were his brother Hyrum, John Taylor, and Willard Richards.

On June 26 the Illinois governor went to Smith's cell for a personal interview. After the meeting, Governor Ford traveled to Nauvoo but left a small contingency of guards known as Carthage Greys, many of whom were hardly sympathetic to the Mormon prophet. In the late afternoon of the next day, a mob attacked the jail, rushing up the stairs to the cell that housed Smith and his colleagues. Leaning against the door, the incarcerated men attempted to defend themselves. Smith, who was armed with a pistol smuggled to him by one of his visitors, opened fire on the attackers. His six-shot pistol[2] discharged only three times, but according to eyewitness John Taylor, all three bullets hit their mark. Still, there was no way that the small group of men could overpower the mob. A musket ball penetrated the cell's wooden door and hit Hyrum in the face. He fell back, with his last words allegedly being "I am a dead man." John Taylor was shot several times but was able to find cover under the bed. According to the official account, Smith then leapt toward the window of the cell and cried out, "Oh Lord, my God." Some believe he was attempting to give the Masonic signal of distress, but his unfinished cry went unheeded. As he reached the window, he was shot several times and fell two stories to the ground below. The mob then finished the deed by shooting Smith one more time. Only Willard Richards escaped without injury. Today Latter-day Saints hail Smith as a martyr, "a lamb led to the slaughter."[3]

None of those involved in the murders were found guilty. For a time, there was an uneasy peace between the Mormons and their non-Mormon neighbors. The problem now facing the Saints was finding a successor to Smith. It came down to two men: Sidney Rigdon and Brigham Young. Rigdon had been a part of the Mormon movement almost from the beginning. He was a former Church of Christ minister who once espoused the teachings of Alexander Campbell. In addition, he was a gifted orator who, after joining the fledgling church in the early 1830s, quickly became the right-hand man of Joseph Smith. Rigdon often was unwilling to avoid controversy, a trait that caused him conflict with both Smith and his colleagues on more than one occasion.

Standing in the way of Rigdon was Brigham Young, a convert to the church in 1832. Young did not see Rigdon's close association with Smith a reason for his becoming Smith's successor. Young claimed that the authority to choose a new prophet lay with the Council of the Twelve. It was decided that both men would have their opportunity to address the Mormon membership. When all was said and done, Young became Mormonism's second prophet, seer, and revelator. Rigdon later fell into obscurity.

The church remained in Nauvoo, and the temple that Smith had begun years earlier was finished and dedicated in April 1846. However, when it seemed apparent that those who were bent on seeing the Saints leave the area would never cease in their efforts, plans were made to move west to

Two pistols were smuggled into the Carthage Jail, one of which was used by Joseph Smith to shoot three people in the gun battle.

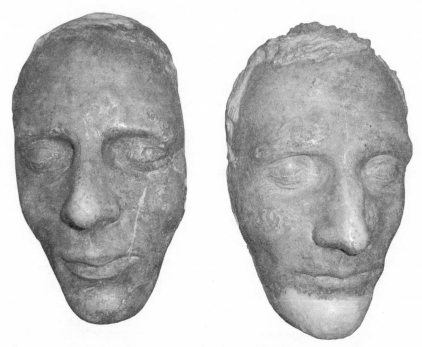

The death masks of Joseph (left) and Hyrum Smith (right) are housed in the Church History Museum in Salt Lake City.

avoid further clashes. On February 24, 1846, hundreds of Latter-day Saints left Nauvoo and crossed the frozen Mississippi River into Iowa. By the middle of May, it was estimated that nearly twelve thousand Mormons had fled.[4]

Many Mormons chose to live on Indian land in Iowa in an encampment that would be called Winter Quarters; others traveled to nearby Council Bluffs. Thousands of Latter-day Saints were scattered in Iowa until the spring of 1847, when the first party of emigrants headed toward the Salt Lake Valley. On July 21, 1847, a detachment of Saints led by apostles Orson Pratt and Erastus Snow was the first to cast eyes on Mormonism's new home. Brigham Young, suffering from an attack of "mountain fever," arrived three days later on July 24. By the time Young arrived, Pratt's company was already busy building irrigation ditches.

Salt Lake City became the new headquarters of the LDS Church; though many of the Mormons set up their abode in the Salt Lake Valley, many more began settlements throughout what is today the state of Utah. Young became the territorial governor in September 1850. Any privacy the Saints once had was soon lost, thanks in large part to the gold rush of 1849 as well as the completion of the transcontinental railroad, both of which brought many non-Mormon "Gentiles" west.

In 1852 Apostle Orson Pratt, under the direction of Brigham Young, proclaimed the doctrine of plural marriage as a belief of the LDS Church. This teaching became so prominent in the Latter-day Saint faith that some leaders even claimed it was necessary for salvation. However, the controversy surrounding this teaching threatened to prevent Utah from achieving statehood in the United States. To alleviate this and other problems, the doctrine was officially abolished in 1890 with what has become known as the Manifesto. But the stigma of polygamy still haunts the Mormon Church today.[5]

Misunderstandings and mistrust plagued the Saints for years following the Mormon emigration to Utah. The most serious conflict took place in 1857 when, unknown to Brigham Young, President James Buchanan had him replaced as territorial governor. Having been led to believe that the Mormons were in a state of rebellion against the United States, President Buchanan sent a contingent of soldiers to ensure that Young would relinquish his position. Apparently the president failed to explain this to Young, who assumed the Mormons were once again going to be forced from their homes. When Captain Stewart Van Vliet entered Salt Lake City to make arrangements for provisions, he was surprised to find that the Mormons were expecting a hostile invasion. Despite denials from Van Vliet that the army had any intention of driving out the Saints, the Mormons continued to prepare their defense. Young devised a strategy that bought the Saints some time. Rather than fight the encroaching army, small units of Mormons delayed their arrival by blocking roads, creating cattle stampedes, and setting fires. These delays prevented the army from arriving in Salt Lake City before winter set in. The tactic worked, and the "Utah War" of 1857 failed to become the potential bloodbath many Mormons feared.

Although tragedy on a military level was diverted, the Utah War did have its casualties. A wagon train of emigrants from Arkansas on their way to California traveled through Utah during this tumultuous time. The Mormons were instructed not to sell supplies to outsiders because of the perceived threat. This circumstance compelled the wagon train to travel south into an area north of St. George, Utah, called the Mountain

Meadows. This treatment served to infuriate the emigrants who began to make their feelings known. Rumors circulated that some of the emigrants had participated in the Missouri persecutions, and it was also rumored that they had the gun that killed Joseph Smith. Soon tensions escalated.

While the Arkansas emigrants camped at the meadows before crossing the desert, local Indians attacked them. This led to a conspiracy between local Mormon leaders and the Indians. As a result, a total of 120 men, women, and children were viciously killed in what has become known as the "Mountain Meadows Massacre." All of the Mormon participants took an oath of silence, and the Indians were blamed for the atrocity. Although Brigham Young knew the details within days of the incident, no one was held accountable for another twenty years. In 1877 John D. Lee became the lone scapegoat for this event. He was executed by a firing squad as he sat on his coffin.

For many years a small monument marked the grave of several victims of the massacre, but few details were given to explain what exactly happened on that day in 1857. In 1990 a new marker was placed on the site, yet no information of the Mormon involvement in the massacre was added. Finally, in what many hail as an effort of reconciliation, the LDS Church dedicated a new memorial in September 1999 that admitted to Mormon participation in the event. On the 150th anniversary of the event (September 11, 2007), Henry B. Eyring, a member of the First Presidency, gave a talk at the site where he expressed "profound regret" for the "undue and untold suffering experienced by the victims and their relatives." However, he stopped short of offering the apology that several of the descendants of massacre victims had hoped would be forthcoming. When some erroneously assumed that his "regret" was actually an apology, LDS "Church leaders were adamant that the statement should not be construed as an apology." Church spokesman Mark Tuttle stated, "We don't use the word 'apology.' We used 'profound regret.'"[6]

It is doubtful that the struggles of the nineteenth century will ever become a vague memory among Latter-day Saints. The suffering and hardships faced by the early Mormon pioneers will continually be pushed to the forefront by LDS leaders who understand that loyalty to heritage is a very powerful force. It is this legacy that compels many Mormons to remain in the faith, regardless of the myriad doctrinal problems. Still, the doctrinal inconsistencies cannot be overlooked, for those who hope to be true worshipers of God must worship Him in truth (John 4:24).

Notes

1. Mormon apologist David J. Ridges explains, "It should be pointed out that for Latter-day Saints, 'Gentile' generally means 'not Latter-day Saint,' although the meaning also extends to include 'not Jewish' and 'not Lamanite.'" David J. Ridges, *Mormon Beliefs and Doctrine Made Easier* (Springville, UT: CFI, 2007), 114.

2. For many years this gun has been displayed at the Church History Museum located across the street west of Temple Square in Salt Lake City, Utah.

3. For more on the topic of Smith's martyrdom, see chapter 36, "Why would Joseph Smith be willing to die as a martyr if he didn't believe God spoke to him?" in our book *Answering Mormons' Questions.*

4. Not all Latter-day Saints ventured west with Brigham Young. Emma Smith, Joseph's widow, had a strong dislike for Young. She remained behind with her three sons. The oldest, Joseph Smith III, later became president of the Reorganized Church of Jesus Christ of Latter Day Saints (RLDS), which is today called the Community of Christ, based in Independence, Missouri.

5. While those found practicing plural marriage are promptly excommunicated from today's LDS Church, we have found that many who have a very limited understanding of Mormonism may think that Mormon men still have more than one living wife. For more information on the subject of plural marriage, see the last part of chapter 16 in this book as well as chapter 6, "Why do so many equate our church to splinter groups when we no longer practice polygamy?" in our book *Answering Mormons' Questions.*

6. Paul Foy, "Mormon Church Regrets 1857 Massacre," September 11, 2007, http://www.foxnews.com/printer_friendly_wires/2007Sep11/0,4675,PioneerMassacre,00.html.

Part I

Examining the LDS Concept of God

1 | God the Father

Some who write anti-Mormon pamphlets insist that the Latter-day Saint concept of Deity is contrary to what is recognized as traditional Christian doctrine. In this they are quite correct.

William O. Nelson, director of the LDS Church's
Melchizedek priesthood department[1]

Holy Ghost: Third member of the Godhead, sometimes described as the Holy Spirit while at other times described as distinct from the Holy Spirit.

intelligences: This can refer to either the preexistent spirit offspring of God or individual eternal entities that existed before the preexistence. At one time every person existed in this state.

Inspired Version of the Bible: Also known as the Joseph Smith Translation. Joseph Smith made "corrections" to the King James Bible and claimed to finish this work on July 2, 1833.

mortality: The "second estate," life on earth, where people have freedom to determine whether or not to follow God.

preexistence/premortality: The "first estate" where the spirit offspring of God existed prior to their mortal existence on earth.

restoration: Since Christianity ceased to exist soon after the deaths of the biblical apostles, God returned the authority of the true church through Joseph Smith in 1830.

Few would debate that the concept of God is paramount in any belief system. If two people hope to consider themselves of the same faith, they need to agree on their definition of the Almighty God. If they cannot agree on this vital point, they would be deceiving themselves and others to say that their faiths are the same.

Many laypeople in the Mormon Church insist that the God they worship is the same God worshiped by millions of Christians throughout the world. The problem with this assumption is that it does not concur with many statements made by the LDS leadership. Speaking about God the Father, the *Gospel Principles* church manual reports, "His eternal spirit is housed in a tangible body of flesh and bones (see D&C 130:22). God's body, however, is perfected and glorified, with a glory beyond all description."[2] Besides quoting anthropomorphic passages (i.e., God taking on human characteristics, such as actions, emotions, and physical features), the Mormon cannot point to any biblical passages to support the case that God the Father has a physical body. Quoting Stephen E. Robinson, BYU professor Charles R. Harrell says "that the doctrine of the corporeality of the Father is not explicitly taught in the Bible."[3]

According to LDS leaders, this version of God is not understood by those outside the LDS Church. Apostle Quentin L. Cook wrote, "Among the first principles lost in the Apostasy was an understanding of God the Father."[4] The misunderstanding of God extends to anyone outside the

LDS Church today. President Gordon B. Hinckley taught, "Other people do not understand the true nature of God. They are still bound by the old Nicene Creed of the fourth century, which I cannot understand. But we have a perfect knowledge of the nature of God that has come through the First Vision of the Prophet Joseph."[5]

Mormon leaders falsely assume that a nonhuman God cannot be a personal God. Yet numerous biblical passages definitively prove how God desires to have an intimate relationship with humankind. In fact He gave His only Son to make it possible! Consider, for instance, 1 Peter 5:7, where Christian believers are told to cast all their cares on God. Why? Because He is a personal God who cares for His creation. To those who have sinned, God lovingly calls them to "reason together" with Him (Isa. 1:18).

When Christians say that God is "incomprehensible," they do not mean that God is an irrational or confusing being. It is difficult, if not impossible, for finite humans to fully understand the infinite God. While describing the greatness of God in 1 Timothy 6:16, Paul explained that God dwells in unapproachable light. Because of our limitations, we can never expect to fully comprehend every aspect of the Creator. As Isaiah 55:8 says, "For my thoughts are not your thoughts, neither are your ways my ways, saith the LORD."

Christian thinker A. W. Tozer wrote,

> A right conception of God is basic not only to systematic theology but to practical Christian living as well. It is to worship what the foundation is to the temple; where it is inadequate or out of plumb the whole structure must sooner or later collapse. I believe there is scarcely an error in doctrine or a failure in applying Christian ethics that cannot be traced finally to imperfect and ignoble thoughts about God. . . . Wrong ideas about God are not only the fountain from which the polluted waters of idolatry flow; they are themselves idolatrous. The idolater simply imagines things about God and acts as if they were true.[6]

Tozer added,

> When we try to imagine what God is like we must out of necessity use that-which-is-not-God as the raw material for our minds to work on; hence, whatever we visualize God to be, He is not, for we have constructed our image out of that which He has made and what He has made is not God. If

33

we insist upon trying to imagine Him, we end with an idol, made not with hands but with thoughts; and an idol of the mind is as offensive to God as an idol of the hand.[7]

When we compare the attributes of the God of the Bible to the attributes that LDS leaders have applied to their God, it is apparent that major differences do exist.

Not Eternally God

Was God always God? Not according to Mormonism. A church manual explains, "It will help us to remember that our Father in Heaven was once a man who lived on an earth, the same as we do. He became our Father in Heaven by overcoming problems, just as we have to do on this earth."[8]

The teaching that God was once a man can be found in a late sermon by Joseph Smith. In 1844 a Mormon elder by the name of King Follett was "crushed in a well by the falling of a tub of rock." At Follett's funeral Smith delivered a sermon that has come to be known as the King Follett discourse. It was later reprinted in its entirety in the May 1971 edition of the official LDS magazine *Ensign*. According to Smith,

> It is the first principle of the Gospel to know for a certainty the Character of God. . . . He was once a man like us; . . . God himself, the Father of us all, dwelt on an earth, the same as Jesus Christ himself did (*Teachings of the Prophet Joseph Smith*, sel. Joseph Fielding Smith [1976], 345–46).[9]

In a 1945 priesthood study course published by the church, Seventy Milton R. Hunter wrote,

> In June of 1840, Lorenzo Snow formulated the following famous couplet: "As man is, God once was; as God is, man may become." This doctrine, when first announced by the Prophet and later restated by Elder Snow, was astounding to Christendom, since the teachers as well as the laity had long ago ceased to regard man as a being of such magnitude. Even today it is still a doctrine understood primarily by members of the Church of Jesus Christ of Latter-day Saints.[10]

One manual explains:

This is a doctrine which delighted President Snow, as it does all of us. Early in his ministry he received by direct, personal revelation the knowledge that (in the Prophet Joseph Smith's language), "God himself was once as we are now, and is an exalted man, and sits enthroned in yonder heavens," and that men "have got to learn how to be Gods . . . the same as all Gods have done before. . . ." [*Teachings*, pp. 345–46.] After this doctrine had been taught by the Prophet, President Snow felt free to teach it also, and he summarized it in one of the best known couplets in the Church in these words: "As man now is, God once was; As God now is, man may be."[11]

Snow's couplet has been repeated many times by LDS leaders and church publications as being true.[12]

God the Father lived on a world similar to this earth. Mormon Apostle Orson Pratt taught:

We were begotten by our Father in heaven; the person of Father in Heaven was begotten on a previous heavenly world by His Father; and again, He was begotten by a still more ancient Father; and so on, from generation to generation.[13]

Apostle Orson Hyde said:

Remember that God, our heavenly Father, was perhaps once a child, and mortal like we ourselves, and rose step by step in the scale of progress, in the school of advancement; has moved forward and overcome, until He has arrived at the point where He now is.[14]

This idea that God was once a human who became God at a certain point in time is foreign to biblical Christianity. Logic would demand that if the Mormon God had to *attain* the position he now holds, then he could not be the eternal God of the Bible. Meanwhile, Mormonism teaches that men and women were created to become gods and goddesses in the next life. A church reference manual explains, "You are a literal child of God, spiritually begotten in the premortal life. As His child, you can be assured that you have divine, eternal potential and that He will help you in your sincere efforts to reach that potential."[15] Another manual reports, "God's work and glory is to bring to pass the immortality and eternal life of His children."[16]

According to the *Ensign* magazine:

The stunning truth, lost to humankind before the Restoration, is that each of us is a god in embryo. We may become as our heavenly parents. We, too, in exalted families, may one day preside in our own realms, under him who is our God and our Father forever.[17]

Despite the limitations that Mormon leaders place on God, the Bible is very clear that God has neither beginning nor end. Words such as *eternal* and *everlasting* emphasize the fact that God's perfection transcends time. He always was God and always will be God. Consider the following verses:

Before the mountains were brought forth, or ever thou hadst formed the earth and the world, even from everlasting to everlasting, thou art God. (Ps. 90:2)

Thy throne is established of old: thou art from everlasting. (Ps. 93:2)

Hast thou not known? hast thou not heard, that the everlasting God, the LORD, the Creator of the ends of the earth, fainteth not, neither is weary? (Isa. 40:28)

For thus saith the high and lofty One that inhabiteth eternity, whose name is Holy. (Isa. 57:15)

Philosopher and mathematician William Dembski, a committed Christian, writes,

God did not depend on any preexisting entity separate from God—no pre-existing stuff, no autonomous principles, no other gods. Indeed, for God to have employed such an entity in the primal act of creation would have meant that something outside of God had a separate existence from God. Orthodox Christian theology, by contrast, affirms that there is but one God, that this God is the source of all being, and that nothing exists self-sufficiently apart from this God.[18]

Not Immutable

According to LDS teaching, God gradually progressed to the position and power he now holds. President Brigham Young explained, "The doctrine that God was once a man and has progressed to become God is unique to this Church. How do you feel, knowing that God, through His own

36

experience, 'knows all that we know regarding the toils [and] sufferings' of mortality?"[19]

If God the Father once lived as man on another world and had a God before Him, then we must wonder whether or not He sinned during His mortality. Acknowledging that some Mormons believe God was a sinner, one LDS apologetic website explains, "Does it really matter all that much? Whether it is true or it is not, does anything change? Knowing details of God's previous mortality doesn't change the fact that our Heavenly Father is still our Heavenly Father, who loves us very much."[20]

Yes, this issue really does matter! Biblically speaking, God's perfection means that He never needs to change in a metaphysical or moral sense. As His nature remains constant, so, too, His desires and purposes never change. As the psalmist correctly pointed out in Psalm 102:27, "But thou art the same, and thy years shall have no end." In an expression that could not be made any clearer, Malachi 3:6 says, "For I am the LORD, I change not." And James 1:17 declares that there is no variation or "shadow of turning" when it comes to the Father of lights.

There is no fluctuation in God's divine character. The perfect God of the Bible has no need to change. If He were to better Himself, it would show that He *was* not perfect. Should He make Himself worse, it would show that He *is* not perfect. In the words of Christian theologian Herman Bavinck, "Whatever changes ceases to be what it was."[21] The idea that God is immutable should bring comfort to His people, since they can be assured that God would never change anything affecting their salvation. While humanity struggles with sin and thus alters its relationship with God, it is not God who wavers, because He is always constant.

Some have asked why the Bible speaks of God as "repenting." It would seem that if God was the one who declared all things to happen in precise order, nothing could possibly catch Him unawares. Was God really unsure if Adam and Eve would sin and produce some of the most evil offspring imaginable? Or was God surprised when the wicked citizens of Nineveh repented in the Old Testament book of Jonah, thus "sidetracking" God's impending judgment? Not at all. The Bible often uses anthropomorphic language—words describing God in human terms.

Since it is God who declares the end from the beginning, it would be inconceivable to think that God could change His mind as humans do. We change our minds as a result of previously unavailable information. God, however, knows all things. There is nothing new for Him to evaluate.

When God chose not to bring judgment on Nineveh, it was not because He literally "changed his mind." Quite the contrary, His decision to spare the city was actually an example of His immutability, or His constant nature. Jonah recognized this, for in his anger he confirmed that God was gracious and merciful, slow to anger and abundant in loving kindness (Jonah 4:1–2). Jonah understood why God would not destroy the city. It was based on the fact that God consistently forgives those who are repentant. Jeremiah 18:7–10 sheds light on this issue:

> If at any time I declare concerning a nation or a kingdom, that I will pluck up and break down and destroy it, and if that nation, concerning which I have spoken, turns from its evil, I will relent of the disaster that I intended to do to it. And if at any time I declare concerning a nation or a kingdom that I will build and plant it, and if it does evil in my sight, not listening to my voice, then I will relent of the good that I had intended to do to it. (ESV)

What appears to be a case of God changing His mind is really nothing more than God's unchangeable response to people changing *their* minds. Should Mormons fail to see this attribute as defined in the Bible, they would do well to read Moroni 8:18 in the Book of Mormon. It says, "For I know that God is not a partial God, neither a changeable being; but he is unchangeable from all eternity to all eternity." Mormon 9:19 strongly adds these words:

> And if there were miracles wrought then, why has God ceased to be a God of miracles and yet be an unchangeable Being? And behold, I say unto you he changeth not; if so he would cease to be God; and he ceaseth not to be God, and is a God of miracles.

According to Mosiah 3:5 and Moroni 7:22, God is God "from all eternity to all eternity" and from "everlasting to everlasting." Third Nephi 24:6 and Mormon 9:9–10 add that He does not vary or change. To explain how LDS apologists try to minimize these verses, BYU professor Charles R. Harrell writes,

> When Mormons today read passages proclaiming that God is "from everlasting to everlasting" (Moro. 7:22), one interpretation given is that God had an eternal existence as an intelligence and eventually became a human being and then a God. But this doesn't really address the several scriptures cited above that suggest that God was *God* from all eternity. Some LDS doctrinal

expositors have expressed the view that God has been eternally God only in a relative sense or from our finite point of view. Others explain that, in the Bible, eternity means "an age" which has a beginning and an end, so he is God from an age past to an age to come. Eternity has also been interpreted to mean "that existence gained by exalted beings," rather than duration of existence.[22]

After providing a few more LDS explanations, Harrell continues, "One wonders if any of these explanations was necessary for the original audience of the scriptures who seemed to be comfortable taking the eternality of God at face value."[23] He's exactly right.

Not Self-Existent

Unique to Mormonism is the idea that all humans (and gods) once existed as undeveloped "intelligences." By following laws and principles that Mormons believe are eternal, each intelligence progresses until godhood becomes possible. Joseph Smith taught that his God, by obedience to these eternal laws, now has "power to institute laws to instruct the weaker intelligences, that they may be exalted with himself, so that they might have one glory upon another."[24] However, Mormonism does not trace this long procession of deities to one specific first cause. Instead, it is assumed that a myriad of gods preceded the LDS God and that he himself is the offspring of one of these gods.

On this subject Brigham Young taught the following:

> How many Gods there are, I do not know. But there never was a time when there were not Gods and worlds, and when men were not passing through the same ordeals that we are now passing through. That course has been from all eternity, and it is and will be to all eternity.[25]

Mormonism also has its share of mysteries. For example, Young admitted that trying to understand how the first God came to be God was difficult.

> Many have tried to penetrate to the First Cause of all things; but it would be as easy for an ant to number the grains of sand on the earth. It is not for man, with his limited intelligence, to grasp eternity in his comprehension. . . . It would be as easy for a gnat to trace the history of man back to his origin as for man to fathom the First Cause of all things, lift the veil of

eternity, and reveal the mysteries that have been sought after by philosophers from the beginning.[26]

While it is admittedly difficult to comprehend the existence of a God who has always existed, it is neither implausible nor unbiblical. On the other hand, Mormonism's view of God is both implausible and unbiblical. It is also illogical since it raises several questions as to how the first intelligence was able to elevate himself to the position of deity. What allowed for this first intelligence to be first out of the "starting gate" toward godhood? How was he able to comply with the many requirements necessary to reach such a position? Following this logic, other questions are raised:

• As mentioned earlier, the Mormon God is subject to laws that are alleged to be eternal. How can this be if there is no such thing as an eternal lawgiver in Mormonism?

• If becoming a human and living in a sin-tainted world is necessary for godhood, how did the first God get his human body? Who made the world that he supposedly lived on?

• If the purpose of going through mortality is to overcome sin, who was it that defined sin? How could this first God overcome something that could not have been defined?

Mormonism's lack of a first cause is what makes understanding this LDS doctrine problematic. Joseph Fielding McConkie and Robert L. Millet claim that "God is the giver of the law, the author and maker of it."[27] This statement could only make sense if the God of Mormonism was eternally God. Since he was not, he cannot be credited with making laws that are eternal.

The Bible teaches that God is *the* First Cause. He is self-existent, or *uncaused*, and therefore not dependent on anything for His existence. God is life, and it is because of Him that we have life. All creation exists due to the purpose and will of God Himself. To assume that there were other gods before the God of the Bible refutes Isaiah 43:10, which declares, "I am he: before me there was no God formed, neither shall there be after me." When God said in Isaiah 48:12, "Hearken unto me, O Jacob and Israel, my called; I am he; I am the first, I also am the last," He allowed no room for any assumption that He came along later in the creation process.

Not Transcendent

God is distinct from His creation and the universe. When discussing the transcendence of God, we need to consider a number of aspects. Not only is the "person" of God unlike human beings, but His moral character is also unique. He is infinitely exalted above all that He has ever created. Mormon leaders have not hidden the fact that they believe God is an exalted human being. Joseph Smith said, "That which is without body or parts is nothing. There is no God in heaven but that God who has flesh and bones."[28] A student manual explains,

> Modern revelation declares that Heavenly Father "has a body of flesh and bones as tangible as man's" (D&C 130:22). The Church of Jesus Christ of Latter-day Saints accepts Genesis 1:26 and Moses 2:26 literally. As children of our Heavenly Father, our physical bodies and our spirit bodies are in His image.[29]

The God of the Bible loathes the idea of being likened to His creation. In Psalm 50:21 He chided His people for trying to make such a comparison when He declared, "These things you have done, and I have been silent; you thought that I was one like yourself. But now I rebuke you and lay the charge before you" (ESV). Numbers 23:19a says, "God is not man, that he should lie, or a son of man, that he should change his mind" (ESV). And in Romans 1:22–23, Paul said only fools attempt to change the glory of the incorruptible God into an image made like corruptible man. While pagan religions tend to make their gods in the fashion of some created thing, the God of the Bible will have none of it. In His prohibition of graven images, God eliminated the possibility of imagining a form that they might suppose represented the true God. Whereas Joseph Smith claimed that He physically saw God, John 1:18 reports, "No one has ever seen God; the only God, who is at the Father's side, he has made him known" (ESV).[30]

Some have used the anthropomorphic language of the Bible to assume that God does in fact inhabit a body similar to ours. However, verses that speak of God having arms (Deut. 33:27), hands (2 Chron. 6:4), feet (Ps. 18:9), ears (2 Sam. 22:7), and so on, are never meant to be taken any more literally than those passages that speak of God having wings (Ps. 17:8) or the ability to breathe smoke out of His nostrils and fire from His mouth (2 Sam. 22:9).[31]

Not Omnipotent

According to Apostle Orson Hyde:

> There are Lords many, and Gods many, for they are called Gods to whom the word of God comes, and the word of God comes to all these kings and priests. But to our branch of the kingdom there is but one God, to whom we all owe the most perfect submission and loyalty; yet our God is just as subject to still higher intelligences, as we should be to him.[32]

While many LDS leaders have taught that their God Elohim is omnipotent (all-powerful), several factors belie this thought. Since Mormonism has reintroduced polytheism to the modern world, the question is, who among the many gods is the "most powerful"? Some Mormons dodge this dilemma by insisting that the word *omnipotent* does not mean "all-powerful" but rather refers to being "unlimited in power." Even this definition does not help solve the problem, since the Mormon God cannot create *ex nihilo,* or out of nothing, which "was not the invention of early Christian theologians who had imbibed too much Greek philosophy. Rather, Jews and Christians alike believed it long before it was formalized as a doctrine."[33] The Mormon God's ability to *create* is limited by the fact that he is only able to organize already existing matter. Apostle John Widtsoe said, "God, the supreme Power, cannot conceivably originate matter; he can only organize matter. Neither can he destroy matter; he can only disorganize it. . . . The doctrine that God made the earth or man from nothing becomes, therefore, an absurdity."[34]

Although faithful Mormons hope to someday achieve the status of deity, they concede that they will never rise above the preeminence of Elohim. Even as gods, exalted Mormons will always be subservient to him. In the same way, Elohim will never rise above those gods who preceded him. Contrary to this opinion, the Old Testament is replete with accounts that demonstrate the superior power of the God of Israel. Whether it was Moses versus Pharaoh's magicians or Elijah against the prophets of Baal on Mt. Carmel, God's authority always reigns supreme. What may be seen as a contest between deities was really nothing of the kind.

The book of Job contains four chapters in which God personally proclaims His omnipotence to His suffering servant. When He was finished, Job had to admit, "I know that you can do all things, and that no purpose of yours can be thwarted" (Job 42:2. ESV). Unlike the deities worshiped by the pagan world, the God of the Bible does whatever He pleases (Ps. 115:3). With Him all things are possible (Matt. 19:26).[35] The God of Christianity is omnipotent and answers to no one.

The Bible also never hides the fact that the God of both the Jews and Christians is the "God of gods." Five times this expression is used to demonstrate that the God of the Bible is the sovereign and powerful God of creation (Deut. 10:17; Josh. 22:22; Ps. 136:2; Dan. 2:47; 11:36). Although it would be easy for a Mormon to misuse this phrase and try to say it proves the existence of other gods, this idea is not consistent with the many passages of Scripture that insist there is no other God than He Himself (Deut. 4:35, 39; Isa. 45:5–6; 46:9; Mark 12:32). Contrary to pagan belief, God is above anything man might think is a god.

Not Omnipresent

According to Mormon theology, no member of the LDS Godhead has the ability to be truly omnipresent. A Mormon educator writes, "There is a false doctrine held by many religions that God, personally, is omnipresent. And this leads to a false belief that He is indefinable and completely indescribable, is everywhere present, fills the immensity of space, and is yet so small that He dwells in everyone's heart, etc."[36] The God of Mormonism cannot be personally present everywhere because he dwells in a finite body. Brigham Young stated, "Some would have us believe that God is present everywhere. It is not so. He is no more every where present in person than the Father and Son are one in person."[37] Not only are Mormonism's versions of God the Father and Jesus unable to be in more than one place at a time, but this limitation also applies to the Holy Ghost. Page 32 of *Gospel Principles* states, "(The Holy Ghost) can be in only one place at a time, but His influence can be everywhere at the same time."

The God of the Bible is described much differently. Explaining God's omnipresence, Christian theologian R. C. Sproul takes particular notice of the prefix *omni*. He writes:

> The "omni" relates not only to the places where God is, but also to how much of Him is in any given place. God is not only present in all places but God is fully present in every place. This is called His immensity. Believers

living in New York enjoy the fullness of the presence of God while believers in Moscow enjoy that same presence. His immensity, then, does not refer to His size, but to His ability to be fully present everywhere.[38]

When Solomon dedicated the Jerusalem temple, he fully recognized that such a building could never actually house the person of God. In his dedicatory prayer, Solomon declared God's omnipresence when he proclaimed, "Behold, the heaven and heaven of heavens cannot contain thee" (1 Kings 8:27). Isaiah 66:1 adds, "Thus saith the LORD, The heaven is my throne, and the earth is my footstool: where is the house that ye build unto me?" In Proverbs 15:3 Solomon expressed both God's omnipresence and omniscience when he stated, "The eyes of the LORD are in every place, beholding the evil and the good." The prophet Jeremiah also extolled God's omnipresence when he wrote Jeremiah 23:23–24: "Am I a God at hand, saith the LORD, and not a God afar off? Can any hide himself in secret places that I shall not see him? saith the LORD."

God's omnipresence is demonstrated by the fact that He has no body. While God is present everywhere, He does not fill space. The concept of a God of spirit is taught ever so precisely in John 4:24, which states that "God is a Spirit." To alleviate this problem, LDS leaders have insisted that this passage was mistranslated. Joseph Smith, in his Inspired Version of the Bible, actually removed the troubling words.

While some Mormons may counter by insisting God *has* a spirit, this passage does not allow for such an interpretation. Since God is Spirit, it stands to reason that He is also invisible (see Col. 1:15; 1 Tim. 1:17; Heb. 11:27).

Conclusion

A Gospel Topics essay ("Are Mormons Christian?") posted on an LDS Church website explains, "Although the doctrine of The Church of Jesus Christ of Latter-day Saints differs from that of the many creedal Christian churches, it is consistent with early Christianity. One who sincerely loves, worships, and follows Christ should be free to claim his or her understanding of the doctrine according to the dictates of his or her conscience without being branded as non-Christian."[39] Yet how can this be? Many claim to "love" and "follow" Jesus—including Muslims and New Age adherents—but if their stated beliefs are not "Christian," can it be said they are "Christian"? If Mormonism's perception of God—arguably the most important teaching to the foundation of any religion—is contrary in every way, shape, and form to biblical Christianity, should Christians readily accept Mormonism as just another "denomination" of Christianity? The answer seems obvious.

Discussion Questions

1. When a Christian says that God is incomprehensible, what does that mean? Does it bother you, as a Christian, that there are some things about God that cannot be understood? How do you reconcile your lack of knowledge with the existence of a God whom we cannot fully grasp with human minds?

2. Brigham Young said that the idea that God was once a man and progressed to be God was "unique to this Church." In what ways is the LDS God unique? How does this version of God differ from what the Bible teaches? Are there any Bible verses you can use in support of your views?

3. What are the implications if God has not always been God? For instance, is it possible that God the Father was a sinner? If something like this is true, would this change the way you viewed and even worshiped God?

Final Thought

The Westminster Confession of Faith says that the chief end of man is to "know God" and "enjoy Him forever." Unfortunately, Latter-day Saint theology tends to simplify God and turns Him into nothing less than a glorified human being. This is a tragic mistake because the God described in the Bible was never a human, has always been God, and is not limited to being in one place at one time. While we may not fully grasp the attributes of God, thus prohibiting humans from putting Him into a box, Latter-day Saints are also limited in their understanding because they cannot explain how God became God. If only former humans can achieve exaltation, we must reject the biblical truth of Genesis 1:1 that God was in the beginning. Mormonism turns this teaching on its head, for if there is a primary cause, it must be a man who started it all.

Notes

1. *A Sure Foundation: Answers to Difficult Gospel Questions* (Salt Lake City: Deseret Book Co., 1988), 93.

2. *Gospel Principles*, 2nd edition (Salt Lake City: The Church of Jesus Christ of Latter-day Saints, 2009), 6. Because it is a very popular church manual that is often used with potential or new converts, we will quote liberally from *Gospel Principles* (updated in 2009) and refer to it in the main text by its title.

3. Charles R. Harrell, *"This Is My Doctrine": The Development of Mormon Theology* (Draper, UT: Greg Kofford Books, 2011), 131. As of this writing, Harrell is a Latter-day Saint who often does not support the traditional LDS interpretations of biblical passages.

4. *Ensign* (February 2012): 33.

5. *Ensign* (February 2007): 8. For more details about the First Vision and how God the Father and Jesus supposedly appeared to Joseph Smith, see chapter 31, "How do you account for Joseph Smith's 'First Vision'?" in our book *Answering Mormons' Questions*.

6. A. W. Tozer, *The Knowledge of the Holy* (New York: HarperOne, 1961), 3–4.

7. Ibid., 8.

8. *Gospel Fundamentals* (Salt Lake City: The Church of Jesus Christ of Latter-day Saints, 2002), 7.

9. *Gospel Principles*, 279; ellipses in original.

10. Milton R. Hunter, *The Gospel through the Ages* (Salt Lake City: Stevens and Wallis, 1945), 105–6. According to this book's preface, "This book is designed primarily for a course of study in the Melchizedek Priesthood quorum of the Church. It is to be used by all high priests', seventies', and elders' classes in their weekly meetings beginning January 1, 1946. . . . The volume has been written and published under the direction of the General Authorities."

11. *The Life and Teachings of Jesus & His Apostles Course Manual Religion 211–212*, 327, as taken from an address by Joseph Fielding Smith at Snow College, May 14, 1971, 1–8; ellipses in original.

12. For example, see *Doctrine and Covenants and Church History Seminary Teacher Resource Manual* (Salt Lake City: The Church of Jesus Christ of Latter-day Saints, 2001), 64; *Teachings of Presidents of the Church: George Albert Smith* (Salt Lake City: The Church of Jesus Christ of Latter-day Saints, 2011), 70–71; and *Teachings of Presidents of the Church: Lorenzo Snow* (Salt Lake City: The Church of Jesus Christ of Latter-day Saints, 2012), 83. In an article in *Ensign* (February 1982): 39–40, Gerald Lund answered the question, "Is President Lorenzo Snow's oft-repeated statement—'As man now is, God once was; as God is, man may be'—accepted as official doctrine by the Church?" He concluded, "It is clear that the teaching of President Lorenzo Snow is both acceptable and accepted doctrine in the Church today."

13. Orson Pratt, *The Seer* (Salt Lake City: Eborn Books, 1990), 132. Being a polygamist, the LDS Elohim physically created spirit children with his heavenly wives. All spirit beings in existence were produced this way. The Heavenly Mother doctrine finds no scriptural support from the four written LDS scriptures. Apostle Bruce R. McConkie said the Heavenly Mother doctrine was an "unspoken truth," Bruce R. McConkie, *Mormon Doctrine*, 2nd ed. (Salt Lake City: Bookcraft, 1966), 516. The *Encyclopedia of Mormonism* admits that Latter-day Saints must "infer from authoritative sources of scripture and modern prophecy that there is a Heavenly Mother as well as a Heavenly Father. . . . Today the belief in a living Mother in Heaven is implicit in Latter-day Saint thought," *Encyclopedia of Mormonism*, Daniel H. Ludlow, ed., s.v. "Mother in Heaven," 2:961.

14. Hunter, *Gospel through the Ages*, 104–5. This originated with Orson Hyde, *Journal of Discourses*, ed. Watt, 1:123.

15. *True to the Faith: A Gospel Reference* (Salt Lake City: The Church of Jesus Christ of Latter-day Saints, 2004), 74.

16. *The Pearl of Great Price Teacher Manual: Religion 327* (Salt Lake City: The Church of Jesus Christ of Latter-day Saints, 2000), 12.

17. *Ensign* (June 1993): 10.

18. *New Dictionary of Christian Apologetics*, s.v. "Transcendence," accessed May 29, 2014, www.designinference.com/documents/2003.10.Transcendence_NDOCApol.pdf.

19. *Teachings of Presidents of the Church: Brigham Young*, 34.

20. "Mormonism and the Nature of God," *FairMormon*, accessed May 29, 2014, http://en.fairmormon.org/Mormonism_and_the_nature_of_God/Was_God_once_a_sinner.

21. Herman Bavinck, *The Doctrine of God* (Edinburgh, United Kingdom: Banner of Truth Trust, 1991), 147.

22. Harrell, *"This Is My Doctrine,"* 128; italics in original.

23. Ibid.

24. *The Pearl of Great Price Student Manual: Religion 327* (Salt Lake City: The Church of Jesus Christ of Latter-day Saints, 2000), 37, which quoted from *History of the Church* (Salt Lake City: Deseret Book Co., 1973), 6:312.

25. Brigham Young, *Journal of Discourses*, ed. Watt, 7:284.

26. *Teachings of Presidents of the Church: Brigham Young*, 31; ellipses in original. This was first reported in Watt, ed., *Journal of Discourses*, 7:284.

27. Joseph Fielding McConkie and Robert L. Millet, *Doctrinal Commentary on the Book of Mormon* (Salt Lake City: Bookcraft, 1987), 1:193.

28. *Teachings of Presidents of the Church: Joseph Smith* (Salt Lake City: The Church of Jesus Christ of Latter-day Saints, 2007), 42.

29. *Pearl of Great Price Student Manual*, 8.

30. To counter the idea that nobody has seen God, some Mormons have responded that Jesus has been seen by humans. Since Jesus is God, therefore they conclude that God has been seen by humans. The logic is faulty. According to the context of the passage, John 1:18 is not referring to Jesus, the Incarnation of God, but rather God the Father. This Word that became flesh (Jesus) was made known by the Father (John 1:1, 14).

31. For more on this topic, see chapter 16, "If God is spirit, why did Moses say he saw God face-to-face?" in our book *Answering Mormons' Questions*.

32. Orson Hyde, "A Diagram of the Kingdom of God," *Millennial Star 9* (January 15, 1847): 23–24, as quoted in Andrew F. Ehat and Lyndon W. Cook, *The Words of Joseph Smith* (Orem, UT: Grandlin Book, 1993), 299. According to Ehat and Cook, there was "probably no clearer statement of Joseph's theology" than this editorial by Orson Hyde, 297.

33. Francis J. Beckwith, et al., ed. *The New Mormon Challenge: Responding to the Latest Defenses of a Fast-Growing Movement* (Grand Rapids: Zondervan, 2002), 97. Paul Copan and William Lane Craig wrote an excellent chapter titled "Craftsman or Creator? An Examination of the Mormon Doctrine of Creation and a Defense of *Creatio ex nihilo*," which we recommend for further research on this important topic.

34. John A. Widtsoe, *A Rational Theology as Taught by the Church of Jesus Christ of Latter-day Saints* (Salt Lake City: Deseret Book Co., 1965), 12.

35. This attribute should not be construed to mean that God, in His infinite perfection, could or would ever do anything contrary to His righteous nature. To be clear, God can do all things that are *possible* but nothing that is *impossible*. Miracles requiring God's intervention are possible only when God is involved, even though the act may go against

natural causes. However, God cannot accomplish illogical acts. For example, He cannot go against His nature by lying, acting contrary to His word, or sinning in any way. Just as it is impossible to create a three-sided *square* or become a married *bachelor*, so God—who is the creator of logic—cannot do the absurd. This is because, by definition, a three-sided object is a triangle, and someone who is married is not a bachelor.

36. Ridges, *Mormon Beliefs and Doctrines Made Easier*, 221. Although he doesn't say so, Ridges is referencing a pre-April 1990 version of the LDS temple ceremony in which Lucifer, Adam, and the apostle Peter are interacting. When Lucifer is asked by Peter what he was doing, Lucifer replied, "Teaching religion . . . a religion made of the philosophies of men, mingled with scripture." Adam, though, said he could not comprehend it, adding, "They preach of a God who is without body, parts, or passions; who is so large that he fills the universe, and yet is so small that he can dwell in my heart; and of a hell, without a bottom, where the wicked are continually burning but are never consumed. To me, it is a mass of confusion." Jerald and Sandra Tanner, *Evolution of the Mormon Temple Ceremony 1842–1990* (Salt Lake City: Utah Lighthouse Ministry, 2005), 81–82.

37. *Teachings of Presidents of the Church: Brigham Young*, 29. See also Brigham Young, *Discourses of Brigham Young*, comp. John A. Widtsoe, (Salt Lake City: Deseret Book Co., 1978), 23–24.

38. R. C. Sproul, *Essential Truths of the Christian Faith* (Wheaton: Tyndale House, 1992), 43.

39. "Are Mormons Christian?," The Church of Jesus Christ of Latter-Day Saints, accessed May 29, 2014, https://www.lds.org/topics/christians.

2 | Jesus

The official doctrine of the Church is that Jesus is the literal offspring of God. He's got 46 chromosomes; 23 came from Mary, 23 came from God the eternal Father.

BYU Professor Stephen E. Robinson[1]

On January 1, 2000, the *Church News* published a declaration signed by the First Presidency and Quorum of the Twelve Apostles that testified to their belief in "The Living Christ." The one-page statement mentioned how Jesus was "the first and the last," "the Firstborn of the Father," "the Only Begotten Son in the flesh," "the Redeemer of the world," and "the immortal Son of God." While on the surface the declaration sounded very orthodox, it conspicuously failed to specifically state what the LDS leaders meant by these terms. Two years later President Gordon B. Hinckley admitted that his Jesus is different from what many Christians might suppose. Speaking to a 2002 general conference audience, he explained, "As a church we have critics, many of them. They say we do not believe in the traditional Christ of Christianity. There is some substance to what they say."[2]

Proper belief in the person of Jesus Christ has always been considered essential to Christian fellowship. History bears out that a biblical view of Christ was imperative if an individual or organization was to be considered part of the Christian fold. The question is, which view of Jesus is true?

A Mythical Jesus

Despite the claim of people who accept that all religions each have a path to God—a system known as Universalism or Pluralism—a belief in a false Jesus is just as dangerous as no Jesus at all because faith is only as good as the object in which it is placed. Indeed, James 2:19 shows that an intellectual belief in God is not the same as true faith.

Paul certainly admonished the Corinthians for accepting a false version of Christ when he said in 2 Corinthians 11:4, "For if someone comes and proclaims another Jesus than the one we proclaimed, or if you receive a different spirit from the one you received, or if you accept a different gospel from the one you accepted, you put up with it readily enough" (ESV). He added in Galatians 1:6–9:

> I am astonished that you are so quickly deserting him who called you in the grace of Christ and are turning to a different gospel—not that there is another one, but there are some who trouble you and want to distort the gospel of Christ. But even if we or an angel from heaven should preach to you a gospel contrary to the one we preached to you, let him be accursed. As we have said before, so now I say again: If anyone is preaching to you a gospel contrary to the one you received, let him be accursed. (ESV)

Heretical views of Christ have plagued Christianity since its beginning. Because of the importance of the belief in Jesus, early heresies (false teachings) needed to be dealt with by the young church. Christian scholar Harold O. J. Brown wrote, "To a degree that is hard for twentieth-century people to grasp, the early church believed that it was absolutely vital to know and accept some very specific statements about the nature and attributes of God and his Son Jesus Christ."[3]

Since belief in the biblical Christ is vital because it affects one's eternal destiny, let's consider the Jesus of Mormonism and compare this version with the Jesus of biblical Christianity.

The Brother of Lucifer

According to Mormonism, Jesus was the firstborn son of God the Father in the First Estate, called the preexistence. Lucifer was another son who wanted to become the savior of the world. One of the more offensive attributes designated to the Jesus of Mormonism is the claim that Jesus is the spirit-brother of Lucifer. Seventy Milton R. Hunter wrote,

> The appointment of Jesus to be the Savior of the world was contested by one of the other sons of God. He was called Lucifer, son of the morning. Haughty, ambitious, and covetous of power and glory, this spirit-brother of Jesus desperately tried to become the Savior of mankind.[4]

Mormon educator Jess L. Christensen said:

> On first hearing, the doctrine that Lucifer and our Lord, Jesus Christ, are brothers may seem surprising to some, especially to those unacquainted with latter-day revelations. But both the scriptures and the prophets affirm that Jesus Christ and Lucifer are indeed offspring of our Heavenly Father and, therefore, spirit brothers. . . . Both Jesus and Lucifer were strong leaders with great knowledge and influence. But as the First-born of the Father, Jesus was Lucifer's older brother.[5]

Ironically, the same passages of the Bible that expound on Christ's eternal deity also show that Lucifer could not be the brother of Christ. John 1:1–3 says that all things (including Lucifer) were made by Jesus, who was, is, and always will be God. Colossians 1:15, the one biblical verse used by Christensen, says that He (Jesus) "is the image of the invisible God, the firstborn of every creature." However, this has nothing to do with Jesus and Satan being brothers. In fact, it proclaims Christ's deity ("image of the invisible God"). Verses 16–17 show that Christ created all things and that He is before all things, holding them together. Just as a person can look into the mirror to see a reflection, so too is Jesus the exact image of God.

51

BYU professor Charles R. Harrell refutes the commonly held LDS notion, writing, "Paul is not referring to premortal spirit birth, but to Christ becoming the firstborn in attaining God's glory, a status which would subsequently be attained by 'many brethren' (i.e., disciples)."[6] The Bible adamantly declares Lucifer to be a creation of Jesus, not in any way the brother of Jesus. Besides, Jesus and Satan are as opposite as light and darkness. Satan merely tries to imitate an angel of light in order to fool as many people as possible (2 Cor. 11:14).

Referring to humanity's premortal existence in heaven, Apostle Robert D. Hales taught that, while we can't remember this time,

> we probably sat in meetings much like this, where the Father's plan for us was explained. We cannot remember that Lucifer, a son of God the Father, a brother of Jesus Christ, rebelled against God's plan and, in his rebellion, promised he would bring us all back home. But Lucifer would have denied us our free agency, the freedom to make decisions. We cannot remember that his plan was not accepted by us because, without choice, there would not have been a purpose for coming to this mortal probation. We would not have had opposition or repentance. We would not have learned obedience.[7]

Gospel Principles says, "After hearing both sons speak, Heavenly Father said, 'I will send the first' (Abraham 3:27)."[8] Unfortunately, one third of the spirits chose Lucifer's plan that denied free choice; everyone who would end up receiving bodies by being born on the earth apparently chose Jesus. Thus,

> In this great rebellion, Satan and all the spirits who followed him were sent away from the presence of God and cast down from heaven. A third part of the hosts of heaven were punished for following Satan (see D&C 29:36). They were denied the right to receive mortal bodies. Because we are here on earth and have mortal bodies, we know that we chose to follow Jesus Christ and our Heavenly Father. . . . In our premortal life, we chose to follow Jesus Christ and accept God's plan.[9]

The Virgin Birth

Since the beginning, Christ's followers have believed that He was born as a result of a miraculous conception, as attested in Matthew 1:18. Mormon leaders have insisted in a belief of the virgin birth, yet they give a description far removed from that held by Christians throughout the centuries. An instructor's guide explains how Mormonism disagrees with the traditional doctrine:

> The teacher might wish to point out that many people in the Christian world want to believe in Jesus, but only as a great human being, only as a great man. They feel uncomfortable about the concept of the miraculous, virgin birth. Yet if this is denied, all of the Atonement must be rejected as well. It was the inheritance that came from a mortal mother and a divine Father that made the Atonement possible.[10]

What exactly does the leadership mean when it refers to a "mortal mother and a divine Father"? Let's allow the LDS leaders and church resources to speak for themselves:

- "Now, we are told in scriptures that Jesus Christ is the only begotten Son of God in the flesh. Well, now for the benefit of the older ones, how are children begotten? I answer just as Jesus Christ was begotten of his father. . . . Jesus is the only person who had our Heavenly Father as the father of his body."[11]
- "The Church of Jesus Christ of Latter-day Saints proclaims that Jesus Christ is the Son of God in the most literal sense. The body in which He performed His mission in the flesh was sired by that same Holy Being we worship as God, our Eternal Father. Jesus was not the son of Joseph, nor was He begotten by the Holy Ghost. He is the Son of the Eternal Father!"[12]
- "To condescend is literally to go down among. The condescension of God lies in the fact that he, an exalted Being, steps down from his eternal throne to become the Father of a mortal Son, a Son born 'after the manner of the flesh.'"[13]
- "He is the Son of God, literally, actually, as men are the sons of mortal parents."[14]
- "Thus, God the Father became the literal father of Jesus Christ. Jesus is the only person on earth to be born of a mortal mother and an immortal father."[15]
- "Our Savior, Jesus Christ, is called the Only Begotten Son because He is the only person on earth to be born of a mortal mother and an

immortal Father. . . . Modern prophets have testified: [Jesus Christ] was . . . the Only Begotten Son in the flesh, the Redeemer of the world."[16]

Since Mormonism teaches that Mary did not have sexual relations with a *mortal* man but instead was impregnated by an *immortal* man (Elohim), many Latter-day Saints have no qualms about using the phrase "virgin birth." Harrell describes the difficulties with this position when he writes:

> Of course, for Latter-day Saints who hold the belief that Christ was literally conceived by God the Father, the idea of a virgin birth becomes a bit problematic as it would presumably change Mary's status as a virgin. Bruce R. McConkie gives his resolution to this conundrum by redefining "virgin" to mean a woman who has not known a *mortal* man: "She conceived and brought forth her Firstborn Son while yet a virgin because the Father of that child was an immortal personage."[17]

When one considers how Mormonism teaches that every human born on earth is a literal child of God, the above quotes become even more disconcerting. Mormon leaders have maintained that all humans, Mary included, are literally God's spirit children, born in the preexistence via a sexual relationship between Heavenly Father and one of his goddess wives. If LDS leaders are telling the truth when they say that God physically impregnated Mary, then we have no other recourse than to assume that the Jesus of Mormonism was created through an incestuous relationship.

The Diminishing of Jesus

There are a number of ways that Mormonism corrupts the very being of Jesus. For example, consider how Jesus—as with everyone born onto this earth—lost His ability to remember anything from the preexistence and had to "progress." Jay E. Jensen, a member of the Presidency of the Seventy, explained, "When the Lord came to earth, He had a veil of forgetfulness placed over His mind, as we do, but He, like us, progressed from grace to grace."[18] One resource traces the teaching back to Mormonism's founder Joseph Smith:

> As Joseph Smith taught, Jesus was born with a veil of forgetfulness common to all who are born to earth, but even as a child he had all the intelligence

necessary to enable him to govern the kingdom of the Jews (see source under Basic Library), because he overcame the veil and came into communication with his Heavenly Father.[19]

Jesus became a god, according to Milton R. Hunter, "through consistent effort and continuous obedience to all the Gospel truths and universal laws." That effort, Hunter continues, included Jesus's own baptism:

> Although John recognized Jesus as a perfect man, the Master made it clear that it was absolutely necessary for even the Son of God to be baptized. He—like the least of us—must obey every law of the Gospel if He was to receive all the blessings predicated on obedience.[20]

This idea that Jesus was under obligation of the law has been taught by a number of leaders. President Joseph F. Smith said, "Even Christ himself was not perfect at first; he received not a fullness at first, but he received grace for grace, and he continued to receive more and more until he received a fullness."[21] Bruce R. McConkie claimed, "Jesus kept the commandments of his Father and thereby worked out his own salvation, and also set an example as to the way and the means whereby all men may be saved."[22] McConkie's use of Philippians 2:12 ("work out your salvation") misses the meaning of the passage. Paul does not use this expression to mean "work *for* your salvation" as so many Mormons will insist. Rather, as the words literally read, it means that believers "should 'conduct' themselves in a manner worthy of their right standing before God at the day of Christ."[23]

Apostle Russell M. Nelson said Jesus achieved His perfection only *after* His resurrection:

> That Jesus attained perfection *following* his resurrection is confirmed in the Book of Mormon. It records the visit of the resurrected Lord to the people of ancient America. There he repeated the important injunction previously cited, but with one very significant addition. He said, "I would that ye should be perfect *even as I,* or your Father who is in heaven is perfect" (3 Nephi 12:48). This time he listed himself along with his Father as a perfected personage. Previously, he had not (See Matt. 5:48).[24]

It is difficult to understand why Jesus, who allegedly became a god before His mortality, would have to work out his own salvation. Such a comment also fails to take into account that only sinners need to be saved in the first place. To say Christ had to do anything to gain His own salvation should rightfully be considered blasphemous by anyone who holds the Bible dear. Problematic also is the fact that the Jesus of Mormonism is but one of many saviors. According to Brigham Young:

> Consequently every earth has its redeemer, and every earth has its tempter; and every earth, and the people thereof, in their turn and time, receive all that we receive, and pass through all the ordeals that we are passing through.[25]

If such a comment was true, we could assume that there are literally millions of saviors on millions of worlds! Despite these false teachings, the Bible states that Jesus is God and has been from all eternity. John 1:1–2, 14 says:

> In the beginning was the Word, and the Word was with God, and the Word was God. The same was in the beginning with God. . . . And the Word was made flesh, and dwelt among us, (and we beheld his glory, the glory as of the only begotten of the Father), full of grace and truth.[26]

Christianity has historically taught that Jesus, as the very God, took upon Himself the form of a man. This is not to say that at any time His Godhood was diminished in any degree after His physical appearance on earth (His incarnation).[27] Jesus was, and is, both divine and human: 100 percent God and 100 percent man. He was conceived through the agency of the Holy Spirit (Matt. 1:18–25; Luke 1:35); He lived a sinless life while subjected to human temptations (John 5:19; Heb. 2:18; 4:15); He died a real death and rose again bodily from the dead to conquer sin (Rom. 5:6–10; 1 Cor. 15:3–4); He will return to judge all humanity (John 5:22); He sent the Holy Spirit to empower the believers (John 14–16; Acts 1:8); and He can be prayed to (Acts 7:59).[28] Finally, He is deserving to receive honor, love, faith, and worship as the Father (Matt. 10:37; John 5:23; 14:1; Heb. 1:6). At the same time, He shares attributes with the Father because Jesus is also God.

The Marriages of Jesus

When plural marriage was being practiced openly in Utah, some early LDS leaders defended this practice by insisting that God the Father and Jesus were also practicing polygamists. Consider the following quotes:

The Scripture says that He, the Lord, came walking in the Temple, with His train; I do not know who they were, unless His wives and children.[29]

From the passage in the forty-fifth Psalm, it will be seen that the great Messiah who was the founder of the Christian religion, was a Polygamist. . . . the Messiah chose to take upon himself his seed; and by marrying many honorable wives himself, show to all future generations that he approbated the plurality of Wives under the Christian dispensation, as well as under the dispensations in which His Polygamist ancestors lived.[30]

It will be borne in mind that once on a time, there was a marriage in Cana of Galilee; and on a careful reading of that transaction, it will be discovered that no less a person than Jesus Christ was married on that occasion. If he was never married, his intimacy with Mary and Martha, and the other Mary also whom Jesus loved, must have been highly unbecoming and improper to say the best of it.[31]

The grand reason of the burst of public sentiment in anathemas upon Christ and his disciples, causing his crucifixion, was evidently based upon polygamy, according to the testimony of the philosophers who rose in that age. A belief in the doctrine of a plurality of wives caused the persecution of Jesus and his followers. We might almost think they were "Mormons."[32]

It is doubtful that many modern Mormons would go out of their way to defend the above statements regarding Jesus's polygamy. However, they cannot consistently ignore the notion that Jesus must have been married to at least one person if He had to "work out His own salvation." It would seem necessary that He was married to at least one woman, since marriage is a very important element in the exaltation process.[33]

Discussion Questions

1. When questioned about whether or not their church is "Christian," Mormon missionaries sometimes point to their badges, showing how "Jesus Christ" is depicted in a large font size. If you had to provide three examples to show how the LDS Jesus is different from the version described in the Bible, what would you say? Provide evidence.

2. In his talk titled "Eternal Life—to know Our Heavenly Father and His Son, Jesus Christ" given at the October 2014 general conference,

Apostle Robert D. Hales described his version of Jesus this way: "Jesus is a God, yet He continually distinguishes Himself as a separate individual being by praying to His Father and by saying that He is doing His Father's will."[34] Based on what he said, describe Jesus as understood in a Mormon mind-set. How is this similar or different from the biblical description of the Savior?

3. Evangelical Christians have consistently held to the idea that it is possible to have a personal relationship with Jesus as their Savior. Part of this intimacy includes conversing with Him in prayer. However, some Mormon leaders have encouraged their people not to pray to Jesus. Is it possible for a person to have a personal relationship with someone to whom they are not allowed to speak? How would your intimacy with Jesus be affected if you were not allowed to talk to Him?

Final Thought

While the name of Jesus is in the LDS Church's title, it is important to know how the leaders have defined that name. Evangelical Christians have long insisted that Jesus's death on the cross was an "all-sufficient" payment made in behalf of sinners. Mormons, on the other hand, feel it is necessary to add "good works" and thus diminish Christ's sacrifice. In addition, the Mormon Jesus, like His Father, is not "eternally God." This version of Jesus is not to be prayed to, contrary to what the martyr Stephen did in Acts 7:59. The Bible says that Jesus desires to have a personal relationship with His bride (the Church) and offers grace to those who, though unworthy, place their trust in His finished work. Those who want to worship the true Jesus as proclaimed in the Bible must take great caution, as 2 Corinthians 11:4 says that it is quite possible to believe in "another Jesus." Seeking after the true Christ really does matter!

Notes

1. *The Mormon Puzzle*, produced by the Southern Baptist Convention (Alpharetta, GA: North American Mission Board, 1997), DVD.
2. *Ensign* (May 2002): 90.
3. Harold O. J. Brown, *Heresies: The Image of Christ in the Mirror of Heresy and Orthodoxy from the Apostles to the Present* (Grand Rapids: Baker, 1984), 21.

4. Hunter, *The Gospel through the Ages*, 15.

5. *A Sure Foundation*, 223–24.

6. Harrell, *"This Is My Doctrine,"* 168. Lest there be confusion over the term *firstborn,* it should be pointed out that the Greek word used is not *protoktistos* (meaning *first created*) but rather *prototokos* (meaning *firstborn*). Both Hebrews 1:3 and 2 Corinthians 4:4 point out that Christ is the exact representation of God. Referring to Colossians 1, Harrell writes that this is "an unmistakable reference to his [Jesus's] preeminence in the resurrection from the dead." He adds that "in the New Testament Christ is the firstborn in the sense of (1) being prior to and the source of all creation; (2) being the first to receive exaltation and glory, and (3) being the first to rise from the dead, 'that in all things he might have the preeminence' (Col. 1:18)," 171.

7. *Ensign* (May 1990): 39.

8. *Gospel Principles*, 15.

9. Ibid., 16–17.

10. *The Life and Teachings of Jesus and His Apostles Instructor's Manual: Religion 211–212*. (Salt Lake City: The Church of Jesus Christ of Latter-day Saints, 1978), 14.

11. Joseph F. Smith, *Family Home Evening Manual* (Salt Lake City: The Church of Jesus Christ of Latter-day Saints, 1972), 125–26.

12. Ezra Benson, *Teachings of Ezra Taft Benson* (Salt Lake City: Bookcraft, 1988), 7. This was quoted in the *Ensign* (April 1997): 15.

13. *Book of Mormon Seminary Student Study Guide* (Salt Lake City: The Church of Jesus Christ of Latter-day Saints, 2000), 22. See also Bruce R. McConkie, *The Mortal Messiah* (Salt Lake City: Deseret Book Co., 1982), 1:314, as well as McConkie and Millet, *Doctrinal Commentary on the Book of Mormon*, 1:78.

14. "What the Mormons Think of Christ," a pamphlet published by the LDS Church, 44.

15. *Gospel Principles*, 53. See also *Ensign* (December 2013): 7.

16. "The Divine Mission of Jesus Christ: The Only Begotten Son," *Ensign* (December 2013): 7; brackets and ellipses in original.

17. Harrell, *"This Is My Doctrine,"* 167. Italics in original.

18. *Ensign* (January 2011): 42.

19. *The Life and Teachings of Jesus and His Apostles Instructor's Manual*, 13.

20. Hunter, *The Gospel through the Ages*, 200. An LDS apologetic website chastised us for using this quote in our original edition of *Mormonism 101*, saying we "insult the intelligence of Latter-day Saints by claiming that Elder Milton Hunter's biblical assertion (Hebrews 5:8) that Jesus Christ is God because of His 'continued obedience to gospel laws' is in fact, a 'diminishing of Jesus.'" See "Response to claims made in Chapter 2: Jesus," *FairMormon*, accessed May 29, 2014, http://en.fairmormon.org/Criticism_of_Mormonism/Books/Mormonism_101/Index/Chapter_2. To the contrary, this quote—which comes from a book used by priesthood holders in 1946—diminishes the Personhood of Jesus because it is absurd to think that our Savior somehow needed to have continual "obedience to gospel laws." We are speaking, after all, about the Creator of the universe. As one creed puts it, He is "very God of very God." By nature, Jesus is holy and perfect.

21. *Teachings of Presidents of the Church: Joseph F. Smith* (Salt Lake City: The Church of Jesus Christ of Latter-day Saints, 1998), 153. See also Joseph F. Smith, *Gospel Doctrine*, comp. John A. Widtsoe (Salt Lake City: Deseret Book Co., 1919), 68.

22. McConkie, *The Mortal Messiah*, 4:434.

23. Frank Thielman, *The NIV Application Commentary: Philippians* (Grand Rapids: Zondervan, 1995), 138.

24. *Ensign* (November 1995): 87; italics in original. Unless it is possible for a god to be imperfect, this would seem to contradict the notion that Jesus became a god in the preexistence.

25. Watt, ed., *Journal of Discourses,* 14:71–72.

26. It should be noted that Joseph Smith radically changed verse 1 in his Inspired Version of the Bible to read: "In the beginning was the gospel preached through the Son. And the gospel was the word, and the word was with the Son, and the Son was with God, and the Son was of God." No ancient biblical manuscript supports such a translation. The idea that Jesus was eternally God can be supported from many other passages, including John 5:17–18; 8:58 (in conjunction with Exod. 3:14); 10:30–33; 14:7–11; 17:5 (in conjunction with Isa. 42:8); 20:28–29; 2 Corinthians 8:9; Colossians 1:19; 2:3, 8–9; Titus 2:13; 2 Peter 1:1; 1 John 5:20.

27. The doctrine of *kenosis* ("empty") as described in Philippians 2:5–11 states that Jesus voluntarily gave up the exercise of those attributes while here on earth.

28. Although some Mormon leaders (including Joseph Fielding Smith in *Doctrines of Salvation, Sermons and Writings of Joseph Fielding Smith,* ed. Bruce R. McConkie [Salt Lake City: Bookcraft, 1954–56], 1:14) say prayers should be offered only to the Father, 3 Nephi 19:17–18 in the Book of Mormon supports praying to Jesus.

29. Brigham Young, *Journal of Discourses,* ed. Watt, 13:309.

30. Pratt, *The Seer,* 172.

31. Orson Hyde, *Journal of Discourses,* ed. Watt, 4:259. See also 2:81–82, 210. The idea that Jesus was married at Cana is an argument from silence, since there is no proof of this whatsoever. It requires the assumption that Jesus was actually the groom at the wedding. The context, however, shows that Jesus was merely a guest. Finally, at the cross, why was Jesus only concerned about the welfare of His mother? If He were married, it would have been logical for Him to have made instructions for the welfare of His wives and children as well.

32. Jedediah M. Grant, *Journal of Discourses,* ed. Watt, 1:346.

33. Joseph Fielding Smith, *Doctrines of Salvation,* 2:43–44; Joseph Fielding Smith, ed., *Teachings of the Prophet Joseph Smith,* 301; Kimball, *The Miracle of Forgiveness,* 245.

34. *Ensign* (November 2014): 81.

3 | The Trinity

Joseph knew, as no other soul living, these absolutes: He knew that God lives, that He is a [glorified] person with flesh and bones and personality, like us or we like Him, in His image. He knew that the long-heralded trinity of three Gods in one was a myth, a deception. He knew that the Father and the Son were two distinct beings with form, voices, and . . . personalities. He knew that the gospel was not on the earth, for by the Deities he had learned it, and the true Church was absent from the earth, for the God of heaven and earth had so informed him.

President Spencer W. Kimball [1]

MORMONESE:

Trinity: Depending on the person, could mean a number of things, including a teaching that was formulated centuries after the Bible was compiled saying how God the Father is the same god as Jesus and the Holy Spirit. Regardless of how this word is interpreted, it is generally rejected as pagan by Latter-day Saints.

One of the doctrines that Mormon leaders have attacked, probably with more venom than any other, is the doctrine of the Trinity. It has been mocked and slandered despite being the heart and soul of Christian theology. According to the LDS Church magazine *Ensign:*

The Prophet Joseph learned early that the sectarian creeds were confusing in their declarations on the nature of God. They held to the notion of the Trinity as conceived in the Nicene and Athanasian Creeds, developed by councils convened in the early centuries of Christianity to settle theological differences. Those creeds portray God as three personages in one and one in three, "neither confounding the persons, nor dividing the substance"; as being uncreated, incomprehensible, and almighty. From these creeds has grown the current orthodox view held by most Christian denominations that "there is but one living and true God, everlasting, without body, parts, or passions; of infinite power, wisdom, and goodness."[2]

Joseph Smith separated himself from the rest of the Christian world when he proclaimed that "always and in all congregations when I have preached on the subject of the Deity, it has been the plurality of Gods." He ridiculed the Trinity, saying:

> Many men say there is one God; the Father, the Son and the Holy Ghost are only one God. I say that is a strange God anyhow—three in one, and one in three! It is a curious organization. . . . All are to be crammed into one God, according to sectarianism. It would make the biggest God in all the world. He would be a wonderfully big God—he would be a giant or a monster.[3]

President Gordon B. Hinckley explained why he also could not believe in the Trinity:

> The world wrestles with the question of who God is, and in what form He is found. Some say that the Father and the Son and the Holy Ghost are one. I wonder how they ever arrive at that. How could Jesus have prayed to Himself when he uttered the Lord's Prayer? How could He have met with Himself when He was on the Mount of Transfiguration? No. He is a separate being. God, our Father, is one. Jesus Christ is two. The Holy Ghost is three. And these three are united in purpose and in working together to bring to pass the immortality and eternal life of man.[4]

Saying how it was absurd that "three persons combined in one substance, a Trinitarian notion never set forth in the scriptures," Apostle Jeffrey R. Holland said the following in a general conference talk:

> Indeed no less a source than the stalwart *Harper's Bible Dictionary* records that "the formal doctrine of the Trinity as it was defined by the great church councils of the fourth and fifth centuries is *not* to be found in the [New Testament]." So any criticism that The Church of Jesus Christ of Latter-day Saints does not hold the contemporary Christian view of God, Jesus, and the

Holy Ghost is *not* a comment about our commitment to Christ but rather a recognition (accurate, I might add) that our view of the Godhead breaks with post-New Testament Christian history and returns to the doctrine taught by Jesus Himself.[5]

BYU professor Joseph Fielding McConkie gave his incorrect assessment of the Trinity: "The men had their turn at the Council of Nicaea, at which philosophical speculation replaced the plain meaning of scripture, Christ became his own Father, and the gospel plan was transformed into an incomprehensible mystery."[6] Another BYU professor, Robert L. Millet, explained the LDS position this way:

> If an acceptance of the doctrine of the Trinity makes one a Christian, then of course Latter-day Saints are not Christians, for they believe the doctrine of the Trinity as expressed in modern Protestant and Catholic theology is the product of the reconciliation of Christian theology with Greek philosophy.[7]

Finally, in a Gospel Topics essay ("Are Mormons Christian?") released in early 2014, the LDS Church explained:

> Latter-day Saints believe the melding of early Christian theology with Greek philosophy was a grave error. Chief among the doctrines lost in this process was the nature of the Godhead. The true nature of God the Father, His Son, Jesus Christ, and the Holy Ghost was restored through the Prophet Joseph Smith. As a consequence, Latter-day Saints hold that God the Father is an embodied being, a belief consistent with the attributes ascribed to God by many early Christians. This Latter-day Saint belief differs from the post-New Testament creeds.[8]

If Mormonism is correct, then the Trinity is nothing more than a pagan teaching and should be rejected. Let's consider the background and history of this most important doctrine.

Church History

The Trinity is a vital doctrine in Christianity. When alternate voices attempted to challenge orthodox positions, the early Christian church leaders felt compelled to define its position and answer the charges being raised against this doctrine. Contrary to LDS belief, the Trinity is not a philosophical invention; rather, early church leaders provided a definitive response explaining the biblical position of the church. Second-century theologian Irenaeus described the Trinity this way:

> This, then, is the order of the rule of our faith. . . . God the Father, not made, not material, invisible; one God, the creator of all things: this is the first point of our faith. The second point is this: the Word of God, Son of God, Christ Jesus our Lord, Who was manifested to the prophets according to the form of their prophesying and according to the method of the Father's dispensation; through Whom (i.e. the Word) all things were made. . . . And the third point is: the Holy Spirit, through Whom the prophets prophesied, and the fathers learned the things of God, and the righteous were led into the way of righteousness; Who at the end of the age was poured out in a new way upon mankind in all the earth, renewing man to God.[9]

It would be incorrect to assume that such teachings were the result of later corruption. Essential doctrines were "implicit in Christian faith from the beginning, even though they did not become explicit until considerably later."[10] The results were the Nicene and Athanasian Creeds, which described orthodoxy. For example, the Athanasian Creed says, in part, that "we worship one God in Trinity, and Trinity in Unity; Neither confounding the Persons; nor dividing the Essence." This idea remains alive and well in Christendom in the twenty-first century!

As for denying the Trinity because it cannot be fully comprehended, we ask: What about Mormons who believe in certain doctrines that they cannot fully understand? For example, in chapter 1 under the section concerning the self-existence of God, we quoted several LDS leaders who admitted that they could not comprehend the first cause of all things. John Widtsoe called the doctrine "mysterious." Joseph Fielding Smith said humankind has a "limited capacity to understand." Brigham Young boldly stated that it was "as easy for an ant to number the grains of sand on the earth" as it was to understand this teaching. If this is the case, and if this doctrine is so hard to comprehend, then why has the doctrine of the Trinity been so often maligned? Our inability to comprehend a teaching is not the basis for its truthfulness. This must be determined by its compatibility with Scripture—specifically, the Holy Bible—which is the Christian's source for all truth.

Saying that he "loves" the Trinity because this doctrine reveals God's nature, Christian apologist James White gives a basic definition of the

Trinity: "Within the one Being that is God, there exists eternally three coequal and coeternal persons, namely, the Father, the Son, and the Holy Spirit."[11] As White puts it, the Trinity consists of three Whos (Persons of God) and one What (the essence of God). Using this formula, let's take a closer look at what the Bible has to say about this important doctrine.

One God

In the first part of the definition, White says "within the One being that is God. . . ." Over and over again the Bible emphasizes the importance of the belief in only one God. This was a major point of separation between the religious system of the Jews and their pagan neighbors. This pattern is found throughout the Old Testament. When God rejected King David's offer to build Him a house, the humble king prayed and said, "O LORD, there is none like thee, neither is there any God beside thee, according to all that we have heard with our ears" (1 Chron. 17:20).

The idea that there is only one God is very clear in the New Testament as well. Consider Mark 12:29 when Jesus quoted Deuteronomy 6:4—it says, "Hear, O Israel: The Lord our God is one Lord"—to an inquiring scribe. In response, the scribe remarked in verse 32, "Well, Master, thou hast said the truth: for there is one God; and there is none other but he." Notice how Jesus responded in verse 34: "And when Jesus saw that he answered discreetly [wisely], he said unto him, Thou art not far from the kingdom of God."

Mormonism emphasizes God as being the Father, but it also teaches that there are many gods in existence. As BYU professor Charles R. Harrell writes,

> One of the most distinctive doctrines of Mormonism is the belief in a plurality of Gods. This is generally understood to mean that there are innumerable Gods besides (and above) the God that we worship, all of whom are creators of worlds and objects of worship. Furthermore, these Gods were all once human, and just as they attained Godhood, so can we. This view goes beyond the traditional Christian doctrine of human divinization or theosis in which the righteous are partakers of God through the indwelling of God's Spirit.[12]

The Latter-day Saint may argue that whenever the Bible declares the existence of only one God, it must be speaking of purpose only and that it merely means they agree in all things. Rex E. Lee, who once served as the president of BYU, explained, "Biblical statements that those three are one mean that they are unified in purpose, action, and belief, not that they are one being."[13]

This certainly is a superficial interpretation, for many passages show this *oneness* far surpasses the mere notion of agreement. For example, the First Commandment strongly warns, "Thou shalt have no other gods before me" (Exod. 20:3). The Mormon may insist his *worship* does not extend beyond the one he calls Elohim, but context demands that this must also involve his faith (he is not to even believe there are other true gods).

The book of Isaiah offers perhaps more verses in defense of monotheism— the belief and worship of only one God—than any other. Throughout chapters 43 through 45, Isaiah emphasizes the existence of one God and one God only (see Isa. 43:10; 44:6; 45:5–6, 14, 21–22; 46:9).[14]

It is difficult to interpret passages such as Isaiah 43:10 as merely referring to several gods being one in purpose since it rejects the possibility of other gods existing either before or after the one true God. One would think that even the God of Mormonism would be aware of the many gods who allegedly exist with him, or for that matter, the god that begat his mortal body. Yet Isaiah 44:8 tells us that the God of the Bible doesn't even know of other gods! Are we to believe in the context of Mormonism that Joseph Smith's God can't remember who his own father was?

A common rebuttal to the Isaiah passages is that these verses speak only of idols. While it is true that idol worship was a problem during the time of Isaiah, the above verses cannot be limited to such an interpretation. Let us assume *idols* are meant in Isaiah 43:10. It could then be understood to read, "Before me there was no *idol* formed, neither shall there be after me." Are we really expected to believe that idols had not been formed *after* God? If only idols were being referred to in Isaiah 44:8, this passage would read, "Is there an *idol* beside me? yea, there is no *idol*; I know not any." Does it make sense to conclude that the God of the Bible was unaware that idols existed? Not likely.

Why does the LDS Church reject the historic church's concept of the Trinity? Not only does the Trinity remove any hope of a Mormon ever achieving godhood, but it also undermines Smith's First Vision account and subsequent teachings regarding a multiplicity of deities. If it can be demonstrated that the Father, Son, and Holy Ghost/Spirit are God, and at the same time be shown that there exists only one God, it would definitely place the integrity of the first Mormon prophet on the line.

Not only does the Bible provide such a teaching, but the Book of Mormon does as well. Were the Nephites practicing polytheists? Alma 11:26–29, which describes a conversation between the righteous prophet Amulek and the wicked lawyer Zeezrom, shows they were not. Before examining this discourse, it must be understood that verse 22 states that Amulek could "say nothing which is contrary to the Spirit of the Lord." With that in mind, Zeezrom and Amulek engage in the following dialogue:

> And Zeezrom said unto him: Thou sayest there is a true and living God?
> And Amulek said: Yea, there is a true and living God.
> Now Zeezrom said: Is there more than one God?
> And he answered, No.

The context revolves around the existence of a "true and living God." Amulek agrees that there is a true and living God, but when asked by Zeezrom if there is more than one (true and living) God, he is told that there is not. With that context in mind, verse 44 goes on to say that the Father, Son, and Holy Spirit "is one Eternal God."[15] Assuming Amulek was giving a correct answer, the Mormon who wishes to insist in the existence of more than one God within the Godhead must resolve the dilemma as to which of the three is not true. Again, according to Amulek's answer, if the Father, Son, and Holy Ghost are, in fact, three separate Gods, two of them must be false Gods. Even if Mormons insist that this means there is only one God for this world whom they should worship, it still does not relieve them of this difficulty since Mormon theology definitely teaches that Jesus and the Holy Ghost play a prominent role when it comes to *this* world.

Three Persons

The second part of White's definition says that "there exists eternally three coequal and coeternal persons, namely, the Father, the Son, and the Holy Spirit." In other words, each member of the Trinity is separate in personhood from the other members. Each member—being fully, 100 percent God in His own right—is not identical to the others.

Jesus was fully God in the very beginning, as described in the previous chapter. Thomas called Him both "Lord" and "God" (John 20:28). And Jesus claimed that, while He was not the Father, He came as God in the flesh who "dwelled" among humanity (John 1:1). Yet critics may argue that

Jesus appears to be somehow lesser in being than the Father. For example, John 14:28 may be cited ("for my Father is greater than I"). However, Jesus was referring to a *position* of authority and not His nature. Consider Philippians 2:6–8, which says how Jesus, who "in the form of God,"

> did not count equality with God a thing to be grasped, but emptied himself, by taking the form of a servant, being born in the likeness of men. And being found in human form, he humbled himself by becoming obedient to the point of death, even death on a cross. (ESV)

According to Paul, Jesus was in the "form" of God but "did not count equality with God a thing to be grasped." In other words, Jesus became a servant even though He was, by nature, God. He came to this earth to serve by becoming a man, even experiencing death as all humans do. Yet the passage continues in verses 9–11:

> Therefore God has highly exalted him and bestowed on him the name that is above every name, so that at the name of Jesus every knee should bow, in heaven and on earth and under the earth, and every tongue confess that Jesus Christ is Lord, to the glory of God the Father. (ESV)

When an ordinary American citizen is compared to the president of the United States, which person has greater authority? While the president is equal in nature (he's human), he's greater in authority (position). To say "here is someone greater than I" when the president walks into the room would be accurate for any American to say. In the same way, Jesus—though He retained His status as deity—humbled Himself to take on a fleshly body, meaning that the Father was "greater" in authority than Jesus. Referring back to John 14:28, it says the Father was *greater* than, not *better* than, Jesus. According to Philippians 2, every person living on this earth has a choice: to call Jesus "my Lord and my God" in this life, as Thomas did when he touched the wounds of Jesus, or to wait until after death when it is too late.

Another objection is the claim that Jesus prayed to Himself. The Trinity does not teach that the Father is Jesus or that Jesus is the Holy Spirit. There are three Persons in the Trinity, and thus there is communication within the Godhead. If one member of the Trinity communicates with another, this does not negate the deity of either one. Jesus was *not* a ventriloquist, as some might claim; instead, He was praying to the Father in the Garden of Gethsemane, to whom He subjected Himself and who is separate in person, though one in nature.

In this short chapter, we cannot pretend to offer every possible answer to the questions that might be opposed by those rejecting the Trinity.[16] However, it behooves each Christian to study this very important doctrine and, while acknowledging that humans are limited in their understanding because God is transcendent as well as incomprehensible, present a biblical response to those who reject this teaching.

Discussion Questions

1. Critics of Christianity seem to enjoy critiquing Christian doctrines such as the Trinity or salvation by grace alone through faith. Why do you think these are two common targets? Are these two doctrines worthy to be defended? Why or why not?

2. Historically, Christians have not pretended to fully comprehend the nuances of the Trinity. While this teaching must remain a mystery in our finite minds, we must accept the Trinitarian formula presented by the biblical evidence. Suppose a Mormon argues that he can't believe in anything he cannot understand. Can you give a reasonable response to this objection?

3. As one LDS resource puts it, the Mormon view of the Godhead "may seem natural and logical to long-time members of the Church. However, this doctrine is very different from the beliefs of most other Christian churches. List and explain three ways that your life—such as your thoughts, behavior, and prayers—is different because you know what the Godhead is really like."[17] Turning the tables, list and explain three ways that your life is different based on *your* Christian understanding of the Godhead.

Final Thought

Although the word "trinity" is not found in the Bible, the concept is. First, the Bible says that God is one God (Deut. 6:4; Mark 12:29). However, it also portrays God the Father, God the Son, and God the Holy Spirit as three separate Persons who do not have the same roles. At first glance, a person may try to think about God as 1 + 1 + 1, which added together comes out to three. However, it is a better illustration of the Trinity to think of this doctrine as 1 x 1 x 1, with the existence of three numbers equaling one. Consider this question: Who created the world? Answer? God did: the Father (Gen. 1:1), the Spirit (Gen. 1:2), and the Son (John 1:3). Or who raised Jesus from the dead? Answer? God did: the Father (Acts 3:15), the Son (John 2:19), and the Spirit (Rom. 8:11). In short, the Trinity is a mystery to our finite minds because God is transcendent; He is *not* an advanced human being. Despite our inability to understand all the nuances of the Trinity, this important teaching helps solve the dilemma of how God could be one in essence and yet three Persons at the same time.

Notes

1. *Teachings of Presidents of the Church: Spencer W. Kimball* (Salt Lake City: The Church of Jesus Christ of Latter-day Saints, 2006), 230; brackets and ellipses in original.

2. Larry Dahl, "The Morning Breaks, the Shadows Flee," *Ensign* (April 1997): 14–15. He quoted Talmage, *Articles of Faith*, 47–48.

3. Joseph Fielding Smith, ed., *Teachings of the Prophet Joseph Smith* (Salt Lake City: Deseret Book Co., 1938), 370, 372.

4. *Church News,* July 4, 1998, 2, from a member meeting in Leon, Mexico, March 11, 1998.

5. *Ensign* (November 2007): 40; italics and brackets in original. Holland failed to note that Thomas R. W. Longstaff, the author of the dictionary article he cited, also said that "the early stages of its development can be seen in the [New Testament]." Longstaff again reiterated this point when, in the same article, he wrote, "Nevertheless, . . . the presence of Trinitarian formulas in 2 Cor. 13:14 (which is strikingly early) and Matt. 28:19 indicate that the origin of this mode of thought may be found very early in Christian history," *Harper's Bible Dictionary* (Atlanta: Society of Bible Literature, 1985), 1098–99.

6. McConkie, *Answers*, 139. What makes McConkie's analysis especially confusing is his correct description of the *straw man* argument described on page 216: "To build a straw man, your critic takes something he knows he can pound the stuffing out of, and he attributes it to you as your belief. He then beats it up as evidence that the doctrines for the Church aren't true." McConkie does not show evidence that he truly understands the historical definition of the Trinity. By slamming this teaching in such a way, he commits the very error that he derides LDS critics for making, which is a faulty attempt to make the opponent's argument look silly (i.e., "Christ became his own Father").

7. Robert L. Millet, *A Different Jesus? The Christ of the Latter-day Saints* (Grand Rapids: Eerdmans, 2005), 171.

8. "Are Mormons Christian?," The Church of Jesus Christ of Latter-Day Saints, accessed May 29, 2014, https://www.lds.org/topics/christians.

9. J. N. D. Kelly, *Early Christian Doctrines* (New York: HarperSanFrancisco, 1978), 89.

10. Brown, *Heresies*, 20.

11. White, *The Forgotten Trinity: Recovering the Heart of Christian Belief* (Minneapolis: Bethany House, 1998), 26.

12. Harrell, *"This Is My Doctrine,"* 114.

13. Rex E. Lee, *What Do Mormons Believe?* (Salt Lake City: Deseret Book Co., 1992), 21.

14. These verses in Isaiah are similar when the King James Version and Joseph Smith's Inspired Version of the Bible are compared. This makes sense since Joseph Smith's view of the Godhead had not yet evolved into a plurality of gods. Moses 1:6 (PoGP) states that "there is no God beside me." Ironically, this is identical to the phrase used in Isaiah 44:6. Without supplying any supporting evidence, a church manual claims that this "should not be interpreted to mean that mankind does not have the eternal potential to become like God," *Pearl of Great Price Student Manual*, 4.

15. In a rebuttal to our use of these verses, one LDS apologetic site explains, "Let's understand the situation first. Zeezrom is a lawyer opposed to the Gospel. He tries to take Amulek into cross-examination. Every word Amulek says he tries to use against him. Would Zeezrom have understood a complex answer? Or would he have made a fool of Amulek? Would he have trampeled upon sacred beliefs? Anybody who has read that passage in Alma knows for sure that this was what Zeezrom intended. In giving a simple answer, even if it is not exact, Alma does not throw his pearls before the swine." See "Response to claims made in Chapter 3: The Trinity," *FairMormon*, accessed May 29, 2014, http://en.fairmormon.org/Criticism_of_Mormonism/Books/Mormonism_101/Index/Chapter_3. It seems that Zeezrom's question was simple. Is the reader of this Book of Mormon passage really supposed to believe that Amulek misled Zeezrom by saying "no" to his question about the existence of multiple gods in order not to be too complex? Or that he lied in order to "not throw his pearls before the swine"? These possibilities seem highly unlikely.

16. For more information on this topic, see chapter 15, "How do you justify the doctrine of the Trinity?" in our book *Answering Mormons' Questions* as well as White, *The Forgotten Trinity*.

17. *Doctrine and Covenants and Church History Seminary Student Study Guide* (Salt Lake City: The Church of Jesus Christ of Latter-day Saints, 2001), 147.

Part II

Examining the LDS Concept of Humankind

4 | Preexistence and the Second Estate

With all this in mind, can we account in any other way for the birth of some of the children of God in darkest Africa, or in flood-ridden China, or among the starving hordes of India, while some of the rest of us are born here in the United States? We cannot escape the conclusion that because of performance in our pre-existence some of us are born as Chinese, some as Japanese, some as Indians, some as Negroes, some as Americans, some as Latter-day Saints. These are rewards and punishments, fully in harmony with His established policy in dealing with sinners and saints, rewarding all according to their deeds.

Apostle Mark E. Petersen[1]

MORMONESE:

agency: The ability for spirits and humans to have freedom to choose between serving or disobeying God, whether in the first or second estates.

Council in Heaven: A meeting of the gods was called by God in the first estate to arrange for the creation and peopling of the earth as well as determining how humankind would be saved.

eternal life: The status given those who meet the conditions for godhood.

eternal progression: Three stages: the first estate (premortality or preexistence), the second estate (mortality), and the third estate (immortality).

exaltation: Synonymous with eternal life.

first estate (preexistence): Also called premortality, the place where spirits existed with our heavenly parents: God the Father and Heavenly Mother. One third of God's spirit offspring were cast out of God's presence because they chose Lucifer, not Jesus, as the savior of the world. The other two thirds of these spirits received physical bodies on earth.

second estate (mortality): Also known as mortal probation, a time of testing for humans to prove their obedience to God the Father.

third estate (postmortality): Eternal existence in one of three levels of glory.

Where did I come from? Why am I here? Where am I going? These are questions every thoughtful human being has asked. The Bible gives much evidence about the final destiny of humankind. However, little is written about our existence before birth. Perhaps this is because there is nothing to talk about, since we did not exist. Mormon leaders, on the other hand, have built an entire doctrine around the idea that, like God, men and women have eternally existed since before the beginning of this world.[2]

The First Estate: Preexistence

The teaching of preexistence (also called premortality) says that "prior to their birth into mortality, all people were begotten spirit children of God and lived with him."[3] In fact, the *Ensign* magazine reports that "of all the major Christian churches, only The Church of Jesus Christ of Latter-day Saints teaches that the human race lived in a premortal existence with God the Father and His Son, Jesus Christ."[4] Seventy Lawrence E. Corbridge explained, "Everything did not begin at birth. You lived before the presence of God as His son or daughter and prepared for this mortal life."[5]

Seventy Adhemar Damiani wrote, "Before this world was organized, we had spirit bodies and lived in a premortal world with Heavenly Father, the father of our spirits. We knew Him personally just as He knows us. He desired that we become as He is—having eternal life and exaltation."[6]

Everything that is living existed in the preexistence:

A distinctive LDS teaching today regarding preexistence is that all living things—humans, animals, plant life, and even the earth itself—had a preexistence as spirits. The idea that the trillions upon trillions of insects and noxious weeds have spirits that existed for aeons prior to their fleeting and seemingly insignificant existence on earth is a curious thought. Even more astounding is the notion that they will be resurrected to immortal glory at some unspecified time in the future.[7]

In an April 2013 general conference talk titled "Your Wonderful Journey Home," Dieter F. Uchtdorf, a member of the First Presidency, taught:

> Back in that first estate, you knew with absolute certainty that God existed because you saw and heard Him. You knew Jesus Christ, who would become the Lamb of God. You had faith in Him. And you knew that your destiny was not to stay in the security of your premortal home. As much as you loved that eternal sphere, you knew you wanted and needed to embark on a journey. You would depart from the arms of your Father, pass through a veil of forgetfulness, receive a mortal body, and learn and experience things that hopefully would help you grow to become more like Father in Heaven and return to His presence.[8]

Uchtdorf claims that every person born on the earth existed in this first estate:

> Nevertheless, everyone you see around you—in this meeting or at any other place, today or at any other time—was valiant in the premortal world. That unassuming and ordinary-looking person sitting next to you may have been one of the great figures you loved and admired in the sphere of spirits. You may have been such a role model yourself! Of one thing you can be certain: every person you see—no matter the race, religion, political beliefs, body type, or appearance—is family.[9]

This unique teaching can be traced to Moses 3:5 (PoGP), which credits God with saying, "For I, the Lord God, created all things, of which I have spoken, spiritually, before they were naturally upon the face of the earth." Heavenly Father became the God of this earth as a result of his worthiness demonstrated on another planet. As far as the creation of this earth goes, his firstborn spirit son Jesus was aided by "many of the noble and great spirit children of the Father." These included Michael (the preincarnate Adam), Enoch, Noah, Abraham, Moses, Peter, James, John, and even Joseph Smith![10]

According to Mormonism, agency prevailed in heaven, which meant that the spirits had a choice.

> In our premortal life we had moral agency. One purpose of earth life is to show what choices we will make (see 2 Nephi 2:15–16). If we were forced to choose the right, we would not be able to show what we would choose for ourselves. Also, we are happier doing things when we have made our own choices. Agency was one of the principal issues to arise in the premortal Council in Heaven. It was one of the main causes of the conflict between the followers of Christ and the followers of Satan.[11]

Apostle Robert D. Hales described Satan's desire to change God's plan delivered to humankind in the preexistence:

> We recognize that when God the Eternal Father presented His plan to us at the beginning of time, Satan wanted to alter the plan. He said he would redeem all mankind. Not one soul would be lost, and Satan was confident he could deliver on his proposal. But there was an unacceptable cost—the destruction of man's agency, which was and is a gift given by God.[12]

Everyone on this earth chose the plan offered by Jesus. Hales explained, "But think of it: in our premortal state we chose to follow the Savior Jesus Christ! And because we did, we were allowed to come to earth."[13] In fact, "Only those who accepted Jesus to be their Savior can have bodies of flesh and bones. We know, because we have bodies of flesh and bones, that we accepted Jesus to be our Savior. We chose the right things in heaven."[14]

As a result of his rebellion, "Lucifer, a spirit in a position of authority in the premortal life, was cast out of God's presence and became Satan because he sought to exalt himself above God and rule over Heavenly Father's other children."[15] One-third of the preexistent spirits who were not wise enough to side against Lucifer will never be worthy of receiving a body on earth and will be forever doomed.

With all of this said, it is worth noting how the doctrine of preexistence was not a teaching during the first few years of the LDS Church's existence.

> Spirits or angels mentioned in the Bible as being with God in the first estate, including Lucifer and the spirits who followed him (Isa. 14:12–15; Jude 6; Rev. 12:3–4), were traditionally viewed as being a separate species from humans, not preexistent spirits. Biblical passages used today to support

preexistence were interpreted differently when cited by the Saints during the first decade of the Church.[16]

It wasn't until the middle of the 1830s that this teaching was further developed in LDS thought. Abraham 3:21–23 (PoGP) provides the best support of this doctrine. It reads in part:

> . . . for I rule in the heavens above, and in the earth beneath, in all wisdom and prudence, over all the intelligences thine eyes have seen from the beginning; I came down in the beginning in the midst of all the intelligences thou hast seen. Now the Lord had shown unto me, Abraham, the intelligences that were organized before the world was; and among all these there were many of the noble and great ones; And God saw these souls that they were good, and he stood in the midst of them, and he said: These I will make my rulers; for he stood among those that were spirits, and he saw that they were good; and he said unto me: Abraham, thou art one of them; thou wast chosen before thou wast born.

According to Mormonism, Abraham, the man divinely appointed as the "father of many nations," pleased God before the creation of the world, so he was chosen to fulfill God's will in the world. Aside from this passage, there is little written support for this important doctrine. This might be the reason why "the Latter-day Saints did not at first deduce the idea of preexistence from the biblical passages so frequently summoned today to prove it." It also does not appear "in the scriptural or other writings and recorded sermons of Joseph Smith."[17]

The Biblical Response to Preexistence

The Bible seems to be adamant that being born upon this earth had nothing to do with a "preexistent" life. Consider, for instance, the story of Jesus healing the blind man in John 9. Verses 1 through 3 read:

> As he passed by, he saw a man blind from birth. And his disciples asked him, "Rabbi, who sinned, this man or his parents, that he was born blind?" Jesus answered, "It was not that this man sinned, or his parents, but that the works of God might be displayed in him." (ESV)

Another passage that ought to be considered is Romans 9:9–12, which indicates that Jacob and Esau had "done nothing either good or bad" prior to their birth "in order that God's purpose of election might continue" (ESV). Notice how neither the blind man nor Jacob and Esau were rewarded or punished based on their good or bad works in a "preexistent" life. According to Mormonism, people are born on this earth based on their performance in a previous life. According to the Bible, life's circumstances are not random; God's sovereignty and His glory are what matters! As Jesus and Paul argued, it is impossible to point to a previous existence to support a mortal's status or destiny.

Certain biblical passages have been used by Latter-day Saints to support the doctrine of premortality, though they have to be taken out of their context to do so. One commonly used proof text is Jeremiah 1:5, which says, "Before I formed thee in the belly I knew thee; and before thou camest forth out of the womb I sanctified thee, and I ordained thee a prophet unto the nations." This verse emphasizes God's foreknowledge ("I knew thee"), *not* humanity's previous knowledge of God. Many LDS leaders have also referred to the book of Job for support of the pre-existence. In Job 38:4, God questions Job and rebukes him for his pride, asking, "Where wast thou when I laid the foundations of the earth?" When God formed the world, Job 38:7 says, "The sons of God shouted for joy." *Gospel Principles* explains, "When we lived as spirit children with our heavenly parents, our Heavenly Father told us about His plan for us to become more like Him. We shouted for joy when we heard His plan (see Job 38:7)."[18]

BYU professor Charles R. Harrell questions this common LDS interpretation when he writes:

> Most biblical scholars, however, see God's question as rhetorical and intended to highlight the fact that Job was nowhere around during the creation. The whole tenor of the Lord's query, when read in context with the entire chapter, is to emphasize the insignificance and fleeting nature of human existence. The Lord does tell Job, however, that the "sons of God" were there and "shouted for joy" (Job 38:7), but there is no indication that Job was numbered among them.[19]

In effect, Job was reminded by God that he wasn't even in existence when God created the world. Just as the clay should not talk back to the potter, so too Job had no business questioning God's work (compare Jer. 18:1–6 with Rom. 9:18–26).

Another verse often brought up is Ecclesiastes 12:7, which states that "the spirit shall return unto God who gave it." The Mormon who holds to the doctrine of preexistence assumes that this is referring to the second leg of a "round trip." This passage, though, merely shows how life exists beyond death. One would have to approach this verse with a preconceived notion of preexistence to draw this conclusion. According to Zechariah 12:1, God gave each person a spirit, so certainly the spirit will return to Him for judgment. It does not imply that humans existed before their mortal existence.

While the Bible does show how all humans are creations of God, becoming a part of His family requires faith in the redemptive work of Jesus Christ. Paul wrote in Galatians 3:26, "For ye are all the children of God by faith in Christ Jesus." He also said in Romans 9:8, "This means that it is not the children of the flesh who are the children of God, but the children of the promise are counted as offspring" (ESV).

Even the Book of Mormon tends to discount the idea of preexistence. Ether 3:14 says, "Behold, I am Jesus Christ. I am the Father and the Son. In me shall all mankind have life, and that eternally, even they who shall believe on my name; and they shall become my sons and my daughters." A Mormon may argue that this only refers to a spiritual sonship. However, this objection has validity only if it can be demonstrated that the Book of Mormon teaches the LDS concept of the preexistence, which it does not.[20]

The Second Estate: Mortality

The "second estate" "refers to mankind's mortal existence on this earth. This estate is a probationary period in which individuals 'prepare to meet God.'"[21] The determining factor for where people are born is how they acted as spirits in the preexistence. In a "Q&A" section, another LDS resource explains,

> QUESTION. Then what determines where and when you are born?
> ANSWER. We don't know in detail all the factors that influence the circumstances into which we are born, but the prophets have clearly taught that the basic rule of obedience to law as the prerequisite for blessings holds true in this matter as well.
> QUESTION. Meaning that the kind of life we lived in the premortal existence influenced where we are now?
> ANSWER. Yes.[22]

Without a body, a spirit could never obtain godhood, which means eternal damnation. So the goal of each spirit would be to leave its Heavenly Father and Mother and graduate to being born as a human being on an earth to physical parents who were once spirits themselves.

All those who chose in the premortal life to follow Heavenly Father's plan gain a physical body by being born on this earth. During our mortal life, we are tested to see whether we are willing to live by faith and obey Heavenly Father's commandments when we are not in His physical presence.[23]

The goal for every human on this earth, then, is to merit eternal life, which can be obtained through obedience to God's commandments as taught by the LDS Church. Thus, it is taught, "Those who keep their second estate, accepting and obeying the gospel in mortality (or in the postmortal spirit world), will receive eternal glory from God."[24]

Until Mormons can show better proof of humanity's eternal existence, Christians will be unable to agree with this unbiblical teaching.

Discussion Questions

1. One LDS tract titled "Your Pre-Earth Life" explains that each person is "a descendant of God" and that God "is your Heavenly Father in a very literal sense. . . . You are the lineage of God." What are some biblical problems with the doctrine that everyone existed as spirits previously to birth on earth, and then each person was born in circumstances defined by good or bad actions done prior to birth? List any Bible verses that support your view.

2. Certain biblical passages are utilized by Latter-day Saints to support the doctrine of a premortal existence, including Jeremiah 1:5 and Job 38:7. Why are these not good references for support of the doctrine of premortality? Formulate an intelligent response to someone who insists that humans once existed as preexistent spirits.

3. If premortality did not take place and human beings did not know God before this world, would this be a major blow to Mormonism? Or could Mormonism still be true despite being wrong on this particular issue? Is there any unique doctrine of Mormonism that, if proven wrong, would undermine the entire religion?

Final Thought

A Mormon may feel very strongly about the doctrine of preexistence because it seems to explain the origins of humankind while providing a reason for why people are born into either good or bad circumstances. This is very similar to the idea of reincarnation, as people in the Eastern religious system believe they bring the previous life's "karma" with them; the goal is to accumulate as much good karma as possible into the next life, all of which is based on one's merits. In Mormonism, a person is born upon the earth in circumstances based on personal "merit" from the preexistence. This world is therefore a place for faithful people to keep the commandments and endure to the end, with the hope that their obedience will qualify the Latter-day Saint for eternal life. Jesus, Paul, and the writers of the Bible seem to reject any possibility of premortality. If this is the case, the idea of preexistence should be rejected as heretical.

Notes

1. Mark E. Petersen, "Race Problems as They Affect the Church," August 27, 1954, 11. To read this speech, see www.mormonhandbook.com/storage/media/Mark_E_Petersen-Race_Problems_as_They_Affect_The_Church.pdf.

2. In a review of our original edition, Mormon apologist Allen Wyatt acknowledged, "It can be stated right up front that the authors do a fairly good job of concisely stating the views of the LDS Church in relation to preexistence and the plan of salvation." See John Divito, response to Allen Wyatt, "Mormonism 201: Chapter 4—Preexistence," Mormonism Research Ministry, http://www.mrm.org/topics/rebuttals-rejoinders/mormonism-201/pre-existence-wyatt.

3. Robert L. Millet et al. *LDS Beliefs: A Doctrinal Reference* (Salt Lake City; Deseret Book Co., 2011), 498. This event presupposes a "Heavenly Mother." As BYU professor Charles R. Harrell astutely points out, "The doctrine that God, through a procreative act involving a heavenly mother, is the literal father of our spirits expresses the most fundamental and important relationship between God and humankind in LDS theology. Surprisingly, however, nowhere is this doctrine explicitly taught in LDS scripture, neither is it found in any of Joseph Smith's recorded teachings." As far as the state of spirits before the first estate, Harrell says, "There is a difference of opinion, however, as to whether we always existed as individual intelligences or were part of a pool of intelligence that became individualized through spirit birth." Harrell, *"This Is My Doctrine,"* 138, 211.

4. *Ensign* (February 2006): 30.

5. *Ensign* (May 2014): 103.

6. *Ensign* (March 2004): 8–9.

7. Harrell, *"This Is My Doctrine,"* 212.

8. *Ensign* (May 2013): 126.

9. Ibid., 128.

10. Joseph Fielding Smith, *Doctrines of Salvation,* 1:74–75.

11. *Gospel Principles,* 17.

12. *Ensign* (May 2013): 86.

13. *Ensign* (November 2010): 25.

14. *Gospel Fundamentals,* 11.

15. *Old Testament Seminary Teacher Resource Manual* (Salt Lake City: The Church of Jesus Christ of Latter-day Saints, 2003), 168.

16. Charles R. Harrell in *BYU Studies* 28, no. 2 (spring 1988): 77.

17. Ibid., 77, 88.

18. *Gospel Principles,* 23.

19. Harrell, *"This Is My Doctrine,"* 203.

20. For more information on premortality, see chapter 13, "Didn't the prophet Jeremiah allude to the premortal existence of mankind?" in our book *Answering Mormons' Questions.*

21. *Pearl of Great Price Student Manual,* 38–39.

22. *The Life and Teachings of Jesus and His Apostles Course Manual: Religion 211–212* (Salt Lake City: The Church of Jesus Christ of Latter-day Saints, 1979), 255.

23. *Endowed from on High: Temple Preparation Seminary Teacher's Manual* (Salt Lake City: The Church of Jesus Christ of Latter-day Saints, 2003), 4.

24. *Pearl of Great Price Teacher Manual,* 44.

5 | The Fall

One of these days, if I ever get where I can speak to Mother Eve, I want to thank her for tempting Adam to partake of the fruit. . . . If she hadn't had that influence over Adam, and if Adam had done according to the commandment first given him, they would still be in the Garden of Eden and we would not be here at all. We wouldn't have come into this world. So the commentators made a great mistake when they put in the Bible . . . "man's shameful fall."

President Joseph Fielding Smith [1]

While Christianity has always viewed the fall of Adam and Eve in the Garden of Eden[2] as a tragic event, the LDS Church describes it as "a vital and planned step in our progression to become like our Heavenly Father."[3] *Gospel Principles* states,

Some people believe Adam and Eve committed a serious sin when they ate of the tree of knowledge of good and evil. However, latter-day scriptures help us understand that their Fall was a necessary step in the plan of life and a great blessing to all of us. Because of the Fall, we are blessed with physical bodies, the right to choose between good and evil, and the opportunity to gain eternal life. None of these privileges would have been ours had Adam and Eve remained in the garden.[4]

The Fall of Adam and Eve

According to church manuals:

- "Adam and Eve were chosen to be the first of Heavenly Father's children to come to earth and were placed in the Garden of Eden. At that time, their bodies were not mortal."[5]
- "Adam and Eve chose to eat the fruit that God had forbidden them to eat. As a result, they were separated from God's presence. This separation is called spiritual death. They became mortal, which means that their physical bodies would eventually die. They also became able to have children. The change to the mortal condition is called the Fall."[6]
- "After being taught the plan of salvation and being baptized, Adam and Eve had the Holy Ghost come upon them and they began to prophesy. Both understood the purpose for the Fall and rejoiced in the Lord's plan."[7]

Without this event, preexistent spirits would never have the chance to take on fleshly bodies. Moses 5:10–11 (PoGP) says:

And in that day Adam blessed God and was filled, and began to prophesy concerning all the families of the earth, saying: Blessed be the name of God, for because of my transgression my eyes are opened, and in this life I shall have joy, and again in the flesh I shall see God. And Eve, his wife, heard all these things and was glad, saying: Were it not for our transgression we never should have had seed, and never should have known good and evil, and the joy of our redemption, and the eternal life which God giveth unto all the obedient.

The joint decision by Adam and Eve to disobey God has been commended by LDS leaders since the very beginning. It is claimed that it would have been tragic if Adam had obeyed God's command to abstain from the fruit of the Tree of Knowledge:

> The Fall of Adam and Eve was not a mistake or a surprise. Had they not chosen to become mortal, neither they nor the rest of Heavenly Father's children could progress to become like God (see 2 Nephi 2:22–25). The Fall was a necessary part of the plan, but there are some negative consequences from which we need to be saved.[8]

In essence, a person could say that Adam played just as important a role as Jesus Christ in the progression of humankind. Without Adam, nobody who existed from Cain and Abel to the generations of today would have been able to receive bodies from the preexistence. The act of transgression by Adam and Eve in the Garden of Eden was an absolute necessity to allow spirit bodies to unite with physical bodies on the earth.

BYU professor Robert L. Millet wrote:

> The Latter-day Saint view of the scenes in Eden is remarkably optimistic when compared to traditional Christian views. We believe that Adam and Eve went into the Garden of Eden to fall, that their actions helped "open the way of the world," and that the Fall was as much a part of the foreordained plan of the Father as was the very Atonement.[9]

Chastising those who might believe that the fall was a negative act, Seventy Bruce Hafen gave a talk titled "The Atonement: All for All" at the April 2004 general conference, explaining:

> Since the fifth century, Christianity taught that Adam and Eve's Fall was a tragic mistake, which led to the belief that humankind has an inherently evil nature. That view is wrong—not only about the Fall and human nature, but about the very purpose of life. The Fall was not a disaster.[10]

Because of the fall, Adam and Eve allegedly received a number of benefits:

- "Adam and Eve were married for time and eternity by Heavenly Father."[11]
- "Adam, Eve, and their children were taught the gospel of Jesus Christ."[12]
- "Adam and Eve were the first Christians."[13]

A Biblical Response

Contrary to the LDS concept of the fall, the Bible shows that this event was the result of disobeying God. The Lord made it clear to Adam and Eve that they could eat from any tree in the Garden of Eden *except* the Tree of Knowledge (Gen. 2:16–17). If partaking of the forbidden fruit was necessary to propagate the human race, then it begs the question as to why God would command Adam and Eve to be fruitful and multiply (Gen. 1:28) before turning right around and forbidding them one of the prime ingredients to do so.

Eve was told by Satan in Genesis 3:5 that she would "be like God" and that she would not die. Some Mormons believe that Satan was telling the truth, even though Satan is called the "father of lies."[14] The physical consequences for the sin committed by Adam and Eve were spelled out in Genesis 3:16–19, including being cast out of the Garden of Eden as well as physical pain and suffering. There were also spiritual consequences to this event: eternal death, making a sinner of every human being (Ps. 51:5; Jer. 17:9; Rom. 3:10, 23; Eph. 2:2–3). Some may claim that Satan was telling a partial truth by saying that Adam and Eve could become "like god." Genesis 3:22 ("And the LORD God said, Behold, the man is become as one of us, to know good and evil") is then cited to show how knowing the difference between good and evil equates to being "like god."

Christian researcher John Divito astutely responded to this argument:

> However, Genesis 3:22 does not show that Adam and Eve will become gods as God is. The verse defines in what way Adam and Eve became "as one of us"; it was "to know good and evil" . . . the "knowledge of good and evil" was God's wisdom that was obtained unlawfully. As a result, they were removed from the Garden of Eden (where God was present and where they would have lived forever). They were also punished in other ways. This is not something to celebrate but to mourn. Even if Genesis 3:22 did mean that Adam and Eve were to be gods, there is still a problem with this text. In Genesis 3:22, God gives this statement as a completed fact. In other words, they had already become "as one of us." As a result, according to what Mormons claim this verse teaches, Adam and Eve became gods at the Fall. However, this would mean that they never went through the deification process, they did not obey the eternal celestial law, and they did not need Christ's atonement for this to occur. Mormons cannot, with consistency, admit that this text teaches what they say it does. Their argument would

prove too much. One must remember that the passage itself defines how humans are "as God"—to know good and evil. Mankind obtained wisdom that God had reserved for Himself. This is the only way it can be said that people are "as God."[15]

Becoming "like God" in Mormonism means godhood and eternal increase, which will be talked about in chapter 12. This verse in Genesis does *not* support the idea that people can become gods, in the sense of taking on the qualities of God; verse 22 merely shows how the eyes of the humans were opened, which was a consequence of the sin. To come up with an interpretation that "Adam fell that men might be" (2 Nephi 2:27, with the "be" referring to receiving bodies that is a necessary ingredient to become eligible for godhood) is nothing more than mere reading into the passage.

Here are some more ideas showing why Satan was not to be trusted:

- Satan is allowed to appear as a helpful servant. Second Corinthians 11:14 says, "And no marvel; for Satan himself is transformed into an angel of light." The Greek word for *transform* means to change in appearance, showing that Satan can mask his appearance and be perceived as innocent so that he might be believed.

- Satan does not want good to come to humanity. Mark 4:15 says, "And these are the ones along the path, where the word is sown: when they hear, Satan immediately comes and takes away the word that is sown in them" (ESV). Seeing how Job worshiped God, Satan sought to torment him to see if he would curse God. Satan even tempted Jesus in the desert to see if He would sin (Matt. 4:1–11).

- Satan is not trustworthy. Jesus told Peter, "Behold, Satan hath desired to have you, that he may sift you as wheat" (Luke 22:31). Peter warned all Christians about Satan when he wrote, "Be sober, be vigilant; because your adversary the devil, as a roaring lion, walketh about, seeking whom he may devour" (1 Pet. 5:8). James says the devil is to be resisted (James 4:7).

- Satan does not want to see the coming of God's kingdom but rather its downfall. Paul said that Satan "hindered" his work (1 Thess. 2:18). Revelation 12:9 says, "And the great dragon was cast out, that old serpent, called the Devil, and Satan, which deceiveth the whole world." One day he shall pay for his evil deeds (Rev. 20:7–10).

Although Jesus dealt with Satan, defeating the great adversary through His death and resurrection, this created being still seeks to disrupt God's plans. In light of this, we are instructed to be cautious when dealing with this formidable foe. As powerful as the archangel Michael was, Jude 9 says he "durst not bring against [Satan] a railing accusation, but said, The Lord rebuke thee."

It might be argued that Adam and Eve, as the first of the human creation, did not have the advantage of either Scripture or historical precedent to guide them in their decision. While this may be true, this does not discount the fact that Satan blatantly contradicted the direct command of God.

Sin versus Transgression

To minimize the severity of Adam's disobedience, Mormonism teaches that what Adam and Eve did "was a transgression of the law, but not a sin in the strict sense, for it was something that Adam and Eve had to do!"[16] Apostle Dallin Oaks differentiated between transgression and sin during a speech in general conference:

> Some acts, like murder, are crimes because they are inherently wrong. Other acts, like operating without a license, are crimes only because they are legally prohibited. Under these distinctions, the act that produced the Fall was not a sin—inherently wrong—but a transgression—wrong because it was formally prohibited.[17]

BYU professor Charles R. Harrell states, "In LDS thought, Adam and Eve's decision to transgress gradually came to be regarded even more favorably than an innocent error in judgment. It is now seen as a wise and righteous decision made with God's full commendation."[18] If transgression is not sin, it would seem strange that the apostle John wrote, "Whosoever committeth sin transgresseth also the law: for sin is the transgression of the law" (1 John 3:4). To insist that transgression is not sin certainly goes against the biblical definition.[19] Even Joseph Smith in D&C 132:26 listed transgression and sin in a way that makes them synonymous:

> Verily, verily, I say unto you, if a man marry a wife according to my word, and they are sealed by the Holy Spirit of promise, according to mine appointment,

and he or she shall commit any sin or transgression of the new and everlasting covenant whatever, and all manner of blasphemies, and if they commit no murder wherein they shed innocent blood, yet they shall come forth in the first resurrection, and enter into their exaltation; but they shall be destroyed in the flesh, and shall be delivered unto the buffetings of Satan unto the day of redemption, saith the Lord God.

The Bible never implies that Adam made a "wise and righteous decision" by disobeying God. In fact, the apostle Paul plainly stated that death was the result of Adam's *sin* when he wrote in Romans 5:12, 15:

Therefore, just as sin came into the world through one man, and death through sin, and so death spread to all men because all sinned. . . . But the free gift is not like the trespass. For if many died through one man's trespass, much more have the grace of God and the free gift by the grace of that one man Jesus Christ abounded for many. (ESV)

Paul compared Adam to Jesus by showing how death came to the world through the former and life through the latter. In verses 18–19, he added:

Therefore, as one trespass led to condemnation for all men, so one act of righteousness leads to justification and life for all men. For as by the one man's disobedience the many were made sinners, so by the one man's obedience the many will be made righteous. (ESV)

Notice the phrase "by the one man's [Adam] disobedience the many were made sinners [not merely *transgressors*]." Since becoming a sinner entitles one to death (Rom. 3:23; 6:23), these verses from Romans 5 effectively show that the disobedient act in the Garden of Eden was not a "wise choice."

Discussion Questions

1. According to the Book of Mormon, "Adam fell that men might be." Is this teaching consistent with what is taught in the Bible?
2. What Christians call "sin" has been called a "fall forward" by some Mormons. What do they mean by this? Read Romans 5:12–21 and summarize how Paul described this fall and how Jesus was able to overcome its effects.

3. Some Mormons have tried to use the word "transgression" instead of "sin" to soften the abruptness of the LDS teaching on the fall. Why should renaming the cause of the fall not minimize its severity?

Final Thought

In Romans chapter 5, Paul explained how sin caused death. He said that "just as sin came into the world through one man, and death through sin, and so death spread to all men because all sinned." In verse 15, Paul shows that Jesus's sacrifice trumps original sin: "For if many died through one man's trespass, much more have the grace of God and the free gift by the grace of that one man Jesus Christ abounded for many" (ESV). While Mormonism teaches that the fall was necessary for the preexistent spirits to be able to obtain bodies, there is no biblical support for such a notion. The fall certainly did not take God by surprise, yet it should not be celebrated as a necessary event in order for humans to exist on earth.

Notes

1. "Adam's Role in Bringing Us Mortality," *Ensign* (January 2006): 52; ellipses in original.

2. Mormon leaders have taught that the Garden of Eden was located in what is today the state of Missouri. President Joseph Fielding Smith said in *Doctrines of Salvation,* 3:74: "In accord with the revelations given to the Prophet Joseph Smith, we teach that the Garden of Eden was on the American continent located where the City Zion, or the New Jerusalem, will be built. When Adam and Eve were driven out of the Garden, they eventually dwelt at a place called Adam-ondi-Ahman, situated in what is now Daviess County, Missouri."

3. Ridges, *Mormon Beliefs and Doctrines Made Easier*, 24.

4. *Gospel Principles*, 29.

5. *Endowed from on High*, 3.

6. Ibid., 3–4.

7. *Old Testament Student Manual: Genesis–2 Samuel: Religion 301* (Salt Lake City: The Church of Jesus Christ of Latter-day Saints, 2003), 52.

8. *Old Testament Seminary Teacher Resource Manual*, 15.

9. *Ensign* (January 1994): 10.

10. *Ensign* (May 2004): 97.

11. *Pearl of Great Price Teacher Manual*, 17.

12. Ibid., 21.

13. Ibid., 22.

14. John 8:44 says, "Ye are of your father the devil, and the lusts of your father ye will do. He was a murderer from the beginning, and abode not in the truth, because there is no truth in him. When he speaketh a lie, he speaketh of his own: for he is a liar and the father of it." Even 2 Nephi 9:9 in the Book of Mormon agrees that Satan is the "father of lies."

15. John Divito, response to Kevin Graham, "Mormonism 201: Chapter 5—The Fall," Mormonism Research Ministry, http://www.mrm.org/topics/rebuttals-rejoinders/mormonism-201/fall-graham.

16. *Pearl of Great Price Student Manual*, 13. See also Smith, *Doctrines of Salvation*, 1:114–15.

17. *Ensign* (November 1993): 73.

18. Harrell, *"This Is My Doctrine,"* 253.

19. For instance, Exodus 34:7 lists iniquity, transgression, and sin as being synonymous. Psalm 32:1 and Micah 6:7 also follow this pattern.

6 | Apostasy

The churches of the world are trying, in their way, to bring peace into the hearts of men. They are possessed of many virtues and many truths, and accomplish much good, but they are not divinely authorized. Neither have their priests been divinely commissioned. The Latter-day Saints are the only ones who bear the authority of our Heavenly Father to administer in the ordinances of the Gospel. The world has need of us.

President George Albert Smith [1]

Mormonism was founded on the premise that the authority initially given to the apostles by Jesus Christ was lost until Joseph Smith restored *true* Christianity in 1830.[2] Because it is believed that there was a complete loss of authority that took place soon after the death of Jesus's apostles, Smith and his establishment of the LDS Church in 1830 was a part of God's providence. Those calling themselves "Christian" outside the LDS Church do not possess the necessary authority to administer the ordinances required for salvation. In fact, in almost a condescending manner, it is taught, "Many in the Christian world are sincere, and their false doctrinal conclusions are not their own fault."[3]

As Apostle Neil L. Andersen put it in a general conference address:

> Some ask, "Aren't there many of other faiths who love Christ?" Of course there are! However, as members of The Church of Jesus Christ of Latter-day Saints, having a witness of His reality not only from the Bible but also from the Book of Mormon; knowing His priesthood has been restored to the earth; having made sacred covenants to follow Him and received the gift of the Holy Ghost; having been endowed with power in His holy temple; and being part of preparing for His glorious return to the earth, we cannot compare what we are to be with those who have not yet received these truths.[4]

Where Did All the Christians Go?

Because there was this perceived loss of authority in the Christian churches, Mormonism teaches that a restoration was needed. When the teenage Joseph Smith began to search for religious truth, he claimed that God told him to not join any of the churches because

> all their creeds were an abomination in his sight; that those professors were all corrupt; that: "they draw near to me with their lips, but their hearts are far from me, they teach for doctrines the commandments of men, having a form of godliness, but they deny the power thereof." He again forbade me to join with any of them.[5]

Gospel Principles explains how the authority was lost:

- "One by one, the Apostles were killed or otherwise taken from the earth. Because of wickedness and apostasy, the apostolic authority and priesthood keys were also taken from the earth. The organization that Jesus Christ had established no longer existed, and confusion resulted. More and more error crept into Church doctrine, and soon the dissolution of the Church was complete. The period of time when the true Church no longer existed on earth is called the Great Apostasy. Soon pagan beliefs dominated the thinking of those called Christians. The Roman emperor adopted this false Christianity as the state religion. The church was very different from the Church Jesus organized. It taught that God was a being without substance. . . . It was the Church of Jesus Christ no longer; it was a church of men."[6]

- "After the Savior ascended into heaven, men changed the ordinances and doctrines that He and His Apostles had established. Because of apostasy, there was no direct revelation from God. The true Church was no longer on the earth. Men organized different churches that claimed to be true but taught conflicting doctrines. There was much confusion and contention over religion. The Lord had foreseen these conditions of apostasy, saying there would be 'a famine in the land, not a famine of bread, nor a thirst for water, but of hearing the words of the Lord. . . . They shall . . . seek the word of the Lord, and shall not find it' (Amos 8:11–12)."[7]

- "The Savior told him not to join any church because the true Church was not on the earth. He also said that the creeds of present churches were 'an abomination in his sight' (Joseph Smith—History 1:19; see also verses 7–18, 20)."[8]

A student manual for missionaries says,

Without revelation or priesthood authority, false doctrines began to be taught and the true Church of Jesus Christ was lost. God allowed truth, as well as His priesthood authority, ordinances, and Church organization to be taken once again from the earth because of the apostasy of His children. This apostasy eventually led to the emergence of many churches. False ideas were taught and knowledge of the true character and nature of the Father, His Son, Jesus Christ, and the Holy Ghost was lost. The doctrine of repentance became distorted. Baptism and other ordinances and covenants were changed or forgotten. The gift of the Holy Ghost was no longer available. This period of time when the true Church no longer existed on the earth has come to be known as the Great Apostasy. It lasted until the Restoration through the Prophet Joseph Smith.[9]

Lost in the Great Apostasy were "the priesthood and its keys, or directing power, the institutional power to perform saving ordinances," as well as the ability to "learn the mind of God, and interpret scripture."[10] Mormonism does not pinpoint when this all took place, although one LDS writer said that "it would have been after the death of the apostles and long before the Council of Nicaea in A.D. 325."[11] The gospel is then said to have been restored through the work of the LDS Church:

> The fullness of the gospel has been restored, and the true Church of Jesus Christ is on the earth again. No other organization can compare to it. It is not the result of a reformation, with well-meaning men and women doing all in their power to bring about change. It is a restoration of the Church established by Jesus Christ. It is the work of Heavenly Father and His Beloved Son. As a member of The Church of Jesus Christ of Latter-day Saints, you can receive blessings that were absent from the earth for almost 2,000 years.[12]

The Predicted "Apostasy"

The New Testament warned that a time would come when people would turn from the true faith and give heed to "seducing spirits, and doctrines of devils" (1 Tim. 4:1). Writing to the Thessalonian church, Paul said, "Let no man deceive you by any means: for that day [the return of Christ] shall not come, except there come a falling away first" (2 Thess. 2:3).

Jesus Himself warned the fledgling church to be aware of false prophets. He said that these prophets would be like wolves in sheep's clothing, seeking those whom they could devour. Impersonators would show great signs and wonders in order to make themselves look authentic in their attempt to deceive the people (Matt. 7:15; 24:24). Peter added that these false prophets would introduce "damnable heresies" and deny God (2 Peter 2:1). Many zealous LDS members have used these passages to describe what they call "modern Christianity," but in light of all the unbiblical teachings brought forth by LDS teachers, what guarantee can Mormons give that these passages are not talking about them?

While *some* apostasies were certainly predicted,[13] a *complete* apostasy where God's authority fully left the earth was never predicted or implied. In 1 Timothy 4:1–3 Paul said a time would come when "some" would depart from the faith. Charles R. Harrell agrees that the Mormon explanation of the apostasy verses tends to overreach the New Testament texts, saying "in understanding Paul's comment to the Ephesians in Acts [20:29–30], it is significant that he would later write to Timothy at Ephesus prophesying that only '*some* shall depart from the faith' (1 Tim. 4:1; emphasis mine). Even assuming that Paul anticipated an entire overthrow of the flock at Ephesus, it isn't clear that he intended his comment for the entire church."[14]

A passage that goes against the complete apostasy theory is Matthew 16:18. It reads, "And I say also unto thee, That thou art Peter, and upon this rock I will build my church; and the gates of hell shall not prevail against it." Because the literal meaning would eliminate the "loss of keys" for the "primitive" Christian church, many Mormons choose to spiritualize this otherwise straightforward verse. For instance, the *Encyclopedia of Mormonism* says:

> The Savior's reference to the "gates of hell" (Hades, or the spirit world; Matt. 16:18) indicates, among other things, that God's priesthood power will penetrate hell and redeem the repentant spirits there. Many have been, and many more will yet be, delivered from hell through hearing, repenting, and obeying the gospel of Jesus Christ in the spirit world after the death of the body.[15]

President Harold B. Lee wrote:

> The gates of hell would have prevailed if the gospel had not been taught to the spirits in prison and to those who had not had ample opportunity to receive the gospel here in its fulness. It would have prevailed if there was not a vicarious work for the dead . . . [or] other vicarious work pertaining to the exaltation which those who accept the gospel might receive, both ordinances for the living and for the dead.[16]

While no one will argue that Peter's response was a result of God's intervention,[17] there is no other passage lending support to the idea that the rock in Matthew 16:18 is revelation. However, the New Testament does support the idea that Christ is the rock upon which the church is built. In Ephesians 2:20, Paul states that Christ Himself is the cornerstone, a rock or stone placed in the corner of a proposed building on which all the other stones must align. The "apostles and prophets" do not necessarily mean offices, as the LDS Church implies; rather this phrase encompasses the teachings of the biblical prophets and the apostles.

In 1 Corinthians 3:10–11, Paul says that the wise master builder builds on the foundation of Christ Himself. In saying this, he warned others who also build on this foundation to "take heed" how they did so. This conclusion (that Christ is the rock) seems to more adequately explain what Peter said in his answer to Christ's question in Matthew 16:15. Peter declared that Jesus was the Christ, the Son of the living God. Because the true church is based on Christ, His sovereign protection would never allow its death; hence, the expression, "the gates of hell [or Hades] would not prevail against it."[18]

The Priesthood in Mormonism

Quoting from a church handbook, Apostle Dallin H. Oaks explained at a general conference: "Priesthood keys are the authority God has given to priesthood [holders] to direct, control, and govern the use of His priesthood on earth. Every act or ordinance performed in the Church is done under the direct or indirect authorization of one holding the keys for that function."[19] Those who have been ordained to the LDS priesthoods also have priesthood authority, as *Gospel Principles* explains,

> We must have priesthood authority to act in the name of God when performing the sacred ordinances of the gospel, such as baptism, confirmation, administration of the sacrament, and temple marriage. If a man does not have the priesthood, even though he may be sincere, the Lord will not recognize ordinances he performs.[20]

If there was no proper authority after the apostles until the time of Joseph Smith, then there must not have been the proper authority on earth to hold the priesthood. This is the reason why Mormonism teaches that the priesthood from biblical times needed to be restored. President Wilford Woodruff taught,

> No man has authority from God to administer to the children of men the ordinances of life and salvation [except] by the power of the Holy Priesthood. The power of that Priesthood is with the Latter-day Saints.[21]

Joseph Smith and Oliver Cowdery claimed to have received the Aaronic priesthood from John the Baptist on May 15, 1829, near Harmony, Pennsylvania:

> This ordination gave the two men authority to baptize, and they immediately performed that ordinance for one another in the Susquehanna River. The Prophet Joseph Smith had received no previous revelations authorizing him to baptize; to perform that ordinance properly required specific authorization

from God. The return of John to bestow the Aaronic priesthood confirmed that divine authority had been lost from the earth and that a heavenly visitation was necessary to restore it.[22]

The Melchizedek priesthood was also promised to Cowdery and Smith by John the Baptist at the bestowing of the Aaronic priesthood, as explained by the *Encyclopedia of Mormonism*:

> Sometime before June 14, 1829, the Lord instructed Joseph Smith and Oliver Cowdery concerning their ordination as elders, which is a Melchizedek Priesthood office (HC 1:60–61). Furthermore, when Peter, James, and John appeared to Joseph and Oliver, they ordained them also as apostles (D&C 27:12) and committed to them "the keys of the kingdom, and of the dispensation of the fulness of times" (D&C 128:20; cf. 27:13).[23]

While a woman cannot hold the priesthood by herself, it has been taught in recent years that she can still have "priesthood authority." In an October 2013 general conference message, Apostle Neil L. Andersen explained, "We sometimes overly associate the power of the priesthood with men in the Church. The priesthood is the power and authority of God given for the salvation and blessing of all—men, women, and children."[24] Using "Church callings" such as missionary work as his example, Apostle Oaks stated that a female "is given priesthood authority to perform a priesthood function. . . . Whoever functions in an office or calling received from one who holds priesthood keys exercises priesthood authority in performing her or his assigned duties. . . . The Lord has directed that only men will be ordained to offices in the priesthood. But, as various Church leaders have emphasized, men are not 'the priesthood.' Men hold the priesthood, with a sacred duty to use it for the blessing of all of the children of God."[25]

Blessings of the priesthood can be received vicariously through a woman's husband:

> A woman can receive the blessings of the Melchizedek Priesthood by receiving the ordinances of the gospel and by being married to a righteous priesthood holder. The blessings that come into a home when a man magnifies his priesthood affect his wife as much as they affect him. Perhaps the most important way a woman participates in the blessings of the priesthood is by receiving her endowment and being married in the temple.[26]

Still, women continue to be denied ordination to the LDS priesthood, which has angered some LDS feminists.[27]

Contrary to LDS teaching, the Bible shows that neither the Aaronic nor the Melchizedek priesthoods are available for believers today. The Aaronic priesthood was for the priests of the biblical temple, as defined in the books of Moses known as the Pentateuch. The New Testament shows no need for such a priesthood for Christian believers. As far as the Melchizedek priesthood, Charles R. Harrell sees the traditional LDS interpretation as an argument from silence by pointing out how

> Hebrews speaks of Christ being a "priest after the order of Melchizedek" (Heb. 5:6–10), but gives no indication that any of Jesus's disciples possessed this priesthood. There is no concept in Hebrews of a general order of the priesthood called the Melchizedek Priesthood. Christ alone is extolled as a priest in the "similitude of Melchizedek" (Heb. 7:15). Drawing on contemporary speculations regarding the king-priest Melchizedek, the writer of Hebrews explains that Melchizedek, as a type of Christ, had "neither beginning of days, nor end of life; but made like unto the Son of God; abideth a priest continually" (Heb. 7:3).[28]

As for the authority of the believers, 1 Peter 2:9 says they are part of "a chosen generation" and "a royal priesthood." The Christian is given the right to be called a child of God. Indeed, when speaking of believers, 1 John 3:2 says that "*now* are we the sons of God." First John 5:5 adds that only those who believe "that Jesus is the Son of God" have overcome the world. They, then, are the ones who have been given divine authority.

John the Apostle and the Three Nephites

Despite holding to a complete Christian apostasy, the Book of Mormon and LDS leaders have taught that three members of the "true church" are still living on the earth. In 3 Nephi 28:7, Jesus supposedly granted that three Nephite apostles would remain alive until He came again.[29] This passage reads:

> Ye shall never taste of death; but ye shall live to behold all the doings of the Father unto the children of men, even until all things shall be fulfilled according to the will of the Father, when I shall come in my glory with the powers of heaven.

101

Note carefully the phrase "when I shall come in my glory with the powers of heaven." No LDS leader has taught that this event has already taken place. Mormon scripture also teaches that the apostle John was to remain until Christ's Second Coming. In the introduction to *Doctrine & Covenants* Section 7, it says:

> Revelation given to Joseph Smith the Prophet, and Oliver Cowdery, at Harmony, Pennsylvania, April, 1829, when they inquired through the Urim and Thummim as to whether John, the beloved disciple, tarried in the flesh or had died. The revelation is a translated version of the record made on parchment by John and hidden up by himself.

It should be noted that it is not known whether Joseph Smith ever personally possessed such a parchment,[30] yet Smith commenced to "reveal" that John the Beloved would be given "power over death," and that he "may live and bring souls unto Christ."[31]

Some Latter-day Saints have used Mormon 1:13 in the Book of Mormon to say that God took the three Nephites away as a result of the wickedness that prevailed "upon the whole face of the land." Where exactly they were taken is not addressed in the passage, and it would seem to be presumptuous to insist they were somehow taken off the earth in light of the many statements from LDS leaders to the contrary. The following quotes from general authorities show their belief about how the three Nephites and John were to remain on earth and continue their mission until Christ reappeared:

President John Taylor:

> Also, John, the revelator, was permitted to live upon the earth until the Savior should come, and the Book of Mormon gives an account of three Nephites, who lived on this American Continent, who asked for the same privilege and it was granted to them.[32]

President Wilford Woodruff:

> The first quorum of apostles were all put to death, except John, and we are informed that he still remains on the earth, though his body has doubtless undergone some change. Three of the Nephites, chosen here by the Lord Jesus as his apostles, had the same promise—that they should not taste death until Christ came, and they still remain on the earth in the flesh.[33]

Apostle Franklin Dewey Richards told an April 1892 general conference audience:

> And these men that have never tasted death—the three Nephites and the Apostle John—are busy working to bring to pass righteousness and to carry out the purposes of God; it won't be long till we or our generations after us will see them and have fellowship with them.[34]

Apostle LeGrand Richards:

> In permitting these Three Nephites to tarry upon the earth until he, Jesus, should come in his glory, he must have had in mind some great things for them to accomplish in bringing about a fulfillment of his promises.[35]

Apostle Joseph B. Wirthlin:

> As a result of his perseverance and righteousness, he [Moroni] was ministered to by the Three Nephites, whom the Savior permitted to tarry until His second coming (see Morm. 8:11).[36]

The thought of a complete apostasy becomes a problem if we assume that these men were successful in making converts. If John and the Nephites did gain converts to their message, this certainly would seem to deny any such apostasy. In other words, the church really didn't cease to exist. If the word *complete* has any meaning when combined with *apostasy* in the English language, then there should not have been even one of these four individuals who remained through this alleged dark period of church history.

Mormon educator David J. Ridges stated that "three of the Savior's Nephite disciples or Apostles were translated and are still alive (3 Nephi 28:7). They will continue to serve here on earth until the Second Coming of Christ, when they will die and be resurrected."[37] Some LDS apologists have focused on the word *translated* and argue that, because their bodies were changed, the ability of these men to bestow the priesthood to others was stripped from them. If that was the case, then how could the apostle John participate in bestowing the Melchizedek priesthood to Joseph Smith? If none of their converts could ever hope to have the necessary priesthood authority for salvation, what difference would there be between the converts of these four men and the professing Christians who make up what Mormons call the apostate church?

Even if the four men could not bestow the priesthood in their translated state, this would have no bearing on their personal priesthood authority since the Mormon priesthood is supposed to be an "everlasting principle."[38] In other words, there would still be at least four priesthood-bearing individuals on the earth.[39]

Discussion Questions

1. Mormon leaders have claimed that there was a "Great Apostasy" and the authority of the church was lost soon after the death of the apostles. How important is this teaching for the Mormon Church? Why? And what reasons can you give your Mormon friend to show how God's authority was *not* lost and thus a restoration of Christianity was *not* needed?

2. The Bible says in 1 Peter 2:9 that believers hold "a royal priesthood." Before June 1978 when the policy was changed, males with black skin were not allowed to hold the LDS priesthood. Today women are prohibited from holding the priesthood. Thus, they depend on their husbands to receive "priesthood blessings." What is the problem with this scenario according to the Bible? And do you think the Mormon Church will ever change its policy just as it did with blacks?

3. Mormon leaders in the past have said that there are four apostles who would remain alive until the Second Coming. If this is true, then what is the dilemma for the Mormon who claims there was a "Great Apostasy"?

Final Thought

According to Joseph Smith—History 1:19 (PoGP), Mormonism's founder said he was told by God that "all" of Christianity's creeds "were an abomination in his sight." Because of this, a restoration of Christianity was supposedly needed. Mormons don't realize how offensive it is to say there was a "great" apostasy. After all, shouldn't Jesus be taken at His word when He said that He would be with His people "always, even unto the end of the world" (Matt. 28:20)? Fortunately for Christians, they no longer need a human priest because they have "one mediator between God and men, the man Jesus Christ" (1 Tim. 2:5). While there have been a variety of apostasies, the Christian can rest assured that God remains alive and well and continues to live among us.

Notes

1. *Teachings of Presidents of the Church: George Albert Smith*, 124–25.

2. According to Apostle L. Tom Perry, "It was the birth of the United States of America that ushered out the Great Apostasy, when the earth was darkened by the absence of prophets and revealed light. It was no coincidence that the lovely morning of the First Vision occurred just a few decades after the establishment of the United States," *Ensign* (December 2012): 29–30.

3. *Old Testament Student Manual: 1 Kings–Malachi: Religion 302* (Salt Lake City: The Church of Jesus Christ of Latter-day Saints, 2003), 166.

4. *Ensign* (November 2010): 41.

5. *Joseph Smith—History*, 1:19-20a in the *Pearl of Great Price*.

6. *Gospel Principles*, 92.

7. Ibid., 95; ellipses in original.

8. Ibid., 96.

9. *Missionary Preparation Student Manual: Religion 130* (Salt Lake City: The Church of Jesus Christ of Latter-Day Saints, 2005), 66.

10. Millet, et al. *LDS Beliefs*, 47. BYU professor Charles R. Harrell says that "throughout the nineteenth century and well into the twentieth century," early Mormonism emphasized an apostasy of "gospel perversion, spiritual darkness and loss of priesthood authority." Contemporary Mormonism, he explains, has shifted the concept of the apostasy "from a loss of spiritual gifts and truths to primarily a loss of priesthood authority." Harrell, *"This Is My Doctrine,"* 42–43.

11. McConkie, *Answers*, 19.

12. *True to the Faith*, 136.

13. These would be the result of persecution (Matt. 24:9–10), false teachers (Matt. 24:11), temptation (Luke 8:13), defective knowledge of Christ (1 John 2:19), moral lapse (Heb. 6:4–6), forsaking spiritual living (Heb. 10:25–31), and unbelief (Heb. 3:12).

14. Harrell, *"This Is My Doctrine,"* 37; brackets in original. See also 2 Peter 2:1–3, where Peter said many (not all) will follow the pernicious ways of false prophets.

15. *Encyclopedia of Mormonism*, s.v. "hell," 2:586. In order to explain Matthew 16:18, Mormons are compelled to spiritualize the passage. For instance, Apostle Orson Pratt stated "that the Church of Christ still exists in heaven and that the gates of hell have not prevailed against her," *Divine Authenticity of the Book of Mormon*, from a series of pamphlets (Liverpool, United Kingdom: n.p., 1851), 44. Many passages in the Doctrine and Covenants give the impression that the church spoken of in Matthew 16:18 now refers to the LDS Church (see sections 10:69, 18:1–5).

16. *Conference Reports* (April 1953): 26. See also *Teachings of Presidents of the Church: Harold B. Lee* (Salt Lake City: The Church of Jesus Christ of Latter-day Saints, 2000), 104.

17. First Corinthians 12:3 says, "Wherefore I give you to understand, that no man speaking by the Spirit of God calleth Jesus accursed: and that no man can say that Jesus is the Lord, but by the Holy Ghost."

18. For more information on the topic of apostasy, see chapter 8, "Didn't the Bible predict the apostasy of the Christian faith?" in our book *Answering Mormons' Questions*.

19. *Ensign* (May 2014): 49.

20. *Gospel Principles*, 67.

21. *Teachings of Presidents of the Church: Wilford Woodruff* (Salt Lake City: The Church of Jesus Christ of Latter-day Saints, 2004), 39.

22. Ludlow, ed., *Encyclopedia of Mormonism*, s.v. "Aaronic Priesthood," 1:4.

23. Ibid., "Melchizedek Priesthood," 2:886.

24. *Ensign* (November 2013): 92.

25. *Ensign* (May 2014): 51.

26. *Duties and Blessings of the Priesthood: Basic Manual for Priesthood Holders, Part* B (Salt Lake City: The Church of Jesus Christ of Latter-day Saints, 2000), 31, 33.

27. For example, a group called Ordain Women ("Mormon Women Seeking Equality and Ordination to the Priesthood") was formed in the spring of 2013; the leaders sponsored attempts to get hundreds of women admitted to the priesthood sessions at the fall 2013 and spring 2014 general conferences that are open only to men. The group's leader, Kate Kelly, was excommunicated by the LDS Church in June 2014.

28. Harrell, *"This Is My Doctrine,"* 376.

29. Although the Book of Mormon does not call these men "apostles," Apostle Bruce R. McConkie does so in *Mormon Doctrine,* 793.

30. The *Encyclopedia of Mormonism* says, "Although it is not known whether Joseph Smith actually had this document, he provided a translation of it," s.v. "Book of Abraham," 1:136.

31. Jesus did tell Peter, "If I will that he [John] tarry till I come, what is that to thee? follow thou me" (John 21:22). John gave a personal note in the next verse to head off any faulty interpretation of Jesus's statement: "Then went this saying abroad among the brethren, that that disciple should not die; yet Jesus said not unto him, He shall not die; but, If I will that he tarry till I come, what is that to thee?" This contradicts Joseph Smith's interpretation.

32. John Taylor, *Journal of Discourses*, ed. Watt, 18:308.

33. Wilford Woodruff, *The Discourses of Wilford Woodruff*, comp. G. Homer Durham (Salt Lake City: Bookcraft, 1946), 95.

34. Franklin Dewey Richards, *Millennial Star* 54, no. 32 (August 8, 1892): 510.

35. *Conference Reports of the Church of Jesus Christ of Latter-day Saints* (Salt Lake City: The Church of Jesus Christ of Latter-day Saints, April 1954), 56.

36. "Never Give Up," *Ensign* (November 1987): 8; brackets in original.

37. Ridges, *Mormon Beliefs and Doctrines Made Easier*, 330.

38. Millet et al. *LDS Beliefs*, 501.

39. For more information on the topic of authority, see chapter 11, "Where do you get your authority?" in our book *Answering Mormons' Questions*.

Part III

Examining the LDS Concept of Scripture

7 | The Bible

Some Christians, in large measure because of their genuine love for the Bible, have declared that there can be no more authorized scripture beyond the Bible. In thus pronouncing the canon of revelation closed, our friends in some other faiths shut the door on divine expression that we in The Church of Jesus Christ of Latter-day Saints hold dear: the Book of Mormon, the Doctrine and Covenants, the Pearl of Great Price, and the ongoing guidance received by God's anointed prophets and apostles. Imputing no ill will to those who take such a position, nevertheless we respectfully but resolutely reject such an unscriptural characterization of true Christianity.

Apostle Jeffrey R. Holland[1]

MORMONESE:

Bible: The sixty-six books—the same as Protestant Bibles. The King James Version is the officially accepted translation of the LDS Church.

The Bible is a perennial bestseller that is accepted by Christians the world over as being the authoritative Word of God. Faithful Christian missionaries throughout the world work full-time translating this book into new languages. While Christians uphold the Bible as the sole written authority for Christ's church, many Mormons have disparaged this Scripture even though it is a part of their official canon.

For example, some have said that the Bible's authority has been diluted over the years. This pessimism and the need for other scriptures to supersede the Bible can be traced to the Book of Mormon itself. First Nephi 13:28

says, "Wherefore, thou seest that after the book hath gone forth through the hands of the great and abominable church, that there are many plain and precious things taken away from the book, which is the book of the Lamb of God." Second Nephi 29:6 adds, "Thou fool, that shall say: A Bible, we have got a Bible, and we need no more Bible. Have ye obtained a Bible save it were by the Jews?"

The Bible—the Christian's Written Authority

According to Christian teaching, God's instructions were handed down through His prophets, apostles, and eyewitnesses. Sixty-six books written by dozens of men over a period of about fifteen hundred years make up this revelation known as the Bible.[2] Christians over the centuries have considered this collection of books to be extraordinary and, in fact, sacred. Christian theologian A. Berkeley Mickelsen wrote:

> Inspiration means the action of God in the lives and utterances of his chosen servants so that what they declare conveys to men what God wants men to know. The Scriptures are the inspired word of God because they represent all that God deemed it necessary to preserve from the past so that succeeding generations could know the truths he conveyed to men of earlier generations. Because the Bible is an inspired book, it is a unique book. The reason for its inspiration is to bring men into a living encounter with the living God. Hence the Bible came into existence for interaction and reflection—for good hard use.[3]

Speaking about the Old Testament, Paul wrote in 2 Timothy 3:16–17, "All Scripture is breathed out by God and profitable for teaching, for reproof, for correction, and for training in righteousness, that the man of God may be complete, equipped for every good work" (ESV). According to this verse, Scripture is useful for:

1. Teaching God's truths and the doctrines we are to believe
2. Rebuking others, such as Jesus's example with Lucifer in Matthew 4:1–11
3. Correcting one another when we stray from God's truth
4. Training for righteousness

110

The theatre in Ephesus talked about in Acts 19 has been excavated in modern-day Turkey. Although biblical archaeology cannot prove the Bible and its historicity, the evidence can assist us in better understanding the people, places, and events that are talked about in Christianity's holy book.

The Bible is more than just men's words, for it reveals God's voice to His people. As to how God's written Word was constructed, 2 Peter 1:20–21 says how "no prophecy of Scripture comes from someone's own interpretation. For no prophecy was ever produced by the will of man, but men spoke from God as they were carried along by the Holy Spirit" (ESV). The early church gave a stamp of authority to the writings of the apostles. This is documented in 2 Peter 3:15–16:

> And count the patience of our Lord as salvation, just as our beloved brother Paul also wrote to you according to the wisdom given him, as he does in all his letters when he speaks in them of these matters. There are some things in them that are hard to understand, which the ignorant and unstable twist to their own destruction, as they do the other Scriptures. (ESV)

Paul wrote in 1 Thessalonians 2:13, "And we also thank God constantly for this, that when you received *the word of God*, which you heard from us, you accepted it not as the word of men but as what it really is, the word of God, which is at work in you believers" (ESV). For the Mormon, authority rests not only in written scriptures but also in *modern-day* revelation. As one LDS writer explained, "We read both the Old and New Testaments by the light of modern revelation. To refuse that light is to read in the dark and to place ourselves and those we teach under condemnation."[4]

Apostle Dallin Oaks said:

> What makes us different from most other Christians in the way we read and use the Bible and other scriptures is our belief in continuing reve-lation. For us, the scriptures are not the ultimate source of knowledge, but what precedes the ultimate source. The ultimate knowledge comes by revelation.[5]

Even more disconcerting than this quote was a letter from the First Presidency that was printed on page three of the June 20, 1992 LDS *Church News*. It read in part, "The most reliable way to measure the accuracy of any biblical passage is not by comparing different texts, but by comparison with the Book of Mormon and modern-day revelations."

Transmission versus Translation

The *Ensign* magazine reported, "Today, English-speaking Church mem-bers use the Latter-day Saint edition of the King James Version of the Bible. Based on the doctrinal clarity of latter-day revelation given to the Prophet Joseph Smith, the Church has held to the King James Version as being doctrinally more accurate than recent versions."[6] Even though they may consider the King James Version to be more "doctrinally accurate," many Mormons still have doubts about their Bibles. As the eighth LDS Article of Faith says, the Bible can be trusted only "as far as it is trans-lated correctly." What does this mean? Translation means to take words from one language and put them into the words of another. If the Bible were true only as far as it is *translated* correctly, we would certainly agree. Unfortunately, those who mistakenly think the Bible cannot be trusted apparently do not understand how the Bible has been *transmitted* since the post-New Testament times.

The Bible was written primarily in Hebrew and Koine Greek. Anytime the words from one language are put into another—whether it is Spanish into English or French into Arabic—there is always the risk of losing something in the translation. It is doubtful that our many modern-day translations were produced by unprincipled people who wanted to keep God's truths hidden. In actuality, quite the opposite is true. The motivation behind a new translation is, in most cases, to give a clearer understanding of what God wants to reveal to His people. Granted, some translations do a better job at achieving this goal than others.

However, does Article Eight correctly state the problem the LDS Church has with the Bible? Some Mormons have recognized that the word translated as used in the Articles of Faith is not entirely correct. Knowledgeable Mormons who have studied the methods of translating languages admit that the transmission, not the translation, of the biblical texts concerns them.

Transmission refers to how the manuscripts were copied and handed down through the centuries. A number of Mormons contend that the manuscripts were corrupted, claiming that unscrupulous people had purposely left out "many plain and precious truths" and inserted their own erroneous philosophies. However, this is an argument from silence, since these same detractors cannot produce any untainted manuscripts against which to measure the "tainted" ones.

Although translations will differ, a good translation will go back to the most accurate manuscripts and then attempt to put the words of the Bible into an understandable language for the audience it addresses. Two translators of any written piece will differ in the choice of words, verb tense, and style. But if two good Spanish translators independently translate this morning's paper, most likely the basic message would be the same despite their numerous differences. There is no such thing as a *perfect* translation. The LDS Church leaders must certainly be aware of this, since their translators have often had to revise not only their English edition of the Book of Mormon but several foreign editions as well.[7]

When it comes to the transmission of the text, the Bible has much going for it. For example, consider the wealth of manuscript evidence for the New Testament:

> There are complete Greek texts of the NT from the fourth century, and many earlier papyri of parts of it have survived, some from as early as the middle of the second century. In all, we have over 5,000 Greek manuscripts of the NT, though the majority of these are later and of lesser value. There is also

a wide variety of manuscript evidence for the early versions in Latin, Syriac, and Coptic, as well as numerous citations from the NT books by early Christian writers whose works are preserved. The NT is thus vastly better attested than any other ancient literature. The works of Tacitus, by contrast, survive in only two incomplete manuscripts written many centuries after his time, between them covering only about half of what he is known to have written.[8]

Christian theologian Ron Rhodes lists some of the incredible statistics of the manuscript support for the Bible, including:

There are more than 24,000 partial and complete manuscript copies of the New Testament. . . . There are also some 86,000 quotations from the early church fathers and several thousand Lectionaries (church-service books containing Scripture quotations used in the early centuries of Christianity). . . . The Dead Sea Scrolls prove the accuracy of the transmission of the (Old Testament). In fact, in those scrolls discovered at Qumran in 1947, we have Old Testament manuscripts that date about a thousand years earlier (150 B.C.) than the other Old Testament manuscripts then in our possession (which dated to A.D. 900). The significant thing is that when one compares the two sets of manuscripts, it is clear that they are essentially the same, with very few changes. The fact that manuscripts separated by a thousand years are essentially the same indicates the incredible accuracy of the Old Testament's manuscript transmission.[9]

As far as the reliability of the Greek and Hebrew manuscripts that we have today, biblical scholar Bruce Metzger said:

The earlier copies are generally closer to the wording of the originals. The translators of the 1611 King James Bible, for instance, used Greek and Hebrew manuscripts from the twelfth and thirteenth centuries. Today Bible translators have access to Greek manuscripts from the third and fourth centuries and Hebrew manuscripts from the era of Jesus. We even have the Ryland's Papyrus, just a torn page with a few verses from John 18, that we can date between A.D. 100 and 150. So today we have access to a text of the Old and New Testaments that is more basic, more fundamental, less open to charges of scribal error or change.[10]

Responding to a question about most surviving New Testament manuscripts hailing from a century or two after the originals were written, Metzger said:

By contrast, our copies of other ancient writings, like those of Virgil or Homer, are often many hundreds of years later than their originals. In some of those writings, we have only one copy! The New Testament, on the other hand, has many copies. No key doctrine of the Christian faith has been invalidated by textual uncertainty. On the other hand, some passages have been affected. For example, take Mark 9:29. Jesus is explaining how he was able to cast out a demon, and in the earliest manuscripts, he is quoted as saying, "This kind can come out only by prayer." In the Greek manuscripts the KJV translators used, the two words "and fasting" are tacked on. I do not think that is an earth-shaking difference, but it is typical of the kind of changes we are talking about.[11]

How Do We Know Anything Is True?

Before Latter-day Saints unduly criticize the accuracy of the Bible,[12] perhaps they should first consider the following:

1. How do we know if James 1:5, the verse that Joseph Smith used to draw him to the "Sacred Grove," was indeed correct? For that matter, how can anyone trust other biblical proof texts used to support Mormonism? It would seem reasonable that whatever test for accuracy that could be applied to James 1:5 could also be applied to every other Bible verse as well.

2. If the LDS Church has a prophet who has direct communication with God, then it would seem plausible for him to fix these alleged errors. After all, D&C 107:92 states that one of the "gifts of God which he bestows upon the head of the church" is the role of translator.[13] If the God of Mormonism was able to help Smith translate the Book of Mormon from the golden plates, he could also be able to help the prophet with these alleged errors. Although the LDS Church does not officially publish the Joseph Smith Translation as a bound volume, Smith's alterations are included as footnotes and endnotes in the LDS-published version of the King James Bible. Many Mormons are unaware that Joseph Smith failed to "correct" many of the so-called problematic verses.

3. If Mormons want to scrutinize the small percentage of questionable material in the Bible—none of which affects essential

doctrine—shouldn't they also have a problem with the many changes made to the Book of Mormon over the years?[14]

Finally, we must understand that if a person were to use the Bible alone with no outside sources, it would be impossible to come away accepting the teachings of Mormonism. As BYU professor Charles R. Harrell writes,

> Few of the doctrines unique to Mormonism, however, are sufficiently elucidated in the Bible to be recognizable. Among these are doctrines of the preexistence, eternal marriage, and salvation for the dead. Referring to these and other distinctive Mormon doctrines, LDS scholar Terryl Givens observed, "In none of these cases, or a dozen others that could be mentioned, could one make a reasonable theological defense of the Prophet's ampler enactment of these principles and practices on the basis of the few paltry biblical allusions that exist."[15]

Perhaps this is the reason why Mormon leaders—while holding the Bible as a standard work—require other scriptures for understanding doctrine. An LDS.org Gospel Topics essay ("Are Mormons' Christian?") explains,

> But to claim that the Bible is the sole and final word of God—more specifically, the final written word of God—is to claim more for the Bible than it claims for itself. Nowhere does the Bible proclaim that all revelations from God would be gathered into a single volume to be forever closed and that no further scriptural revelation could be received.[16]

With a proverbial wave of the hand, the LDS leaders want to legitimize their additional scriptures at the expense of being able to trust the Bible. However, one's spiritual detector should go off when realizing the major differences between the basic tenets of the LDS religion—supposedly the "restored" gospel—and the message of the Bible. The best way to do biblical study is approach God's Word as a little child, with as few presuppositions as possible.[17] If you honestly see how the Bible is contradicted by LDS teaching, then we recommend running, not walking, away from such a religious institution, no matter how "Christian" it may sound.

Discussion Questions

1. One former Latter-day Saint once wrote to us to say, "Every single time I talk to a TBM ["true-believing Mormon"] about the things I discovered about Mormonism and the Book of Mormon, instead of defending the indefensible, they begin to try to tear down the Bible." Indeed, much ire can be directed toward the pages of the Bible by Latter-day Saints in their attempt to defend their faith. When Mormons say they believe the Bible only as far as it is "translated" correctly, they probably are referring to the transmission of the text. Why do you think so many Mormons critique the Bible's authenticity—even though it's part of their church's canon? Based on your study, is it possible to trust the Bible? Give reasons why or why not.

2. President Joseph F. Smith explained, "All members of the Church of Jesus Christ of Latter-day Saints should be as familiar as possible with the words that are recorded in the New Testament, especially with reference to those things spoken as recorded by the apostles, and the Savior Himself."[18] What advantages are there for a truth seeker to be "as familiar as possible with the words that are recorded in the New Testament"? For the Mormon, what could possibly happen by studying the New Testament books (say, the epistles) by themselves?

3. Suppose someone says that the Bible is filled with errors because corrupt translators incorporated their pagan ideas into the text. How can having a basic understanding of how the Bible came into existence enhance our ability to evangelize?

Final Thought

The most important tool in the Christian's arsenal when sharing the Christian faith with Latter-day Saints is the Bible. This is because Mormons also accept it to be Scripture, even though they might consider their other scriptural books to be more accurate. When we understand how the Bible was carefully transmitted throughout the centuries and see the care taken to preserve its message, we can rest assured that we can trust its words. The key, then, is to determine just what the Bible says and learn what God intends for people to know about Him and ultimate truth. Whenever in doubt about what you should say to a Latter-day Saint, go to your Bible and explain why you believe the way you do.

Notes

1. "My Words . . . Never Cease," *Ensign* (May 2008): 91.
2. We see no need to debate the validity of the apocryphal books in this book for the reason that Mormons, like Protestants, do not consider them authoritative. In D&C 91:3, Joseph Smith was supposedly told by God that "it is not needful that the Apocrypha should be translated" in his Inspired Version because, as the previous verse says, "there are many things contained therein that are not true, which are interpolations by the hands of men."
3. A. Berkeley Mickelsen, *Interpreting the Bible* (Grand Rapids: Eerdmans, 1963), 94–95.
4. McConkie, *Answers*, 8.
5. *Ensign* (January 1995): 7.
6. *Ensign* (August 2011): 45.
7. Not even LDS Church leaders can claim that their non-English Book of Mormon translations are taken from a first-generation source since the original gold plates are no longer available. All of the dozens of foreign translations of the Book of Mormon have been derived from the admittedly second-generation English rendition (see *Ensign* [May 1995]: 10), making these translations third-generation texts. It would therefore appear that those who mistakenly claim that the Bible is nothing more than a translation of a translation of a translation would better apply their criticism to the Book of Mormon. See "15 Myths about Bible Translation" written by biblical scholar Daniel B. Wallace, http://danielbwallace.com/2012/10/08/fifteen-myths-about-bible-translation/. For more information on this topic, see chapter 25, "Why should a rational person trust in a Bible that has been corrupted?" in our book *Answering Mormons' Questions*.
8. Glen Scorgie et al., eds., *The Challenge of Bible Translation: Communicating God's Word to the World* (Grand Rapids: Zonderan, 2003), 179.
9. Ron Rhodes, "Manuscript Support for the Bible's Reliability," Reasoning from the Scriptures Ministries, accessed May 29, 2014, http://home.earthlink.net/~ronrhodes/Manuscript.html. Additional New Testament manuscripts continue to be found and cataloged. For up-to-date information on this fascinating topic, see the website for the Center for the Study of New Testament Manuscripts (CSNTM), www.csntm.org.
10. Bruce Metzger, "How We Got Our Bible," *Christian History*, no. 43 (1994): 38.
11. Ibid., 39.
12. For more on this issue, see chapter 26, "Why do you trust the Bible when it has so many contradictions?" in our book *Answering Mormons' Questions*.
13. See also Talmage, *The Articles of Faith*, 210.
14. For instance, the name of King Benjamin was later changed to King Mosiah in Mosiah 21:28 and Ether 4:1; the phrase "son of" was added in passages such as 1 Nephi 11:18, 21, 32, and 13:40; the word *not* was inserted in 2 Nephi 12:9 to completely change the meaning.
15. Harrell, *"This Is My Doctrine,"* 91. Harrell quotes from Terry L. Givens's book *By the Hand of Mormon: The American Scripture that Launched a New World Religion* (Oxford: Oxford University Press, 2003), 48.
16. "Are Mormons Christian?," The Church of Jesus Christ of Latter-Day Saints, accessed May 29, 2014, https://www.lds.org/topics/christians.
17. If you're interested, we recommend taking the "Romans challenge" on our website: http://www.mrm.org/romans-road.
18. *Teachings of Presidents of the Church: Joseph F. Smith*, 45.

8 | The Book of Mormon

If the claims regarding the Book of Mormon are accurate, then the book is genuine scripture. If, however, the Book of Mormon is an invention of human origin—in short, a forgery—then the Church itself is a fraud.

Bob Bennett, former Utah senator[1]

MORMONESE:

Book of Mormon: "Another Testament of Jesus Christ" that is believed to have been compiled by the Nephite prophet Mormon on gold plates and buried by his son Moroni, who came back to earth as an angel in 1823; he appeared to Joseph Smith and eventually gave him the plates that were later translated by Smith and then first printed in 1830.

brethren: Generally used to denote the Mormon leadership, though it could refer to the general membership.

gold plates: The original source for the Book of Mormon, a compilation of stories and theology handed down by ancient inhabitants of America.

Jaredites: A Book of Mormon people group that came to the Western Hemisphere around the time when God confounded the languages at the Tower of Babel.

Lamanites: A dark-skinned Book of Mormon people group that descended through Laman, the son of Lehi. They were generally evil and eventually defeated the Nephites, causing them to become extinct.

Mormon: Two possible meanings: 1) An ancient Nephite prophet who abridged and compiled the records of his people known today as the Book of Mormon. 2) A nickname used to describe a follower of Mormonism.

Moroni: The last living Nephite and the son of Mormon who buried the gold plates in the Hill Cumorah.

Nephites: A Book of Mormon people group that descended through Nephi, the son of Lehi. They were generally good and were eventually defeated in the fifth century AD by their Lamanite counterparts.

Through several vigorous campaigns, the LDS Church has been successful at giving away millions of copies of a book touted as "Another Testament of Jesus Christ." "Read this book and pray about it" is the common challenge made by the missionaries to prospective converts. As one article titled "Marvelous Book" in the *Church News* put it, "There seems to be no end to the enthusiasm members feel for the Book of Mormon, the most correct of any book on the earth, the book that will lead a man 'closer to God by abiding by its precepts than any other book.'"[2] And President Gordon B. Hinckley exclaimed, "I can't understand why those of other faiths cannot accept the Book of Mormon. One would think that they would be looking for additional witnesses to the great and solemn truths of the Bible."[3] What is this book all about? And what makes it so special to the Latter-day Saint?

The Preeminent Book

In 1823 Joseph Smith claimed to have been visited by an angel named Moroni. This heavenly being told him about gold plates that contained a record of ancient inhabitants of the American continent, the very plates which he had buried centuries earlier when he had lived on the earth. Smith would not be allowed to retrieve the gold record for another four years. In 1827 Smith claimed that he went to a small hill not far from his New York home and dug up the record spoken of by the angel. He reported:

> These records were engraven on plates which had the appearance of gold, each plate was six inches wide and eight inches long, and not quite so thick as common tin. They were filled with engravings, in Egyptian characters, and bound together in a volume as the leaves of a book, with three rings running through the whole. The volume was something near six inches in thickness, a part of which was sealed. The characters on the unsealed part were small, and beautifully engraved. The whole book exhibited many marks

of antiquity in its construction, and much skill in the art of engraving. With the records was found a curious instrument, which the ancients called "Urim and Thummim," which consisted of two transparent stones set in the rim of a bow fastened to a breast plate. Through the medium of the Urim and Thummim I translated the record by the gift and power of God.[4]

This "translation" became the Book of Mormon, which is said to contain the story of primarily two groups of people who came to the Americas. The first group was known as the Jaredites. *The Encyclopedia of Mormonism* describes their history:

This particular people left the Tower of Babel at the time of the confusion of tongues. Their prophet-leaders were led to the ocean, where they constructed eight peculiar barges. These were driven by the wind across the waters to America, where the Jaredites became a large and powerful nation. After many centuries, wickedness and wars led to a final war of annihilation. During that final war, Ether, a prophet of God, wrote their history and spiritual experiences on twenty-four gold plates, perhaps relying on earlier Jaredite records.[5]

The second group arrived in the Americas approximately six hundred years before the birth of Christ. Lehi, a Jewish prophet from Jerusalem, claimed that God told him to flee the city prior to the Babylonian captivity. He fled with his wife, Sariah, and their four sons: Laman, Lemuel, Sam, and Nephi. Also joining Lehi were Zoram, Ishmael, and Ishmael's family. They sailed across the ocean, landed in the Western Hemisphere, and commenced to build cities and a large civilization. After Lehi's death, some of the people accepted Nephi as their leader, while the rest gave allegiance to Laman.

The Book of Mormon narrative describes how these two groups were known as Nephites and Lamanites. Much of the story tells about the hatred between the two groups and the wars they fought. It also records Jesus's appearance to these civilizations after he was resurrected from the dead in Palestine. By the fifth century AD, the Lamanites had completely annihilated the Nephite people at the battle of Hill Cumorah.

According to Mormonism, the descendants of the Lamanites are the American Indians. Moroni, who was the son of Mormon, was the last living Nephite. He buried the record of his people in the Hill Cumorah, which is located near present-day Palmyra in upstate New York. This record on gold plates was later discovered and translated into the Book of Mormon by Joseph Smith.

Both former and contemporary Mormon authorities and scholars have upheld the prominent place the Book of Mormon has in the Latter-day Saint religion. Asserting the supremacy of the Book of Mormon, Apostle Bruce R. McConkie bluntly stated:

> Almost all of the doctrines of the gospel are taught in the Book of Mormon *with much greater clarity and perfection* than those same doctrines are revealed in the Bible. Anyone who will place in parallel columns the teachings of these two great books on such subjects as the atonement, plan of salvation, gathering of Israel, baptism, gifts of the Spirit, miracles, revelation, faith, charity, (or any of a hundred other subjects), will find conclusive proof of the *superiority* of Book of Mormon teachings.[6]

Ezra Taft Benson agreed, adding in a 1978 address, "There will be more people saved in the kingdom of God—ten thousand times over—because of the Book of Mormon than there will be because of the Bible."[7]

"Translating" the Book of Mormon

Many paintings depict Joseph Smith looking directly at the gold plates during the translation process. However, testimony from his contemporaries provides another picture as to how the "Reformed Egyptian" language was translated into English. Seventy B. H. Roberts explained that Joseph Smith had in his possession a "chocolate-colored, somewhat egg-shaped stone which the Prophet . . . was able to translate the characters engraven on the plates."[8] David Whitmer, one of the "three witnesses" whose name is found in every edition of the Book of Mormon, described the method in which Joseph Smith translated the plates into English:

> I will now give you a description of the manner in which the Book of Mormon was translated. Joseph Smith would put the seer stone into a hat, and put his face in the hat, drawing it closely around his face to exclude the light; and in the darkness the spiritual light would shine. A piece of something resembling parchment would appear, and on that appeared the writing. One character at a time would appear, and under it was the interpretation in English. Brother Joseph would read off the English to Oliver Cowdery, who was

his principle scribe, and when it was written down and repeated to Brother Joseph to see if it was correct, then it would disappear, and another character with the interpretation would appear. Thus the Book of Mormon was translated by the gift and power of God, and not by any power of man.[9]

Martin Harris, also one of the three witnesses mentioned in the Book of Mormon, gave a similar account:

By aid of the Seer Stone, sentences would appear and were read by the Prophet and written by Martin, and when finished he would say "written"; and if correctly written, the sentence would disappear and another appear in its place; but if not written correctly it remained until corrected, so that the translation was just as it was engraven on the plates, precisely in the language then used.[10]

Although Mormon history explains the translation of the Book of Mormon taking place with a Urim and Thummim, this painting found in a Salt Lake City visitor's center gives the mistaken impression that Joseph Smith looked directly at the gold plates and gave an oral translation to Oliver Cowdery, who then wrote the words down.

According to the January 2013 *Ensign* magazine:

After using this early in his "translation" history, Smith supposedly stopped using the stones. Gerrit Dirkmaat, a member of the church's history department, reported, "Records indicate that soon after the founding of the Church in 1830, the Prophet stopped using the seer stones as a regular means of receiving revelations after inquiring of the Lord without employing an external instrument."[11]

While this explanation may comfort some members who are uncomfortable with Smith translating a sacred work by means of folk magic, it does not negate the fact that Smith did use this method for a period of time.

The Book of Mormon Witnesses: What about Credibility?

An introductory page found in every copy of the Book of Mormon lists the two combined testimonies made by eleven men who belonged to five families: Cowdery, Whitmer, Harris, Page, and Smith. Their testimonies are said to verify the story. Without the witness of these men, Smith's word alone is all there is to show how this translation was real.

As far as the eight men who signed a short statement called "The Testimony of the Eight Witnesses," four belonged to the Whitmer family and three were from Joseph Smith's immediate family (his father and two brothers). The eighth person was Hiram Page, who was married to a Whitmer. While eight witnesses may sound like a strong testimonial support to Smith's story, only three families are represented. Besides Smith's own family, the other witnesses were close friends of the LDS prophet.

Oliver Cowdery, David Whitmer, and Martin Harris were three of Smith's most trusted men who signed "The Testimony of the Three Witnesses," another statement testifying to the authenticity of the Book of Mormon. Many Mormons do not realize the dubious background of these men. Former LDS historian D. Michael Quinn wrote that folk magic and seer stone divination were quite popular among the Book of Mormon witnesses:

> The Three Witnesses to the Book of Mormon were also involved in folk magic. Oliver Cowdery was a rodsman before he met Smith in 1829 and was soon authorized by divine revelation to continue the revelatory use of his "rod of nature." David Whitmer revered Smith's use of a seer stone, may have possessed one of his own, and authorized a later spokesman for his own religious organization to obtain revelations through a stone. Martin Harris endorsed Smith's use of a seer stone for divination and treasure seeking, and participated in treasure digging himself after the discovery of the gold plates. Of the remaining Eight Witnesses, John Whitmer possessed a seer stone which his descendants preserved, his brothers Christian, Jacob, and Peter were included in their pastor's accusation of magic belief, and Hiram Page, their brother-in-law, had a stone for revelations.[12]

In 1838 Cowdery was excommunicated from the Mormon Church after he accused Smith of adultery, lying, and teaching false doctrines. The Mormon founder classified Cowdery as one who was "too mean to mention." Cowdery charged Smith with having an affair with a woman named Fanny Alger.[13] After his excommunication, Cowdery was accused of a number of crimes, including "denying the faith," "persecuting the brethren," "urging on vexatious lawsuits," "falsely insinuating [Joseph Smith] was guilty of adultery," and dishonesty.[14] Cowdery later joined the Methodist church, a Christian denomination that adheres to the early church creeds and therefore had been condemned by God.[15] He is said to have returned to the LDS Church in 1848 and died two years later at the young age of forty-three.

David Whitmer claimed that none of the three witnesses ever denied the truthfulness of the Book of Mormon. However, Whitmer did believe Joseph Smith was a fallen prophet when he wrote:

Many of the Latter Day Saints believe that it was impossible for Brother Joseph to have fallen. I will give you some evidence upon this matter which I suppose you will certainly accept, showing that Brother Joseph belonged to the class of men who could fall into error and blindness. From the following you will see that Brother Joseph belonged to the weakest class—the class that were very liable to fall. . . . All of you who believe the revelations of Joseph Smith as if they were from the mouth of God. You should have acknowledged belief in the errors of Joseph Smith, and not tried to hide them when there is so much evidence that he did go into error and blindness. . . . I am doing God's will in bringing the truth to light concerning the errors of Brother Joseph. They will see that it is necessary, as he is the man who introduced many doctrines of error into the Church of Christ; and his errors must be made manifest and the truth brought to light, in order that all Latter Day Saints shall cease to put their trust in this man, believing his doctrines as if they were from the mouth of God.[16]

Whitmer—whom Smith called a "dumb ass" and "mean man," saying "Satan deceiveth [Whitmer]"[17]—believed Joseph Smith intentionally changed the very revelations that God had supposedly given him.[18] Believing that God told him to leave the Mormon faith, Whitmer walked away and never returned. He wrote:

If you believe my testimony to the Book of Mormon; if you believe that God spake to us three witnesses by his own voice, then I tell you that in June, 1838, God spake to me again by his own voice from the heavens, and told me to "separate myself from among the Latter Day Saints, for as they sought to do unto me, so should it be done unto them."[19]

Toward the end of his life, Whitmer joined an offshoot of Mormonism called the Church of Christ, a group that accepted the Book of Mormon.[20]

Meanwhile, Martin Harris more than once upset the Mormon founder, for which Smith retaliated by twice referring to him as a "wicked man" in Mormon scripture.[21] It was for these sins that Harris was supposedly commanded in D&C 19:20 by Christ Himself to repent. Harris expressed his worship to God in unique ways. Regarding this, Smith said:

> Martin Harris having boasted to the brethren that he could handle snakes with perfect safety, while fooling with a black snake with his bare feet, he received a bite on his left foot. The fact was communicated to me, and I took occasion to reprove him, and exhort the brethren never to trifle with the promises of God.[22]

Harris left the Mormon movement and joined several other groups, among them the Shakers and the Strangites.[23] While Harris eventually returned to the LDS Church, he apparently never found peace. He told one early Mormon writer that he "never believed that the Brighamite branch of the Mormon church, nor the Josephite church, was right, because in his opinion, God had rejected them." As to why he went to the LDS temple in Salt Lake City, he apparently was curious to discover "what was going on in there."[24] Regarding their testimony to the Book of Mormon, each of these three "witnesses" had questionable qualifications since, as Joseph Smith said, they all fell into error.[25] They were gullible, and their credibility was stained with cases of counterfeiting, dowsing, false prophecies, money digging, and lying.[26]

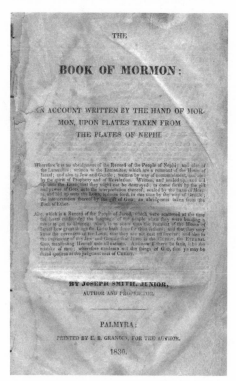

The title page of the 1830 Book of Mormon says that Joseph Smith was the "author and proprietor" of the LDS scripture.

Historical Problems with the Book of Mormon

Across the street from Temple Square in Salt Lake City is a museum owned by the Mormon Church where artifacts dating back to the early years of the church are displayed. Museum pieces include pioneer tools and weapons, handwritten manuscripts from the Book of Mormon, a replica of the Nauvoo Sunstone, and even the gun Joseph Smith used to shoot three people during his last moments at Carthage Jail. One thing that cannot be found in this museum is any artifact that can be clearly traced to the Nephite culture mentioned in the Book of Mormon.

If the Book of Mormon depicts real people who lived in real places and participated in real events, surely there should be at least an archaeological trace. With so many people who supposedly lived on the American continent, artifacts should abound. As President Spencer W. Kimball wrote, "The Lamanite population of the Americas, at the greatest number, must have run into many millions, for in certain periods of Book of Mormon history, wars continued almost unabated and the soil was covered with the bodies of the slain."[27] In Ether 15:2 in the Book of Mormon, the Jaredites alone had "two millions of mighty men, and also their wives and their children."

Meanwhile, a student manual explains:

> Some students of the Book of Mormon are interested in geographical, textual, or archaeological evidences of the book's ancient origin. While these are often fascinating and helpful, it must be remembered that these kinds of discoveries do not constitute the substance and truth of the Book of Mormon. President Gordon B. Hinckley (1910–2008) counseled against relying solely on these discoveries for our testimony of the Book of Mormon.[28]

If the Book of Mormon is *not* a historical book because the events it records never happened, shouldn't a Mormon want to know? Because there is no archaeological or historical evidence to support the scripture, there is controversy within Mormon circles as to where the Book of Mormon story actually took place. These lands are probably most commonly believed to be somewhere in Central America. Supporting this view, a popular LDS apologetic website reports that "nearly all informed Book of Mormon scholars agree that Book of Mormon events would have taken place in Mesoamerica."[29]

Those holding to a North American setting for the Book of Mormon, known today as the Heartland model, would certainly disagree with this conclusion. President Joseph Fielding Smith wrote:

> Within recent years there has arisen among certain students of the *Book of Mormon* a *theory* to the effect that within the period covered by the *Book of Mormon*, the Nephites and Lamanites were confined almost entirely within the borders of the territory comprising Central America and the southern portion of Mexico—the isthmus of Tehauntepec probably being the "narrow neck" of land spoken of in the *Book of Mormon* rather than the isthmus of Panama. . . . In the face of this evidence coming from the Prophet Joseph Smith, Oliver Cowdery, and David Whitmer, we cannot say that the Nephites and Lamanites did not possess the territory of the United States and that the Hill Cumorah is in Central America. Neither can we say that the great struggle which resulted in the destruction of the Nephites took place in Central America.[30]

Smith also said:

> It must be conceded that this description fits perfectly the land of Cumorah in New York, as it has been known since the visitation of Moroni to the Prophet Joseph Smith, for the hill is in the proximity of the Great Lakes and also in the land of many rivers and fountains. *Moreover, the Prophet Joseph Smith himself is on record, definitely declaring the present hill called Cumorah to be the exact hill spoken of in the Book of Mormon.* . . . It is difficult for a reasonable person to believe that such men as Oliver Cowdery, Brigham Young, Parley P. Pratt, Orson Pratt, David Whitmer, and many others, could speak frequently of the Spot where the Prophet Joseph Smith obtained the plates as the Hill Cumorah, and not be corrected by the Prophet, if that were not the fact. That they did speak of this hill in the days of the Prophet in this definite manner is an established record of history.[31]

Apostle James Talmage also placed the Nephite people in North America when he wrote:

> At that time North America was inhabited by two great peoples, the Nephites and the Lamanites, each named after an early leader, and both originally of one family stock. Except for brief periods of comparative peace the two nations lived in a state of hostility due to Lamanite aggression.[32]

President Ezra Taft Benson insisted that not only did the alleged Nephites live in the area of the United States, but that Adam and the Jaredites lived there as well.

Consider how very fortunate we are to be living in this land of America. The destiny of this country was forged long before the earth was even created. . . . This was the place of three former civilizations: that of Adam, that of the Jaredites, and that of the Nephites.[33]

Despite the above comments, many modern LDS scholars have since abandoned the idea that the Book of Mormon lands include areas of North America. In doing so they have claimed that such leaders as those above were misinformed.[34] Yet a message from the First Presidency in 1930 stated:

Jesus Christ, referring to the time when he would manifest himself in the latter days, declared that whereas he manifested himself to his own people in the meridian of time and they rejected him, in the latter days he would come first to the Gentiles, and then to the house of Israel. He says: "And behold, this people (the Nephites) will I establish in this land, (America) and it shall be a new Jerusalem."[35]

In a declaration made by the First Presidency on May 1, 1911, and printed in the *Deseret News* a few days later, President Joseph F. Smith and his counselors Anthon Lund and John Henry Smith stated that it was Moroni himself who claimed to have "ministered to a people called Nephites, a branch of the house of Israel, formerly inhabiting *this land*."[36] Conflicting information of this sort must certainly be confusing to the average Latter-day Saint, especially since there is, for example, an LDS Church marker located north of Gallatin, Missouri, stating how a Nephite altar once existed near the place Joseph Smith called Adam-ondi-Ahman. If the Nephites were relegated to an area in Central America, how did one of their altars appear as far north as the state of Missouri?

While most LDS scholars would feel that there is historical and scientific value in the Book of Mormon, we have found no scientist or historian outside the Mormon faith who would support such a notion. On August 25, 1984, John Carlson addressed a Sunstone Symposium in Salt Lake City where he noted, "The Book of Mormon itself has not made a significant contribution to New World archaeology. Ask any New World archaeologist." When asked on June 16, 1999 if he had changed this position, he said, "No, I have not changed my opinion and would stand by what I said." Carlson, the founder and director for the Center for Archaeoastronomy, did note that "interest in the Book of Mormon by believers has stimulated interest in the ancient Americas and promoted archaeological research." While he stated that much of this research is good and unbiased, "there are also plenty of examples of highly biased research designed to support the Book of Mormon."[37]

Michael D. Coe, a non-Mormon professor emeritus of anthropology at Yale University, is an expert in the early history of Mesoamerica. He wrote a paper in 1973 that discussed the lack of historical evidence in the Book of Mormon. Said Coe:

> Mormon archaeologists over the years have almost unanimously accepted the Book of Mormon as an accurate, historical account of the New World peoples between about 2000 B.C. and A.D. 421. They believe that Smith could translate hieroglyphs, whether "Reformed Egyptian" or ancient American. . . . Let me now state uncategorically that as far as I know there is not one professionally trained archaeologist, who is not a Mormon, who sees any scientific justification for believing the foregoing to be true, and I would like to state that there are quite a few Mormon archaeologists who join this group. . . . The bare facts of the matter are that nothing, absolutely nothing, has ever shown up in any New World excavation which would suggest to a dispassionate observer that the Book of Mormon, as claimed by Joseph Smith, is a historical document relating to the history of the early migrants to our hemisphere.[38]

With a hint of sarcasm, Coe concluded with these suggestions:

> Forget the so-far fruitless quest for the Jaredites, Nephites, Mulekites, and the lands of Zarahemla and Bountiful: there is no more chance of finding them than of discovering the ruins of the bottomless pit described in the book of Revelations. . . . Continue the praiseworthy excavations in Mexico, remembering that little or nothing pertaining to the Book of Mormon will ever result from them.[39]

We wrote Coe in 1993 to see if he still believed twenty years later what he had written in 1973. He responded:

> I haven't changed my views about the Book of Mormon since my 1973 article. I have seen no archaeological evidence before or since that date which would

convince me that it is anything but a fanciful creation by an unusually gifted individual living in upstate New York in the early 19th century.[40]

In a PBS television documentary broadcast in 2007, Coe reiterated his view when he said,

> In the case of the Book of Mormon, you've got a much bigger problem. You really do. We have another part of the world where the archaeology is really very well-known now; we know a lot about people like the Maya and their predecessors. So to try to find unlikely evidence in an unlikely spot, you've got a problem. And of course none of the finds that biblical archaeologists are rightly proud about, no finds on that level have ever come up for Mormon archaeologists, which makes it a big problem.[41]

Mormon apologist L. Ara Norwood claims that the analysis by Coe (and any other non-LDS scholar, for that matter) should be rejected because he is not Mormon. He writes:

> So we have a non-Latter-day Saint archaeologist who does not believe in the supernatural claims of the coming forth of the Book of Mormon due to the lack of "scientific evidence"? Is that significant? If a non-Latter-day Saint individual were to come to believe in the supernatural/spiritual claims of the Book of Mormon, would not that person then in all likelihood join the Latter-day Saint church?[42]

Consider how many discoveries have helped archaeologists ascertain places, names, and events found in the Bible. To name a few, an ossuary (bone box) found in Jerusalem provides evidence for the existence of the high priest Caiaphas, an inscription from Caesarea proves the Roman procurator Pontius Pilate was a real person, and the Tel Dan inscription supports the very existence of King David. For Herod the Great, extensive excavations performed in Caesarea, Herodium, Jericho, and Masada lend credence to the idea that this man was a master builder who indeed built the Second Temple. In addition, discoveries in cities such as Ephesus (Turkey), Corinth (Greece), and Rome (Italy) provide a clearer picture of Paul's missionary journeys and his epistles.[43] Please don't mistake what we're saying. We're not suggesting archaeology can replace faith by proving the Virgin Birth, the resurrection of Christ, and the existence of heaven. At the same time, archaeological discoveries provide reasons to believe the Bible is the historical book it claims to be and is not filled with mythology.

Many biblical archaeological discoveries are made every year; if not for the lack of funding and laborers, there is so much more waiting to be discovered. For instance, the authors have hiked up a tell (a small hill) at Colossae in Turkey. At the time of this writing, no serious archaeology of this important biblical city has been attempted, even though the site has been known for many years. Who knows what will be uncovered once the work begins!

When the Book of Mormon is considered, however, there is nothing that can be positively identified to support the names, places, and events written by ancient Americans. Someone may think that biblical archaeologists have had a head start and that, eventually, evidence for the Book of Mormon will be uncovered. While biblical archaeology in the Holy Land and Turkey has taken place for several hundred years, serious work really didn't begin until the 1920s. Until Book of Mormon evidence moves beyond the realm of faith, it can be rightly classified as a myth, legend, or story without any basis in historical fact.[44]

"Fulness of the Everlasting Gospel"

One of Mormonism's primary arguments against the Bible is that "many plain and precious truths" have been taken away from it. According to Ezra Taft Benson:

> The Book of Mormon is a second witness to Jesus Christ because it contains the plain and precious truths of His gospel. Within this sacred record is the fulness of the gospel of Jesus Christ; in other words, the Lord's requirements for salvation. . . . Not all truths are of equal value, nor are all scriptures of the same worth. What better way to nourish the spirit than to frequently feast from the book which the Prophet Joseph Smith said would get a man "nearer to God by abiding by its precepts than by any other book."[45]

Benson's comment says two things. First, he says that "the plain and precious truths" apparently not found in the Bible are found in the "sacred record" of the Book of Mormon. Second, he claims that "the Lord's requirements for salvation" can be found there as well. In other words, whatever is necessary in order to achieve complete salvation should be found in the pages of the Book of Mormon. Benson echoes Joseph Smith, who said,

"I told the brethren that the Book of Mormon was the most correct of any book on earth, and the keystone of our religion, and a man would get nearer to God by abiding by its precepts, than by any other book."[46]

Where Are the Precepts?

Getting nearer to God has been associated in Mormonism with eternal life, which is also called exaltation or godhood. According to Joseph F. Smith,

> We may become the sons and daughters of God, in the fullest sense of the word, being heirs of God and joint heirs with Jesus Christ [see Romans 8:14–17], to be kings and priests unto God, to inherit glory, dominion, exaltation, thrones and every power and attribute developed and possessed by our Heavenly Father. This is the object of our being on this earth. In order to attain unto this exalted position, it is necessary that we go through this mortal experience, or probation, by which we may prove ourselves worthy, through the aid of our elder brother Jesus.[47]

In order to receive this "exalted position," the following is necessary:

1. We must be baptized.
2. We must receive the laying on of hands to be confirmed a member of the Church of Jesus Christ and to receive the gift of the Holy Ghost.
3. Brethren must receive the Melchizedek priesthood and magnify their callings in the priesthood.
4. We must receive the temple endowments.
5. We must be married for eternity, either in this life or in the next.[48]

In addition to receiving the required ordinances, the Lord commands all of us to:

1. Love God and our neighbors.
2. Keep the commandments.
3. Repent of our wrongdoings.
4. Search out our kindred dead and receive the saving ordinances of the gospel for them.
5. Attend our Church meetings as regularly as possible so we can renew our baptismal covenants by partaking of the covenants.

6. Love our family members and strengthen them in the ways of the Lord.
7. Have family and individual prayers every day.
8. Teach the gospel to others by word and example.
9. Study the scriptures.
10. Listen to and obey the inspired words of the prophets of the Lord.[49]

Numerous requirements not mentioned at all in the Book of Mormon must be met. In addition, the Book of Mormon does not discuss other important LDS doctrines, including:

- The Mormon Church organization, on which its leaders place so much emphasis
- The Melchizedek priesthood order
- The Aaronic priesthood order
- A plurality of gods
- God is an exalted man
- The potential for humans to attain godhood
- Three degrees of glory
- Preexistence
- Eternal progression
- Heavenly Mother
- Temporary hell

In all actuality, there is no evidence to suggest that the Nephites mentioned in the Book of Mormon believed or practiced much of what modern-day Mormons believe and practice today. Harrell notes, "It is noteworthy that the doctrines expressed in the Book of Mormon tend to bear closer similarity to those found in early nineteenth-century Protestantism than to those in later Mormonism."[50]

Praying about the Book of Mormon

One of the most common approaches Mormon missionaries may take with prospective new converts involves opening the Book of Mormon to Moroni 10:4. It reads,

And when ye shall receive these things, I would exhort you that ye would ask God, the Eternal Father, in the name of Christ, if these things are not true; and if ye shall ask with a sincere heart with real intent, having faith in Christ, he will manifest the truth of it unto you, by the power of the Holy Ghost.

A missionary resource explains, "In order to know that the Book of Mormon is true, a person must read, ponder, and pray about it. The honest seeker of truth will soon come to feel that the Book of Mormon is the word of God."[51] Another church manual says, "A sincere reader may not immediately gain a testimony when reading the Book of Mormon. Further, some people may not recognize the testimony that is growing as they study and pray over this tremendous text. But the promise of Moroni will come."[52]

Yet there are problems with this challenge. First of all, the test is skewed. A person who "prays" but doesn't get the same answer as the missionary is viewed as not getting it correct. If prayer is the correct means of testing the book's authenticity, why is a negative outcome immediately rejected as a plausible response? Though the Mormons may not say so, it is likely that they would question whether or not such a person had a "sincere heart" or "real intent." It could also imply that the person lacked a necessary "faith in Christ." However, Jeremiah 17:9 says a feeling that one has can be disastrously wrong because "the heart is desperately wicked." Praying about a religious book, especially if it is fictional and not historical, is hardly an objective test.

If the Book of Mormon is just one of four LDS scriptures, why should *it* be prayed over and not the other three scriptures? For that matter, why shouldn't a seeker after truth pray about the Qu'ran (Islam), the Vedas (Hinduism), or the Tripitaka (Buddhism)? Where does praying about a particular religion's scripture stop? If praying about a book is a way to determine truth, then why have many Mormons never even thought about expanding their prayers to more than just one religion's scripture?

While Christians believe in prayer, they don't believe it is appropriate to approach communication with God in such a cavalier manner. First Thessalonians 5:21 tells believers to "test everything" (ESV). The Bereans were considered to be more righteous than the Thessalonians in Acts 17:11 because they searched the Scriptures (Old Testament) to see if what Paul taught was consistent. While the Mormon missionaries may want potential converts to obtain a subjective feeling that the Book of Mormon (and ultimately, Mormonism) is true, they should instead request their audience to read the

Bible for itself—not in light of "modern-day revelation"—and see if what Mormonism teaches is consistent with the special revelation already given.[53]

Discussion Questions

1. Joseph Smith said that the Book of Mormon was the "most correct book on earth." Suppose a Mormon asked you why you have problems with this LDS scripture. If you only had five minutes to provide three reasons for your view, what would you say?

2. Apostle Jeffrey R. Holland said, "Either the Book of Mormon is what the Prophet Joseph said it is, or this Church and its founder are false, a deception from the first instance onward."[54] Is this general authority correct? What would you say to those Mormons who say it doesn't matter if the events in the Book of Mormon never took place as long as it provides them with spiritual comfort?

3. It is often stressed that a person ought to pray about the Book of Mormon to see if it is true. Should Christians be willing to take this test for themselves? Describe the advantages or consequences to praying about the Book of Mormon.

Final Thought

Many of us have been invited to receive a spiritual witness that the Book of Mormon is true. We have been told to read it for ourselves and then pray about its message. Yet this LDS scripture has many problematic areas. For one, the archaeology of the New World does not support its details. Some of the doctrines in the book do not reflect the teachings of the current Latter-day Saint leaders. Even the manner in how the book was supposedly translated is troublesome. One thing is for sure, though. If the Book of Mormon is *not* the most correct book on earth, then Mormonism and its teachings should not be taken seriously by those who value truth.

Notes

1. Bob Bennett, *Leap of Faith* (Salt Lake City: Deseret Book Co., 2009), 9.
2. *Church News* (3 Jan. 2004): 3.

3. *Ensign* (January 2004): 7. Originally given at a meeting in Baltimore, Maryland, November 15, 1998; also quoted in "Recurring Themes of President Hinckley," *Ensign* (June 2000): 18–19.

4. *History of the Church*, 4:537.

5. Ludlow, ed., *Encyclopedia of Mormonism*, s.v. "Book of Mormon plates and records," 1:200.

6. McConkie, *Mormon Doctrine*, 99; italics added.

7. *Ensign* (November 1984): 7.

8. B. H. Roberts, comp., *Comprehensive History of the Church* (1930; repr. Orem, UT: Sonos Publishing, 1991), 1:129.

9. David Whitmer, *An Address to All Believers in Christ* (Richmond, MO: David Whitmer, 1887), 12. This story is quoted and confirmed by LDS Apostle Russell M. Nelson in *Ensign* (July 1993): 62.

10. B. H. Roberts, comp., *Comprehensive History of the Church*, 1:129. The biblical description of the Urim and Thummim is very vague. What is known is that the name implies *light* and *perfection*. While there is no description of what they looked like, Exodus 28:30 and Leviticus 8:8 state that they were stored in the high priest's breastpiece, which was attached to the ephod, a sleeveless vest. In *Joseph Smith—History* 1:35 (PoGP), Joseph Smith reported that "these stones, fastened to a breastplate," were "deposited with the [Book of Mormon plates.]" While not much is written in church manuals about the origin of the stones, it appears that this Urim and Thummim were different from the pair referred to in the Old Testament.

11. *Ensign* (January 2013): 46.

12. D. Michael Quinn, *Early Mormonism and the Magic World View* (Salt Lake City: Signature Books, 1987), 194.

13. Smith did in fact have an affair with fourteen-year-old Fanny Alger. Mormon historian Todd Compton cited an 1872 letter from William McLellin, who explained that Smith's wife, Emma, "missed Joseph and Fanny Alger. She went to the barn and saw him and Fanny in the barn together alone. She looked through a crack and saw the transaction!!" We can only imagine Emma's reaction. Although Compton places some doubt on the barn story, he believes that Alger became Smith's first plural wife "in February or March 1833." Todd Compton, *In Sacred Loneliness: The Plural Wives of Joseph Smith* (Salt Lake City: Signature Books, 1997), 35.

14. Andrew Jenson, *Latter-day Saint Biographical Encyclopedia: A Compilation of Biographical Sketches of Prominent Men and Women in the Church of Jesus Christ of Latter-day Saints* (Salt Lake City: A. Jensen History, 1901–36), s.v. "Cowdery, Oliver," 1:246.

15. *Joseph Smith—History*, 1:19 (PoGP). See also 1 Nephi 14:10 (BOM) and D&C 1:30.

16. Whitmer, *An Address to All Believers in Christ*, 36, 39.

17. *History of the Church*, 3:228; D&C 28:11.

18. David Whitmer, *An Address to All Believers in the Book of Mormon* (Richmond, MO: David Whitmer, 1887), 56–62.

19. Whitmer, *An Address to All Believers in Christ*, 27.

20. Even LDS scholars do not dispute that Whitmer was an LDS apostate "who never returned to the Church." See *A Sure Foundation*, 41.

21. D&C 3:12–13; 10:6–7. For example, Harris reported "that Joseph drank too much liquor when he was translating the Book of Mormon" (*History of the Church*, 2:26), a fact supported by another witness. See Dan Vogel, ed., *Early Mormon Documents* (Salt Lake City: Signature Books, 1999), 2:282n3.

22. *History of the Church*, 2:95.

23. The Shakers were officially known as the United Society of Believers in Christ's Second Appearing. Led by Ann Lee, this faith came to America from England in 1774. The name "Shaker" was given to the group because of the way the members shook and trembled to rid themselves of evil. After the death of Joseph Smith, James Strang claimed that the slain prophet had written a letter making him his successor. When his claim was rejected, he left to form a splinter group of Latter-day Saints that settled on Beaver Island, Michigan. Steven L. Shields notes, "For several years prior to his death, Strang's following rivaled that of Brigham Young!" *Divergent Paths of the Restoration* (Los Angeles: Restoration Research, 1990), 42. Strang was murdered on June 16, 1856.

24. Anthony Metcalf, *Ten Years before the Mast* (Malad City, ID: Research Publications, 1888), as quoted in Francis W. Kirkham, *A New Witness for Christ in America* (Salt Lake City: Utah Printing Company, 1960), 2:348–49. The Brighamite branch refers to the Salt Lake City church, while the Josephite church refers to the former Restored Church of Jesus Christ of Latter Day Saints (today known as the Community of Christ) based in Independence, Missouri.

25. *History of the Church*, 3:16–20.

26. For information about whether or not the witnesses ever saw the gold plates, see chapter 32, "What about the witnesses who claimed they saw the gold plates?" in our book *Answering Mormons' Questions*.

27. Spencer W. Kimball, *Faith Precedes the Miracle* (Salt Lake City: Deseret Book Co., 1978), 345.

28. *Book of Mormon Student Manual*, 9.

39. "Response to claims made in 'Chapter 8: The Book of Mormon,'" *FairMormon*, accessed May 29, 2014, http://en.fairmormon.org/Criticism_of_Mormonism/Books/Mormonism_101/Index/Chapter_8.

30. Joseph Fielding Smith, *Doctrines of Salvation*, 3:232, 239–40; italics in original.

31. Ibid., 3:233–34; italics in original.

32. James E. Talmage, *The Vitality of Mormonism* (Boston: Gorham Press, 1919), 199.

33. Benson, *Teachings of Ezra Taft Benson*, 587–88.

34. In a personal letter to Bill McKeever on June 11, 1992, John Sorenson stated that Joseph Fielding Smith "misread relevant historical documents." While it is certainly possible that Smith could have done so, we must bear in mind that he held the position of a trusted LDS Church historian for nearly half a century, and he later became Mormonism's tenth president.

35. James R. Clark, ed., *Messages of the First Presidency of the Church of Jesus Christ of Latter-day Saints (1833–1951)*, 6 vols., 5:285.

36. Ibid., 4:232; italics added.

37. John Carlson, e-mail to Bill McKeever, June 16, 1999. According to his website, Carlson is an expert in Native American astronomy who specializes in studies of pre-Colombian Mesoamerica.

38. Michael D. Coe, "Mormons and Archaeology: An Outside View," *Dialogue* 8 (summer 1973): 41, 42, 46.

39. Ibid., 48.

40. Michael Coe, personal letter to Bill McKeever, August 17, 1993.

41. Michael Coe, May 16, 2006, interview transcript, *PBS Frontline/American Experience*, accessed May 29, 2014, http://www.pbs.org/mormons/interviews/coe.html.

42. L. Ara Norwood, *Review of Books on the Book of Mormon* (Provo, UT: FARMS, 1989–97), 5:329. Norwood seems to miss the point. Coe is not basing his conclusion on the *spiritual* significance of the Book of Mormon but on the lack of *historical* significance.

43. For more information on the names and places mentioned in this paragraph, do an Internet search on any of these examples and see what we're talking about.

44. For more information on this issue, see chapter 34, "What about the archaeology supporting the Book of Mormon?" in our book *Answering Mormons' Questions.*

45. Benson, *Teachings of Ezra Taft Benson,* 55, 60.

46. Joseph Fielding Smith, ed., *Teachings of the Prophet Joseph Smith,* 194. *Joseph Smith History* 1:34 (PoGP) says the Book of Mormon is the "fulness of the everlasting gospel."

47. *Teachings of Presidents of the Church: Joseph F. Smith,* 150.

48. Ibid., 278. Except for baptism, none of these ordinances are ever mentioned in the Book of Mormon.

49. Ibid.

50. Harrell, *"This Is My Doctrine,"* 20.

51. *Preach My Gospel: A Guide to Missionary Service* (Salt Lake City: The Church of Jesus Christ of Latter-day Saints, 2004), 38.

52. *Book of Mormon Student Manual,* 8.

53. For more information on praying about the Book of Mormon, see chapter 27, "Doesn't James 1:5 say we should pray for wisdom? Why won't you pray about the truth claims of Mormonism?" in our book *Answering Mormons' Questions.*

54. Jeffrey R. Holland, *Christ and the New Covenant* (Salt Lake City: Deseret Book Co., 2003), 334.

9 | The Doctrine and Covenants and the Pearl of Great Price

I wish that every honest soul in this world would read the Book of Mormon; would read the Doctrine and Covenants, the Pearl of Great Price, besides reading the Bible. What a glorious privilege is ours. The so-called Christian world, divided and subdivided maintains that the Bible contains all of the word of God. To them the Lord has never given a revelation. According to its teachings nothing has come from the heavens by way of counsel and advice or revelation, comparable to that which we find in what they are pleased to call the canon of scripture.

President Joseph Fielding Smith [1]

MORMONESE:

Book of Abraham: A portion of the Pearl of Great Price taken from papyrus said to be written by the patriarch Abraham.

Doctrine and Covenants (D&C): A part of the LDS Church canon, made up of revelations and teachings that Mormon leaders (especially Joseph Smith) received from God, more than half of them coming before 1833.

Pearl of Great Price (PoGP): A part of the LDS Church canon, which was accepted as scripture in 1880. Includes five books as well as a retranslated portion of the Bible.

standard works: The four written scriptures of Mormonism: the Bible (the King James Version is officially accepted, "as far as it is translated correctly"); the Book of Mormon; the Doctrine and Covenants; and the Pearl of Great Price.

B esides the Book of Mormon, Mormonism has two additional books in what is known as the standard works of the LDS Church. These are the Doctrine and Covenants (D&C) and the Pearl of Great Price (PoGP). Many important and unique doctrines come from the pages of the D&C, which is mainly the teachings of Joseph Smith plus several added declarations given to Mormon prophets, such as the abolishment of polygamy and allowing blacks to hold the LDS priesthood.

The Pearl of Great Price, meanwhile, is comprised primarily of two smaller works, the Book of Moses and the Book of Abraham. The Book of Moses is "an extract from the translation of the Bible as revealed to Joseph Smith the Prophet, June 1830–February 1831." The Book of Abraham was allegedly translated from an Egyptian papyrus that Smith obtained in 1835. The Pearl of Great Price includes thirteen articles of faith, a brief history of Smith, and extracts from the Gospel of Matthew that were revised by Joseph Smith in his "translation" of the Bible.

The Doctrine and Covenants: A Modern-day Revelation?

In a 2009 article titled "Enriching Your Study of the Doctrine and Covenants," the *Ensign* magazine reported, "We testify that the Doctrine and Covenants is truly the Lord's voice in our time to each child of God and that great blessings come to those who study it."[2] According to the explanatory introduction to the D&C:

> The Doctrine and Covenants is a collection of divine revelations and inspired declarations. . . . Although most of the sections are directed to members of The Church of Jesus Christ of Latter-day Saints, the messages, warnings, and exhortations are for the benefit of all mankind. . . . [It] is unique because it is not a translation of an ancient document, but is of modern origin and was given of God through his chosen prophets for the restoration of his holy work and the establishment of the kingdom of God on the earth in these days.[3]

President Ezra Taft Benson taught that the D&C "brings men to Christ" as it

> is the binding link between the Book of Mormon and the continuing work of the Restoration through the Prophet Joseph Smith and his successors. . . . The Book of Mormon is the "keystone" of our religion, and the Doctrine and Covenants is the capstone, with continuing latter-day revelation.[4]

The D&C was first put together as the *Book of Commandments*:

By the fall of 1831, Joseph Smith had recorded seventy or more revelations, most of which contained instructions to Church members. In a special conference held November 1, 1831, in Hiram, Ohio, the Church decided to publish a selection of these revelations, or "commandments." . . . Shortly after the unsuccessful 1833 effort to print the Book of Commandments was stopped, plans were made to publish the revelations in Kirtland, Ohio. Renamed the *Doctrine and Covenants of the Church of the Latter Day Saints,* the book was presented to, and accepted by, the members of the Church in an August 1835 conference as the word of God.[5]

Some of the more important doctrines and events recorded in the D&C include:

- the claim that there is only one true church (Section 1)
- words of the angel Moroni to Smith in 1823 (Section 2)
- an explanation of how Smith needed to repent for having lost the first 116 pages of the "Book of Lehi" (which was supposed to be a part of the Book of Mormon) to Martin Harris's wife and that he was not to retranslate these pages because wicked men sought to destroy Smith and the Mormon movement (Sections 3, 10)
- the assertion that the apostle John continues to live until today (Section 7)
- the way God wanted His church organized (Section 20)
- the establishment of Smith as the church's "seer, translator, prophet, apostle, and elder" (given on the first day of the church's existence, April 6, 1830, Section 21)
- the need to be rebaptized, no matter in which church a person had been previously baptized (Section 22)
- how only Smith could receive revelations, and that Hiram Page, one of the Book of Mormon's eight witnesses, was receiving false revelations from Satan (Section 28)
- how Independence, Missouri, was to be the place for the City of Zion and the first LDS temple (Section 57)
- the way the devil and sons of perdition fell, how all receive some type of salvation, and the three kingdoms of "heaven" (Section 76)
- New Jerusalem would be built in Missouri (Section 84)

- the Word of Wisdom, a health code that, when obeyed, brings "temporal and spiritual blessings" (Section 89)[6]
- only the descendants of Aaron are to hold Aaronic priesthood (Section 107)
- the name of Jesus was returned to "The Church of Jesus Christ of Latter-day Saints," previously named the "Church of the Latter-day Saints" (Section 115)
- Spring Hill in Daviess County, Missouri, is named by God as "Adam-ondi-Ahman" because "it is the place where Adam shall come to visit his people" (Section 116)
- baptisms for the dead should be performed in LDS temples (Sections 124, 127, 128)
- God has a body of flesh and bone and, along with Jesus, may make appearances to men (Section 130)
- celestial marriage is required to achieve godhood and continue one's family into eternity (Sections 131–32)
- plural marriage (polygamy) is allowed (Section 132)
- the "martyrdom" of Smith and his brother Hyrum (Section 135)
- the plans for the "Camp of Israel" to head west were made in 1847 in order to search for a new place to reside (Section 136)
- the doctrines of salvation for the dead and how all children are saved in the celestial kingdom (Section 137)
- a vision sixth LDS President Joseph F. Smith had in 1918, including Christ's visit to the spirits of the dead while His body was in the tomb (Section 138)
- the 1890 "Manifesto" officially overturning the practice of polygamy (Official Declaration 1)
- the 1978 revelation declaring all worthy male members eligible to hold the Mormon priesthood (Official Declaration 2)[7]

The Pearl of Great Price

One church manual states how "the Pearl of Great Price testifies that Jesus is the Christ, that Joseph Smith was a prophet of God, and that The Church of Jesus Christ of Latter-day Saints is the only true and living church on earth."[8] According to the introductory note found at the beginning of this LDS scripture:

> The Pearl of Great Price is a selection of choice materials touching many significant aspects of the faith and doctrine. . . . These items were produced by the Prophet Joseph Smith and were published in the Church periodicals of his day.

Apostle Franklin D. Richards put the first collection of materials together in 1851. Over the years revisions were made, including sections that were taken out of the Pearl of Great Price in 1979 and moved to the D&C (Sections 137 and 138). According to Apostle Bruce R. McConkie, the Pearl of Great Price has five sections:

1. Selections from the Book of Moses. This is an extract from the Book of Genesis of Joseph Smith's translation of the Bible.
2. Joseph Smith—Matthew. A one-chapter reinterpretation of Matthew 23:39 and chapter 24.
3. Joseph Smith—History. This includes "excerpts from Joseph Smith's official testimony and history, which he prepared in 1838 . . ."
4. The Articles of Faith. Written by Smith and originally known as the Wentworth Letter, these are the thirteen major points of LDS doctrine.
5. The Book of Abraham. Joseph Smith took Egyptian papyri and translated them, publishing this serially in the *Times and Seasons* beginning in 1842. It is said to contain "priceless information about the gospel, pre-existence, the nature of Deity, the creation, and priesthood, information which is not otherwise available in any other revelation now extant."[9]

The History of the Book of Abraham

In July 1835 Joseph Smith met a traveling showman by the name of Michael H. Chandler who was displaying four Egyptian mummies in Kirtland, Ohio. Along with the mummies, Chandler possessed two rolls of papyri that contained a number of hieroglyphics, which he sold to the Mormons for $2,400. The next day, Smith proclaimed that the manuscripts were actually written by none other than two Old Testament patriarchs: "I commenced the translation of some of the characters or hieroglyphics, and much to our joy found that one of the rolls contained the writings of Abraham, another the writings of Joseph of Egypt, etc."[10] To stumble on such an incredible find was, in itself, an amazing stroke of what Mormons would view as divine providence. Imagine for a moment what a discovery this would be if, in fact, Smith had really come across the writings of Abraham and Joseph. They would be priceless! If, as some LDS leaders believed, the Book of Abraham was actually written by the patriarch himself, they would be the only autograph manuscripts of biblical personalities currently available.[11] If authentic, the Book of Abraham would predate the book of Genesis by about five hundred years.

Truth or Fiction?

Few people in 1835 could have been considered experts in the field of Egyptology. The famous Rosetta Stone, currently on display at the British Museum in London, was discovered accidentally in 1799 by Napoleon's army in Egypt. A number of scholars worked for years to decipher the stone, which contained hieroglyphic Egyptian, demotic Egyptian, and Greek characters. Finally, Jean Francois Champollion announced his results in 1822, and the mystery of the Egyptian language came to an end. The LDS Church acknowledges that "Joseph Smith claimed no expertise in any language. . . . the Lord did not require Joseph Smith to have knowledge of Egyptian." As with the Book of Mormon, the papyri were allegedly translated by the "gift and power of God. . . . Joseph Smith did not claim to know the ancient languages of the records he was translating."[12]

Of the two papyri, Smith chose to focus on the one he claimed was written by Abraham. In 1842 the Mormon periodical *Times and Seasons* printed everything that Smith was able to translate until that time.[13] Circumstances would prohibit him from "translating" the rest of the Book of Abraham papyrus or the other papyrus that he called the Book of Joseph. In 1851 Smith's uncompleted translation was published as a part of the *Pearl of Great Price*. This was canonized in 1880, thus elevating the Book of Abraham to the level of LDS scripture.

The Book of Abraham contains three facsimiles or drawings that Smith attempts to interpret, as this Pearl of Great Price resource explains:

Facsimile 1 shows that Abraham overcame the tests and trials of earth life; Facsimile 2 shows that Abraham obtained the knowledge that would help him return to God's presence and become like Him; and Facsimile 3 shows that Abraham entered the presence of God and obtained eternal life.[14]

The Rediscovered Pagan Papyri

For more than a century, the actual papyri from which Smith "translated" were believed to be lost. Thus, just like the Book of Mormon, nobody could go back to the original manuscripts to see what he had translated. They had remained the property of Emma Smith, Joseph's widow, following his death in 1844. According to LDS historian William E. Berrett, Emma sold the manuscripts to a museum in St. Louis. The papyri eventually found their way to the Chicago Museum. When the Great Chicago Fire occurred in 1871, it was assumed that the manuscripts were destroyed along with the museum.

In 1967 interest in the Book of Abraham again surfaced when the papyri Smith used in 1835 were found in the Metropolitan Museum of Art in New York. These were eventually given back to the LDS Church. With the manuscript of the Book of Abraham now available, scholars could investigate the actual Egyptian that Smith "translated."

If Joseph Smith was indeed a prophet inspired by God who had the ability to translate the Book of Abraham, here was the perfect opportunity to demonstrate it. However, Egyptologists agree that Smith's "translation" was not at all accurate and that his source was an Egyptian myth known as the Book of Breathings, a funerary papyrus dating around the time of Christ, long after the Egyptian dynasty when Abraham lived. It is, in fact, of pagan origin and has nothing to do with Abraham.

Smith's papyrus was both torn and attached to a backing that held it in place. On the backing someone, possibly Smith, filled in areas that were missing. An examination of Joseph Smith's Facsimile No. 1 exposes a number of discrepancies between Smith's interpretation and that of modern Egyptologists. Smith claimed that the facsimile portrays Abraham lying on an altar. Standing next to him is the idolatrous priest Elkanah who holds a knife in his hand. Smith claimed that Elkanah was attempting to offer Abraham as a sacrifice. Below the altar are figures that Smith describes as idolatrous gods. Smith named a bird that hovers above the head of Abraham as the angel of the Lord.

Richard A. Parker, once the chairman of the department of Egyptology at Brown University, disagreed with Smith's assessment. He claimed:

> This is a well-known scene from the Osiris mysteries, with Anubis, the jackal-headed god, on the left ministering to the dead Osiris on the bier. The pencilled(?) restoration is incorrect. Anubis should be jackal-headed. The left arm of Osiris is in reality lying at his side under him. The apparent upper hand is part of the wing of a second bird which is hovering over the erect phallus of Osiris (now broken away). The second bird is Isis and she is magically impregnated by the dead Osiris and then later gives birth to Horus who avenges his father and takes over his inheritance. The complete bird represents Nephthys, sister to Osiris and Isis. Beneath the bier are the four canopic jars with heads representative of the four sons of Horus, human-headed Imseti, baboon-headed Hapy, jackal-headed Duamutef and falcon-headed Kebehsenuf.[15]

Other problems develop when Facsimile No. 2 is considered. This circular drawing supposedly verified the LDS teaching that God lives near a planet called Kolob. Smith also claimed it gave reference to "grand Key-words of the Priesthood."[16] According to Egyptologist Stephen E. Thompson:

> Facsimile 2 is a drawing of an Egyptian funerary amulet known as a hypocephalus, which was placed under the head of the mummy and was intended to protect the head of the deceased, provide him with the sun's life-giving warmth, and to make it possible for him to join the sun god Re in his celestial boat, and thereby insure his continued, pleasant existence in the next life.[17]

Thompson went on to say:

> Concerning Joseph Smith's interpretations of the figures in this facsimile, it has been stated that "his explanations, are, in general, reasonable in light of modern Egyptological knowledge." A comparison of Smith's interpretations with current Egyptological scholarship shows that this statement is also incorrect.[18]

In a documentary called *The Lost Book of Abraham*, Robert K. Ritter, a professor of Egyptology at the University of Chicago, was equally critical of Smith's "translation," saying:

147

I want to be absolutely clear on this. There simply is no justification for the kind of interpretations that appear in facsimile one or facsimile three. They are wrong with regard to the hieroglyphs, they are wrong with regard to the gender, they are wrong with regard to the understanding of what the scene actually represents and where they are used in the body of the text. They are wrong there as well. In short there is no historical validity for the interpretations in that book. None whatsoever.[19]

Doubts about the 1967 Discovery

Because of the vast evidence that shows Smith did not know how to translate Egyptian, some LDS apologists have tried to raise doubts about the 1967 papyri discovered in New York. Was this the same papyri that Smith had in his possession? BYU professor Daniel Peterson wrote:

Critics have long attempted to make a case against the Book of Abraham. They argue that some ancient texts do not support the book. They point to the fragments of the Joseph Smith papyri that we now possess and claim that since the contents of these papyri bear little obvious relationship to the book of Abraham, the book is a fraud; but Hugh Nibley has made an exhaustive study of these claims and has shown that the papyri we now have were probably not the ones from which Joseph Smith translated the book of Abraham.[20]

Christian researcher Charles Larson challenges this claim:

And there could be no question that the Metropolitan papyri were indeed none other than the ones which Joseph Smith had once purchased and used. The reverse sides of the paper to which they were glued contained such things as architectural drawings of a temple and maps of the Kirtland, Ohio area.[21]

Indeed, we know of no official LDS Church pronouncement that denies the authenticity of these documents.

It is obvious why the Mormon Church needs to maintain the Book of Abraham as authentic. As B. H. Roberts noted:

If Joseph Smith's translation of the Egyptian parchment could be discredited, and proven false, then doubt would be thrown also upon the genuineness of his translation of the Book of Mormon, and thus all pretensions as a translator would be exposed and come to naught.[22]

Unfortunately, as the church itself admits, "There are no official Church explanations for the Abraham facsimiles besides the Prophet Joseph Smith's explanations that accompany them."[23] Knowing if it is a book really written by Abraham requires great faith, as a church history manual says that, "like the Book of Mormon, the book of Abraham is its own evidence that it came about through the gift and power of God."[24]

If Smith did not have the academic ability to properly "translate" a common piece of Egyptian funerary papyrus, it would be doubtful that he had the translating ability to decipher the "Reformed Egyptian" supposedly contained in the Book of Mormon. The discovery of the papyri that Smith used for the Book of Abraham puts serious doubt on Smith's translating ability and his claim to being a prophet.[25]

Discussion Questions

1. According to President Ezra Taft Benson, "The Doctrine and Covenants brings men to Christ's kingdom, even The Church of Jesus Christ of Latter-day Saints, 'the only true and living church upon the face of the whole earth' (verse 30). I know that."[26] Is Benson's statement reasonable? Why or why not?

2. Except for Section 138 and the two "official declarations," nothing has been added to the Doctrine and Covenants since the nineteenth century. In your opinion, why doesn't the church add more teachings and revelations if God is still speaking to LDS leaders today?

3. In your mind, does the Book of Abraham help or hinder the idea that Joseph Smith knew how to translate ancient languages? Explain your reasoning.

Final Thought

The Doctrine and Covenants and the Pearl of Great Price are pointed to by Mormons as scripture, showing that God has revealed Himself in the latter-days. However, much trust must be given to Joseph Smith, the originator of these books, in order to accept the extrabiblical writings as authoritative. To be able to entertain this proposal, Smith must be considered as someone who is trustworthy and reliable. Then we need to see if these "scriptures" agree or disagree with God's revealed Word, the Bible. If there are discrepancies, warning bells ought to sound, as Mormonism cannot be true if these writings are nothing more than the product of imagined creativity.

Notes

1. *Conference Reports* (October 1950): 10.

2. "*Ensign* (January 2009): 47.

3. Mormon President Ezra Taft Benson said that the D&C was "the only book in the world that has a preface written by the Lord Himself," *Ensign* (November 1986): 79; brackets in original.

4. *Ensign* (May 1987): 83.

5. Ludlow, ed., *Encyclopedia of Mormonism*, s.v. "Doctrine and Covenant Editions," 1:425.

6. See chapter 14 for a full description of the Word of Wisdom.

7. For more information about inaccurate prophecies found in the D&C, please see chapter 35, "Why do you have difficulty accepting Joseph Smith as a true prophet of God?" in our book *Answering Mormons' Questions*.

8. *Pearl of Great Price Teacher Manual*, 6.

9. McConkie, *Mormon Doctrine*, 564.

10. *History of the Church*, 2:235–36.

11. For example, President Wilford Woodruff said, "The Lord is Blessing Joseph with Power to reveal mysteries of the kingdom of God; to translate through the urim and Thummim Ancient records & Hyeroglyphics as old as Abraham or Adam. . . . Joseph the Seer has presented us some of the Book of Abraham which was written by his own hand but hid from the knowledge of man for the last four thousand years. . . ." Susan Staker, ed., *Waiting for World's End: The Diaries of Wilford Woodruff* (Salt Lake City, UT: Signature Books, 1993), 50–51; ellipses and spelling in original. For more information on this topic, see Luke P. Wilson, "Did Joseph Smith claim his Abraham papyrus was an autograph?," Institute for Religious Research, http://irr.org/files/abraham-autograph.pdf.

12. "Translation and Ancient Historicity of the Book of Abraham," The Church of Jesus Christ of Latter-Day Saints, accessed August 26, 2014, https://www.lds.org/topics/translation-and-historicity-of-the-book-of-abraham.

13. These were the March 1, March 15, and May 16, 1842, issues of the *Times and Seasons*.

14. *Pearl of Great Price Teacher Manual*, 36.

15. Richard A. Parker, "The Joseph Smith Papyri: A Preliminary Report," *Dialogue* 3, no. 2 (summer 1968): 86.

16. Explanation of figure seven opposite Facsimile No. 2. Key words are an essential part of the LDS temple ceremony.

17. Stephen Thompson, "Egyptology and the *Book of Mormon*," *Dialogue* 28, no. 1 (spring 1995): 149–50.

18. Ibid., 150.

19. "The Lost Book of Abraham," 56:31, www.bookofabraham.info.

20. *Ensign* (January 1994): 20.

21. Charles M. Larson, *By His Own Hand upon Papyrus* (Grand Rapids: Institute for Religious Research, 1992), 36. For further study on a fascinating issue, we highly recommend Larson's book, which includes a wonderful pull-out picture of the papyrus.

22. Roberts, comp., *Comprehensive History of the Church*, 2:138.

23. *Pearl of Great Price Teacher Manual*, 35.

24. *Church History in the Fulness of Times Student Manual: Religion 341–343* (Salt Lake City: The Church of Jesus Christ of Latter-day Saints, 2003), 258.

25. For more information on this topic, we highly recommend the DVD titled *The Lost Book of Abraham*, which can be viewed for free at www.bookofabraham.info.

26. Benson, *Teachings of Ezra Taft Benson*, 41.

Part IV

Examining the LDS Concept of Salvation

10 | The Atonement

The demands of justice for broken law can be satisfied through mercy, earned by your continual repentance and obedience to the laws of God. Such repentance and obedience are absolutely essential for the Atonement to work its complete miracle in your life.

Apostle Richard G. Scott[1]

MORMONESE:

atonement: The sacrifice made by Jesus that allows people to be resurrected and gain eternal life if they repent and keep the commandments.
repentance: The process by which a member receives forgiveness. True repentance involves six steps, including confession and a successful abandonment of sins.

Jesus Christ paid a tremendous price when He sacrificed His life at the hands of the Romans and the Jewish leaders. There is no question about the costly nature of this unselfish act. While Christians and Mormons would both accept the atonement of Christ, they disagree as to what this sacrifice actually accomplished and even, for some, where it took place.

The Atonement according to Mormonism

Mormon leaders have taught that the atonement of Jesus Christ releases the "human family" from the consequences of Adam's fall and allows a general resurrection from the dead. The atonement began in the Garden of Gethsemane. This teaching is drawn from two passages within the LDS standard works. Mosiah 3:7 (BOM) gives a description of Christ's suffering similar to what the biblical Gospels say He experienced in the Garden of Gethsemane:

> And lo, he shall suffer temptations, and pain of body, hunger, thirst, and fatigue, even more than man can suffer, except it be unto death; for behold, blood cometh from every pore, so great shall be his anguish for the wickedness and the abominations of his people.

D&C 19:15–19 adds:

> Therefore I command you to repent—repent, lest I smite you by the rod of my mouth, and by my wrath, and by my anger, and your sufferings be sore—how sore you know not, how exquisite you know not, yea, how hard to bear you know not. For behold, I, God, have suffered these things for all, that they might not suffer if they would repent; but if they would not repent they must suffer even as I; which suffering caused myself, even God, the greatest of all, to tremble because of pain, and to bleed at every pore, and to suffer both body and spirit—and would that I might not drink the bitter cup, and shrink—nevertheless, glory be to the Father, and I partook and finished my preparations unto the children of men.

The atonement makes available the forgiveness of personal sins on the condition of repentance.

> Through the Atonement, Jesus Christ redeems all people from the effects of the Fall. All people who have ever lived on the earth and who ever will live on the earth will be resurrected and brought back into the presence of God to be judged (see 2 Nephi 2:5–10; Helaman 14:15–17). Through the Savior's gift of mercy and redeeming grace, we will all receive the gift of immortality and live forever in glorified, resurrected bodies.[2]

The full benefit of the atonement does not come without a cost. Responding to the title of his article ("What Does the Atonement Mean to You?"), Seventy Cecil O. Samuelson Jr. explained,

> The Atonement makes the Resurrection a reality for everyone. However, with respect to our individual transgressions and sins, conditional aspects of the

Atonement require our faith in the Lord Jesus Christ, our repentance, and our compliance with the laws and ordinances of the gospel.[3]

President Spencer W. Kimball said, "The Savior came 'to bring to pass the immortality and eternal life of man' (Moses 1:39). His birth, death, and resurrection brought about the first. But we must join our efforts with his to bring about the second, to attain eternal life."[4] Referring to 2 Nephi 25:23 in the Book of Mormon in his general conference talk "Attempting the Impossible," Seventy Jorge F. Zeballos taught,

> Salvation and eternal life would not be possible if it were not for the Atonement, brought about by our Savior, to whom we owe everything. But in order for these supreme blessings to be effective in our lives, we should first do our part, "for we know that it is by grace that we are saved, after all we can do." Let us with faith, enthusiasm, dedication, responsibility, and love do all that is within our reach, and we will be doing all that is possible to achieve the impossible—that is, to achieve what for the human mind is impossible but with the divine intervention of our loving Father and the infinite sacrifice brought about by our Savior becomes the greatest gift, the most glorious of realities, to live forever with God and with our families.[5]

Apostle Dallin Oaks used this same verse in a 2010 general conference talk:

> Because of what He accomplished by His atoning sacrifice, Jesus Christ has the power to prescribe the conditions we must fulfill to qualify for the blessings of His Atonement. That is why we have commandments and ordinances. That is why we make covenants. That is how we qualify for the promised blessings. They all come through the mercy and grace of the Holy One of Israel, "after all we can do" (2 Nephi 25:23).[6]

What should truly scare every Latter-day Saint is a general conference quote from Henry B. Eyring, a member of the First Presidency, when he said, "It is hard to know when we have done enough for the Atonement to change our natures and so qualify us for eternal life."[7]

The Garden or the Cross?

While the blood shed by Jesus on Calvary's cross completed the atonement, Mormonism clearly teaches that the Garden of Gethsemane is the place where the efficacious atonement took place. As a result, the cross almost seems to be an afterthought. *Gospel Principles* reports, "The Savior atoned for our sins by suffering in Gethsemane and by giving His life on the cross. It is impossible for us to fully understand how He suffered for all of our sins. In the Garden of Gethsemane, the weight of our sins caused Him to feel such agony that He bled from every pore."[8] While he acknowledged that Jesus would eventually go to the cross, President Joseph Fielding Smith implored,

> I wish we could impress this fact upon the minds of every member of this Church: His great suffering occurred before he ever went to the cross. It was in the Garden of Gethsemane, so the scriptures tell us, that blood oozed from every pore of his body; and in the extreme agony of his soul, he cried to his Father. It was not the nails driven into his hands and feet. Now do not ask me how that was done because I do not know. Nobody knows. All we know is that in some way he took upon himself that extreme penalty. He took upon him our transgressions, and paid a price, a price of torment.[9]

Other leaders have taught about Gethsemane in a similar fashion, including:

- Seventy Wolfgang H. Paul, 2007: "It was there that the Savior paid the price for all the sorrows, sins, and transgressions of every human being who ever lived or ever will live. There He drank the bitter cup and suffered so that all who repent may not suffer."[10]
- Seventy Lawrence E. Corbridge, 2008: "Jesus Christ entered a garden called Gethsemane, where He overcame sin for us. He took upon Himself our sins. He suffered the penalty of our wrongs. He paid the price of our education. I don't know how He did what He did. I only know that He did and that because He did, you and I may be forgiven of our sins that we may be endowed with His power."[11]
- Apostle Russell M. Nelson, 2013: "The Savior began shedding His blood for all mankind not on the cross, where the agony of the Atonement was completed, but in the Garden of Gethsemane. There He took upon Himself the weight of the sins of all who would ever live."[12]

A garden atonement seems odd for a couple of reasons. One, Paul always points to the cross where this event happened; never does he give any indication that the atonement was divided over two locations. In addition, the Bible only refers to the garden twice—never once in association with the atonement. Two, if Christ actually atoned for *all* of the sins of mankind in the garden, what would be left for Him to atone for on the cross?

Christianity's Definition of Atonement

The atonement is the act of bringing people together with God by means of a sacrifice. Since all men and women are inherently sinful by nature as well as action,[13] Philippians 2:7 reports that Christ made Himself of no reputation by taking "the form of a servant." He was made in human likeness and humbled Himself, becoming "obedient unto death, even the death of the cross" (v. 8). Hebrews 2:17 says this was done in order that He might make "reconciliation for the sins of the people."

Matthew 1:21 says that Jesus would come to "save his people from their sins." No other conclusion can be made except that only God's personal intervention would be able to overcome humanity's sinful condition. If our personal merit could satisfy the penalty of sin, then no atonement would have even been necessary. Galatians 2:21 says, "I do not frustrate the grace of God: for if righteousness come by the law, then Christ is dead in vain."

In Old Testament times, redemption was demonstrated through the ceremonial sacrifice. God made it clear that forgiveness would be provided only through the death of an innocent substitute that represented the payment for the penalty of sin. Sacrifices were made in the Jerusalem temple on a regular basis for the sins of individuals; however, the people of Israel celebrated the Day of Atonement, or Yom Kippur, once a year. On this sacred day, the Jewish high priest would offer sacrifice for Israel as a nation, which sought reconciliation with the God whom they had offended.

Still, the mere act itself of killing an animal for one's sins did not appease God. Through many examples, the Bible states that redemption was based on an individual's faith in what the sacrifice represented. This faith would lead to the obvious act of repentance, thereby making the sacrifice satisfactory. God had no pleasure in sacrifice without these two important elements.

This principle can be seen in the example of Cain and Abel. Genesis 4:3–5 says that both Cain and Abel offered sacrifices to the Lord, "but unto Cain and to his offering he had not respect." The writer of Hebrews explained that Abel's sacrifice was accepted because, unlike Cain's, it was offered in righteous faith (Heb. 11:4). Since the wages of sin is death (both physical and spiritual), the repentant sinner sees the sacrifice as a vicarious substitute. The animal was symbolically taking on itself the penalty due sinful people. Christian theologian Leon Morris wrote:

> Nobody who came thoughtfully to God by the way of sacrifice could be in any doubt but that sin was a serious matter. It could not be put aside by a lighthearted wave of the hand but required the shedding of blood. . . . No-one who came to God by the way of offering the best in his flock would put a low value on the privilege of such an approach. He would realize, as many of us today do not, that the service of God must cost us something.[14]

Unfortunately, as time went on, many Jews offered sacrifice out of mere protocol, not by faith. To many the significance of what the sacrifice represented was lost in legalistic attitudes. The New Testament book of Hebrews explains that the animal sacrificial system typified what Christ would do when He would voluntarily pay the price of sin through His own death. Morris adds:

> The high priest could do no more than enter the Holy of Holies himself. He could not take anyone with him. And he could enter only on the one day in the year. The fullest exercise of his ministry with all the solemnity at his command obtained only a very limited access: access on one day for him only. The people must forever be content with access by proxy. But in Hebrews there is emphasis on two wonderful truths: Christ secured access into the very presence of God in heaven (as we have just seen, Heb. 9:11–12, 24) and access not for himself only but for all his people as well. . . . Because Christ's blood was shed, all who believe in him have access into the very holiest of all.[15]

Another Christian theologian, A. W. Tozer, wrote,

> The theme of bloodguiltiness is a recurring theme in the Bible and here we have two concepts. The Old Testament picture is that of the blood of murdered Abel crying out for justice; the New Testament picture is that of the blood of Jesus Christ the Savior and mediator crying from the throne of God for mercy![16]

To be sure, Christians throughout the centuries have seen the atonement of Christ as God's way of reconciling sinful humanity to Himself. Through the sacrifice of God's Son, those who were once enemies of God can now know that the barrier that separated them from their Creator has been removed. So powerful is this sacrificial act that believers can be assured that *all* their sins—past, present, and future—are now forgiven. Colossians 2:13–14 reads:

And you, who were dead in your trespasses and the uncircumcision of your flesh, God made alive together with him, having forgiven us all our trespasses, by canceling the record of debt that stood against us with its legal demands. This he set aside, nailing it to the cross. (ESV)

Christians have long maintained that this glorious act of sacrifice took place on Golgotha, known as the Place of the Skull. This area outside the walls of Jerusalem was reserved for the execution of prisoners, both political and criminal. It was here that God Himself was subject to the humiliating death of a common criminal.

The Cross, Not the Garden

By emphasizing what took place in the Garden of Gethsemane, LDS leaders miss a significant point regarding the atonement. The expiation of sin (making amends for wrongdoing) was not based on the substitute's perspiration; rather, it was based on his expiration. Christ's atonement for the sins of the believer was accomplished in His death, not in the short time that He spent in the garden.

Paul stressed that Christ's death was of primary importance in the atonement. In 1 Corinthians 15:3 he wrote, "I delivered unto you *first of all . . .* that Christ *died* for our sins." Throughout the New Testament, the *death* of Christ is emphasized. Referring to Christ's reconciliation, Paul told the Christians in Romans 5:8, "But God commendeth his love toward us, in that, while we were yet sinners, Christ *died* for us." In verse 10, he added, "For if, when we were enemies, we were reconciled to God by the *death* of his Son, much more, being reconciled, we shall be saved by his life."

Meanwhile, Hebrews 9:22 states that there is no remission of sins without the shedding (not sweating) of blood. According to verse 26, Christ came in order to do away with sin by His own sacrifice. Referring to this passage, Christian theologian Leon Morris wrote:

Animal sacrifice can never produce a purification valid in heaven. But Christ's sacrifice can. . . . The sacrifice of himself means an infinitely better sacrifice than any that was possible under the Levitical system. . . . That is one point that this author emphasizes. Another is the finality of Christ's atoning sacrifice. Repeatedly he tells us that Christ offered himself "once and for all" or the like. Believers have been made holy "through the sacrifice of the body of

Jesus Christ once for all" (Heb. 10:10); he "offered for all time one sacrifice for sins" (verse 12); "by one sacrifice he has made perfect for ever those who are being made holy" (verse 14). And he removes decisively the possibility of any further offering by saying that, when sins have been forgiven (as they have been through what Christ has done), "there is no longer any sacrifice for sin" (Heb. 10:18). The utter finality of Christ's sacrifice is an important truth.[17]

The sacrifice spoken of was the death that Jesus suffered. The cross—not the Garden of Gethsemane—is given preeminence, as the following texts attest:

But God forbid that I should glory, save in *the cross* of our Lord Jesus Christ, by whom the world is crucified unto me, and I unto the world (Gal. 6:14, emphasis added).

And that he might reconcile both unto God in one body *by the cross,* having slain the enmity thereby (Eph. 2:16, emphasis added).

And being found in fashion as a man, he humbled himself, and became obedient unto death, even the death of *the cross* (Phil. 2:8, emphasis added).

And, having made peace *through the blood of his cross,* by him to reconcile all things unto himself; by him, I say, whether they be things in earth, or things in heaven (Col. 1:20, emphasis added).

Looking unto Jesus the author and finisher of our faith; who for the joy that was set before him *endured the cross,* despising the shame, and is set down at the right hand of the throne of God (Heb. 12:2, emphasis added).

Unlike LDS leaders, Paul gloried in the cross, not the garden, for it was on the cross that Jesus provided for the Christian's future salvation.

At the Cross Where I First Saw the Light

While Jesus's death on the cross is not totally ignored by LDS leaders, the implication is that this method of execution was only a necessary evil so that the resurrection could take place. During a conference speech in 1953, Marion Romney, a member of the First Presidency under David O. McKay, stated:

Jesus then went into the Garden of Gethsemane. There he suffered most. He suffered greatly on the cross, of course, but other men had died by crucifixion; in fact, a man hung on either side of him as he died on the cross.

But no man, nor set of men, nor all men put together, ever suffered what the Redeemer suffered in the garden. He went there to pray and suffer.[18]

While we would never imply that it is required for a Christian church to have a cross on display, no Latter-day Saint chapel or other building has one. In fact, in the mind of many Latter-day Saints, the symbolism of the cross is not nearly as important as it is to the Christian. A reference manual reports,

> The cross is used in many Christian churches as a symbol of the Savior's death and Resurrection and as a sincere expression of faith. As members of The Church of Jesus Christ of Latter-day Saints, we also remember with reverence the suffering of the Savior. But because the Savior lives, we do not use the symbol of His death as the symbol of our faith.[19]

Misunderstanding the Christian symbol of the cross, such as one strategically placed in a church sanctuary, President Joseph Fielding Smith wrote:

> However, to bow down before a cross or to look upon it as an emblem to be revered because of the fact that our Savior died upon a cross is repugnant to members of The Church of Jesus Christ of Latter-day Saints. . . . To many, like the writer, such a custom is repugnant and contrary to the true worship of our Redeemer. Why should we bow down before a cross or use it as a symbol? Because our Savior died on the cross, the wearing of crosses is to most Latter-day Saints in very poor taste and inconsistent to our worship. . . . We may be definitely sure that if our Lord had been killed with a dagger or with a sword, it would have been very strange indeed if religious people of this day would have graced such a weapon by wearing it and adoring it because it was by such a means that our Lord was put to death.[20]

For those who teach that there is atonement available in the blood of Christ, an LDS Church tract proclaims:

> Christians speak often of the blood of Christ and its cleansing power. Much that is believed and taught on this subject, however, is such utter nonsense and so palpably false that to believe it is to lose one's salvation. For instance, many believe or pretend to believe that if we confess Christ with our lips and avow that we accept him as our personal Savior, we are thereby saved. They say that his blood, without any other act than mere belief, makes us clean.[21]

Obviously these Mormons have missed the point of the atonement of Christ. It was at the cross of Christ that the death of God's own Son was given in payment for the believer's sins. For more than a century Christians have sung the hymn "At the Cross," which portrays the importance of the atonement. Its chorus is:

> At the cross, at the cross, where I first saw the light,
> And the burden of my heart rolled away (rolled away),
> It was there by faith I received my sight,
> And now I am happy all the day.[22]

Discussion Questions

1. In Mormonism, the Garden of Gethsemane is given preeminence when mentioned by general authorities in reference to the atonement. Why do Christians stress the cross rather than the garden as the place where Jesus atoned for the sins of all believers?
2. Some Mormons, including Gordon B. Hinckley, said that they don't like displaying the cross because "it is the symbol of the dying Christ, while our message is a declaration of a Living Christ."[23] Is this description accurate with what the biblical writers said?
3. Joseph Fielding Smith said that he disliked a physical image of the cross because it could end up being bowed down to and possibly worshiped. What parameters should there be in Christian worship with displaying a cross around one's neck or a decoration on the wall? How would you respond to Smith's accusation?

Final Thought

Christians realize that salvation is a result of what Jesus did for them on the cross; namely, providing forgiveness of sins. To even insinuate that the atonement took place in the Garden of Gethsemane is a foreign concept to the Christian. True freedom in Christ can only be found when a person understands what Jesus did on the cross. We who hold the Bible dear to our hearts have no choice but to concur with Paul as he declared in 1 Corinthians 1:18: "The preaching of the cross is to them that perish foolishness; but unto us which are saved it is the power of God."

Notes

1. "The Atonement Can Secure Your Peace and Happiness," *Ensign* (November 2006): 42.
2. *True to the Faith*, 18.
3. *Ensign* (April 2009): 47.
4. *Teachings of Presidents of the Church: Spencer W. Kimball*, 29.
5. *Ensign* (November 2009): 34.
6. *Ensign* (November 2010): 84. As far as 2 Nephi 25:23 is concerned, the question is, "How much can a person do?" If it is possible to devote ten minutes in prayer, isn't it possible to dedicate just five additional minutes? Or in addition to mowing a neighbor's yard, couldn't vacuuming the house and painting the shed also have been completed? For more information, see the next chapter on grace and works. See also chapter 19, "Doesn't the book of James say that 'faith without works is dead'?" in our book *Answering Mormons' Questions*.
7. *Ensign* (May 2007): 90.
8. *Gospel Principles*, 61.
9. *Teachings of Presidents of the Church: Joseph Fielding Smith*, 63.
10. *Ensign* (June 2007): 15.
11. *Ensign* (November 2008): 35.
12. *Ensign* (April 2013): 35.
13. Romans 3:23 says that "all have sinned" and have therefore broken God's law. "Man's heart is evil from his youth" (Gen. 8:21), "full of evil" (Eccles. 9:3), and "deceitful above all things, and desperately wicked" (Jer. 17:9).
14. Morris, *The Atonement: Its Meaning and Significance* (Downers Grove, IL: Inter-Varsity Press, 1983), 50–51.
15. Ibid., 84.
16. A.W. Tozer, *Echoes from Eden: The Voices of God Calling Man* (Harrisburg, PA: Christian Publications, 1981), 41.
17. Morris, *The Atonement*, 64–65.
18. *Conference Reports* (October 1953): 35.
19. *True to the Faith*, 45–46.
20. Joseph Fielding Smith, *Answers to Gospel Questions*, 4:17–18. While Christians revere the symbol, Smith creates a "straw man" argument since most do not "bow down" to the cross. To make it appear that they do turns the cross into a pagan idol, something that certainly should be abhorred.
21. Bruce R. McConkie, *What the Mormons Think of Christ* (Salt Lake City: The Church of Jesus Christ of Latter-Day Saints, 1976),19–20. While McConkie may not like salvation being so simplified, Romans 10:9–10 states that "if you confess with your mouth that Jesus is Lord and believe in your heart that God raised him from the dead, you will be saved. For with the heart one believes and is justified, and with the mouth one confesses and is saved" (ESV). For more information about the cross and its importance to salvation, see chapter 17, "Why do you emphasize the cross? Why highlight Christ's suffering and death?" in our book *Answering Mormons' Questions*.
22. For more information about forgiveness of sins, see chapter 20, "Isn't it arrogant to think you already have forgiveness of sins?" in our book *Answering Mormons' Questions*.
23. *Ensign* (April 2005): 3.

11 | Grace and Works

We are told that faith without works is dead; that as the body without the spirit is dead, so also is faith without works dead [see James 2:17, 26], and I am sorry to say that there are many professed Latter-day Saints who are spiritually dead.

President Heber J. Grant [1]

Many Christians have become understandably confused when their Mormon acquaintances tell them how salvation comes by "grace coupled with gospel obedience."[2] As one Mormon put it, "some Christians make the mistake of taking some of Paul's writing out of context, including the context of the whole Bible, and teaching that we are saved by grace, and not by works at all. . . . when it comes to going to the heaven (the celestial) where God and Christ dwell (D&C 76:112), specific works are

166

required, including baptism (Mark 16:16) and faithfully living the gospel of Jesus Christ."[3] The problem lies in the fact that Mormon leaders have redefined the word *salvation* and given it a split definition that is certainly not taught by the Bible.

According to LDS teaching, salvation by grace is synonymous with mere resurrection from the dead. President Harold B. Lee referred to this concept as "general salvation," saying how this is given to every person on the earth, "whether they are good or bad, rich or poor, when they have lived—it makes no difference. All have the blessings of the Atonement and the blessings of the resurrection given to them as a free gift because of the Savior's atoning sacrifice."[4] Apostle Russell M. Nelson told a general conference audience, "To be saved—or to gain salvation—means to be saved from physical and spiritual death. Because of the Resurrection of Jesus Christ, all people will be resurrected and saved from physical death."[5] In Mormonism, the Atonement allows for all humans to be qualified for one of three levels of heaven:

> Because of the Fall of Adam we will all die (physical death), we are all cut off from the presence of God (spiritual death) and cannot get back to Him on our own, and we live in a world of toil, sin, and sorrow. The Atonement of Jesus Christ provides for the resurrection of all mankind, with immortal physical bodies, thus overcoming physical death.[6]

On the other hand, "individual salvation," otherwise known as exaltation or godhood, goes far beyond a mere resurrection from the dead. Stephen L. Richards, a member of the First Presidency, explained the difference to a general conference audience:

> They [Mormon missionaries] made clear distinction between general salvation or resurrection from the grave and individual salvation or exaltation earned by a man through his compliance with the laws of God. They taught that there are preferential places in heaven as there are on earth and that the highest place or Celestial Kingdom could be attained only by those who faithfully subscribe to and keep all the laws and ordinances of the Gospel of Jesus Christ and thereby entitle themselves to come into the presence of our God and Jesus Christ, His Son.[7]

Unlike resurrection from the dead, exaltation requires a concerted effort on the part of the individual to live according to all of the commandments. In the end, the Mormon will not be able to resort to excuses for justification.

In a 2012 general conference talk titled "What Shall a Man Give in Exchange for His Soul?" Seventy Robert C. Gay addressed the issue this way:

> This is the exchange the Savior is asking of us: we are to give up all our sins, big or small, for the Father's reward of eternal life. We are to forget self-justifying stories, excuses, rationalizations, defense mechanisms, procrastinations, appearances, personal pride, judgmental thoughts, and doing things our way. We are to separate ourselves from all worldliness and take upon us the image of God in our countenances.[8]

Mormons can never have the assurance that all their sins are forgiven, as President Spencer W. Kimball stated,

> It is true that many Latter-day Saints, having been baptized and confirmed members of the Church, and some even having received their endowments and having been married and sealed in the holy temple, have felt that they were thus guaranteed the blessings of exaltation and eternal life. But this is not so. There are two basic requirements every soul must fulfill or he cannot attain to the great blessings offered. He *must* receive the ordinances and he *must* be faithful, overcoming his weaknesses. Hence, not all who claim to be Latter-day Saints will be exalted.[9]

Can the Mormon Do Everything Commanded?

While the LDS missionaries may liberally use the term "grace," Mormonism mandates that one's efforts are required for any hope to attain godhood in the celestial kingdom. Doctrine and Covenants 25:15 says, "Keep my commandments continually, and a crown of righteousness thou shalt receive. And except thou do this, where I am you cannot come."[10] As Henry B. Eyring, a member of the First Presidency, put it, "To receive the gift of living with Him forever in families in the celestial kingdom, we must be able to live the laws of that kingdom (see D&C 88:22). He has given us commandments in this life to help us develop that capacity."[11]

Over and over again, Mormon Church leaders have stated that, by itself, God's grace—though vital for the "atonement"—cannot fully "save" people from their sins. An unattributed article in the *Ensign* magazine stated, "What do Latter-day Saints believe about grace? We believe that God's grace is what ultimately saves us; yet it does not save us without our doing all that we can to live God's commandments and follow Jesus Christ's teachings. We do not believe salvation comes by simply confessing belief in Christ as our Savior. Faith, works, ordinances, and grace are all necessary."[12]

To make our point, consider these quotes from the church presidents themselves about the importance of obedience required to attain celestial glory:

- Wilford Woodruff: "If a man does right, is valiant in the testimony of Jesus Christ, obeys the gospel, and keeps his covenants, when he passes to the other side of the veil he has an entrance into the presence of God and the Lamb; having kept celestial law he enters into celestial glory, he is preserved by that law, and he participates in that glory through the endless ages of eternity. It pays any man under heaven to obey and be faithful to the law of God the few days he spends in the flesh."[13]

- Joseph F. Smith: "Every blessing, privilege, glory, or exaltation is obtained only through obedience to the law upon which the same is promised. If we will abide the law, we shall receive the reward; but we can receive it on no other ground."[14]

- Heber J. Grant: "If you want to know how to be saved, I can tell you; it is by keeping the commandments of God. No power on earth, no power beneath the earth, will ever prevent you or me or any Latter-day Saint from being saved, except ourselves. We are the architects of our own lives, not only of the lives here, but the lives to come in the eternity. We ourselves are able to perform every duty and obligation that God has required of men. No commandment was ever given to us but that God has given us the power to keep that commandment. If we fail, we, and we alone, are responsible for the failure, because God endows His servants, from the President of the Church down to the humblest member, with all the ability, all the knowledge, all the power that is necessary, faithfully, diligently, and properly to discharge every duty and every obligation that rests upon them, and we, and we alone, will have to answer if we fail in this regard."[15]

- George Albert Smith: "Being a member of the Church and holding the Priesthood will not get us anywhere unless we are worthy. The Lord has said that every blessing that we desire is predicated upon obedience to His commandments. We may deceive our neighbors, and we may deceive ourselves with the idea that we are going through all right, but unless we keep the commandments of our Heavenly Father, unless we bear worthily this holy Priesthood that is so precious, we will not find our place in the celestial kingdom."[16]

• Joseph Fielding Smith: "Through obedience to those commandments which are set forth in the Gospel of Jesus Christ, and by continuance therein, we shall receive immortality, glory, eternal life, and dwell in the presence of God the Father and his Son Jesus Christ, where we shall truly know them."[17]

• Harold B. Lee: "The greatest message that one in this position could give to the membership of the Church is to keep the commandments of God, for therein lies the safety of the Church and the safety of the individual. Keep the commandments. There could be nothing that I could say that would be a more powerful or important message today."[18]

• Ezra Taft Benson: "Listen to the spiritual promise: 'All saints who remember to keep and do these sayings, walking in obedience *to the commandments.* . . . shall find wisdom and great treasures of knowledge, even hidden treasures' (D&C 89:18, 19; italics added). Some have thought this promise was contingent on just keeping the provisions of the Word of Wisdom. But you will notice we must walk in obedience to *all* the commandments. Then we shall receive specific spiritual promises. This means we must obey the law of tithing, keep the Sabbath day holy, keep morally clean and chaste, and obey all other commandments."[19]

• Thomas S. Monson: "Don't put your eternal life at risk. Keep the commandments of God."[20]

While some Mormons don't pretend to be perfect and claim to regularly repent, obeying just *some* of the commandments is not an option, according to Apostle Russell M. Nelson:

Teach of faith to keep *all* the commandments of God, knowing that they are given to bless His children and bring them joy. Warn them that they will encounter people who pick which commandments they will keep and ignore others that they choose to break. I call this the cafeteria approach to obedience. This practice of picking and choosing will not work. It will lead to misery. To prepare to meet God, one keeps *all* of His commandments. It takes faith to obey them, and keeping His commandments will strengthen that faith.[21]

Bemoaning the fact that many Latter-day Saints don't follow through on the promises they make every week, Joseph Fielding Smith said, "I wish we could get the members of the Church to understand more clearly the covenants they make when they partake of the sacrament at our sacrament meetings."[22] As Apostle Robert D. Hales explained, "Each week as we participate in the ordinance of the sacrament, we renew the promise of the Savior's birth in our own lives. We take His name upon us, and we renew our covenant of obedience and our promise that we will always remember Him."[23]

In a talk titled "Obedience to Law is Liberty" at the April 2013 general conference, Apostle L. Tom Perry stated, "We must not pick and choose which commandments we think are important to keep but acknowledge all of God's commandments."[24] Apostle Dallin H. Oaks stated in that same general conference, "From modern revelation, unique to the restored gospel, we know that the commandment to seek perfection is part of God the Father's plan for the salvation of His children."[25] Seventy Bruce C. Hafen taught, "If we must give all that we have, then our giving only *almost* everything is not enough. If we *almost* keep the commandments, we *almost* receive the blessings."[26]

Certainly official church manuals are in alignment with this attitude:

- "Latter-day Saints are Abraham's seed of the latter days. Their exaltation or eternal life depends on their obedience to the covenants they have made and kept with God."[27]

- "The Atonement of Jesus Christ assures each of us that we will be resurrected and live forever. But if we are to live forever with our families in Heavenly Father's presence, we must do all that the Savior commands us to do. This includes being baptized and confirmed and receiving the ordinances of the temple."[28]

- "Full obedience brings the complete power of the gospel into your life, including increased strength to overcome your weaknesses. This obedience includes actions you might not initially consider part of repentance, such as attending meetings, paying tithing, giving service, and forgiving others. The Lord promised, 'He that repents and does the commandments of the Lord shall be forgiven' (D&C 1:32)."[29]

- "The Lord keeps His promises: 'I, the Lord, am bound when ye do what I say; but when ye do not what I say, ye have no promise' (D&C 82:10). We must do our part to qualify for the blessings (see D&C 130:20–22). We should also remember that God determines the *then* part according to His wisdom and not according to our expectations."[30]

- "Have class members find and read Moroni 10:32. [It reads: "Yea, come unto Christ, and be perfected in him, and deny yourselves of all ungodliness; and if ye shall deny yourselves of all ungodliness, and love God with all your might, mind and strength, then is his grace sufficient for you, that by his grace ye may be perfect in Christ; and if by the grace of God ye are perfect in Christ, ye can in no wise deny the power of God."] According to this verse, what must we do to 'come unto Christ, and be perfected in him?' ('Deny [ourselves] of all ungodliness, and love God with all [our] might, mind, and strength.') Explain that 'deny yourselves of all ungodliness' means 'give up your sins.' We must strive to give up our sins and demonstrate that we love God with all our might, mind, and strength. If we do this throughout our lives, then Jesus Christ, through his Atonement, will help us become perfect."[31]

- "Receiving ordinances and keeping covenants are essential to Heavenly Father's plan. The scriptures often refer to His people as a 'covenant people.' The Lord's blessings exceed our mortal expectations. To live in the presence of our Heavenly Father, we must receive all of the necessary ordinances and keep all of the required covenants."[32]

There are implications in making covenants with God. In a straight-forward address given in the *Ensign* magazine titled "Understanding our Covenants with God," readers were told:

A covenant is a two-way promise, the conditions of which are set by God. When we enter into a covenant with God, we promise to keep those conditions. He promises us certain blessings in return. When we receive these saving ordinances and keep the associated covenants, the Atonement of Jesus Christ becomes effective in our lives, and we can receive the great blessing God can give us—eternal life (see D&C 14:7). Because keeping our covenants is essential to our happiness now and to eventually receiving eternal life, it is important to understand what we have promised our Heavenly Father.[33]

"I Can Do It Later"

Several Mormon leaders have cautioned members about procrastinating in regards to their salvation while criticizing the concept of a "death-bed" repentance. President David O. McKay warned that "the fallacy that Jesus has done all for us, and live as we may, if on our deathbed, we only believe, we shall be saved in his glorious presence, is most pernicious."[34] Ironically, some Latter-day Saints have even told us that they can make up for lost time after death. Such thinking undermines the LDS concept of a mortal probation, which is the short time on this earth "linking the eternity past with the eternity future." Joseph Fielding Smith taught, "This life is the most vital period in our eternal existence."[35] As Alma 34:32–33 in the Book of Mormon states,

> For behold, this life is the time for men to prepare to meet God; yea, behold the day of this life is the day for men to perform their labors. And now, as I said unto you before, as ye have had so many witnesses, therefore, I beseech of you that ye do not procrastinate the day of your repentance until the end; for after this day of life, which is given us to prepare for eternity, behold, if we do not improve our time while in this life, then cometh the night of darkness wherein there can be no labor performed.[36]

Referring to this passage in Alma, one student manual shows the importance of obedience:

> Amulek made it clear that we are, by our daily choices, ultimately giving ourselves over to the control or influence of either the Spirit of the Lord or the spirit of the devil. President Harold B. Lee (1899–1973) gave the following explanation of Alma 34:34: "To those who die in their wicked state, not having repented, the scriptures say the devil shall seal them as his own (see Alma 34:34), which means that until they have paid the uttermost farthing for what they have done, they shall not be redeemed from his grasp. When they shall have been subjected to the buffetings of Satan sufficient to have satisfied justice, then they shall be brought forth out of the grasp of Satan and shall be assigned to that place in our Father's celestial, terrestrial, or telestial world merited by their life upon this earth." (*The Teachings of Harold B. Lee,* ed., Clyde J. Williams [1996], 59). Elder Melvin J. Ballard (1873–1939) of the Quorum of the Twelve Apostles emphasized the importance of repenting during mortality: "This life is the time in which men are to repent. Do not let any of us imagine that we can go down to the grave not having overcome the corruptions of the flesh and then lose in the grave all our sins and evil tendencies. They will be with us. They will be with the spirit when separated from the body. Amulek made it clear that we are, by our daily choices, ultimately giving ourselves over to the control or influence of either the Spirit of the Lord or the spirit of the devil. . . .

[Mortality] is the time when men are more pliable and susceptible" [Sept 22, 1922], 11–12.[37]

Spencer W. Kimball stated:

Only as we overcome shall we become perfect and move toward godhood. As I have indicated previously, the time to do this is *now*, in mortality. Someone once said: "A fellow who is planning to reform is one step behind. He ought to quit planning and get on with the job. *Today* is the day."[38]

Kimball also said:

Because men are prone to postpone action and ignore directions, the Lord has repeatedly given strict injunctions and issued solemn warnings. Again and again in different phraseology and throughout the centuries the Lord has reminded man so that he could never have excuse. And the burden of the prophetic warning has been that *the time to act is now, in this mortal life.* One cannot with impunity delay his compliance with God's commandments.[39]

"That Is Why We Have Repentance"

When Mormons are confronted with the fact that they cannot keep all of the commandments, many find refuge in their ability to repent. Repentance, they say, erases the transgression and makes everything all right. This attitude is certainly frowned upon in church teachings. For instance, "abandonment of sin" is continually stressed: "although confession is an essential element of repentance, it is not enough. The Lord has said, 'By this ye may know if a man repenteth of his sins—behold, he will confess them and forsake them' (D&C 58:43)."[40]

Utilizing this verse, *Gospel Principles* states, "Our sincere sorrow should lead us to forsake (stop) our sins. If we have stolen something, we will steal no more. If we have lied, we will lie no more. If we have committed adultery, we will stop."[41] Kimball said, "The forsaking of sin must be a permanent one. True repentance does not permit making the same mistake again."[42] Brian D. Garner of the Church Correlation Department utilized a number of LDS scriptural verses to show how "this principle with a promise" requires both repentance and good works, as he italicized the word *and* in each reference to emphasize how forgiveness does not happen without both parts.[43] A student manual explains,

> **D&C 58:42–43. The Lord Promises Complete Forgiveness to Those Who Truly Repent.** The Lord forgives those who truly repent of their sins. This blessing comes through the Atonement of Christ, who "suffered . . . for all, that they might not suffer if they would repent" (D&C 19:16). The Lord promises that He will no more remember the sins of those who repent (see Ezekiel 18:21–22). Repentance, however, requires that we forsake and turn completely from our sins and confess them.[44]

While Seventy Claudio D. Zivic told an April 2014 general conference audience that "there is a need of constant repentance,"[45] such a philosophy seems self-defeating because a person who has to constantly repent must not be doing what should be possible. After all, the Mormon prophet Nephi supposedly said in 1 Nephi 3:7 how he knew "that the Lord giveth no commandments unto the children of men, save he shall prepare a way for them that they may accomplish the thing which he commandeth them."

Another verse that ought to bring consternation to the sincere Latter-day Saint is D&C 82:7, which says, "And now, verily I say unto you, I, the Lord, will not lay any sin to your charge; go your ways and sin no more; but unto that soul who sinneth shall the former sins return, saith the Lord your God." A Doctrine and Covenants resource provides guidance for the instructor:

> **Doctrine and Covenants 82:7. We are commanded to forsake sin. If we sin again after repenting, our former sins return.** (5–10 minutes) Bring several rocks to class that are all labeled with the same sin (for example, breaking the Word of Wisdom). Tell students a story about an imaginary person who commits this sin. Invent details to embellish your story. Each time the imaginary person commits the sin, pick up a rock, until you are holding several of them. Set all the rocks you are holding aside and ask: What might setting the rocks aside represent? (Repentance.) What happens to our sins when we repent? (The Lord forgives them.) Read Doctrine and Covenants 82:7 and look for what happens when we sin again. Ask: How many rocks would a person need to pick up if he sins after repenting? (All that you were previously holding plus a new one.) Why do you think our former sins return? What does that teach you about the importance of forsaking sin? How can knowing this doctrine help you avoid sin?[46]

There is no doubt that, in Mormonism, keeping commandments after repentance is not just a suggestion but a concrete requirement. Quoting D&C 1:31, a reference handbook states,

> The Lord has said that He "cannot look upon sin with the least degree of allowance" (D&C 1:31). The result of sin is the withdrawal of the Holy Ghost and, in eternity, being unable to dwell in the presence of our Heavenly Father, for "no unclean thing can dwell with God" (1 Nephi 10:21).[47]

Referring to this same D&C passage, Kimball said,

> In his preface to modern revelation, the Lord outlined what is one of the most difficult requirements in true repentance. For some it is the hardest part of repentance, because it puts one on guard for the remainder of his life. . . . This scripture is most precise. First, one repents. Having gained that ground he then must live the commandments of the Lord to retain his vantage point. This is necessary to secure complete forgiveness.[48]

Kimball also said that the "repentance which merits forgiveness" is the kind in which

> the former transgressor must have reached a "point of no return" to sin wherein there is not merely a renunciation but also a deep abhorrence of the sin—where the sin becomes most distasteful to him and where the desire or urge to sin is cleared out of his life.[49]

Quoting Alma 11:37 (BOM), a reference manual explains that

> repentance is much more than just acknowledging wrongdoings. . . . The Lord has declared that "no unclean thing can inherit the kingdom of heaven" (Alma 11:37). Your sins make you unclean—unworthy to return and dwell in the presence of your Heavenly Father. They also bring anguish to your soul in this life.[50]

Former Mormon Mark Champneys summarized Mormonism's teaching with two sentences: "In Mormonism, before you can be forgiven of a particular sin by the atonement, you must successfully stop that sin permanently. So, in order to be forgiven of all sin for time and all eternity, you must successfully stop all sin permanently."[51]

Saying that "after doing all they can to repent, some [Mormons] worry whether they have been forgiven," Brian D. Garner of the Church Correlation Department said it's possible for Mormons to know that repentance has taken place. How? "When we regularly feel the influence of the Holy Ghost in our lives, we can be assured that the Lord has forgiven us."[52] Heber J. Grant taught that "many Latter-day Saints" are "building their houses upon the sand. They are failing to carry out the commandments of our Heavenly Father that come to us from time to time through His inspired servants."[53]

Let's be honest, no sinner who has lived has found success in permanently ceasing from sin. For any Mormon to think it is possible to consistently obey God's commandments is to demonstrate the epitome of prideful arrogance.[54] To such a person comes the condemnation of Alma 5:27–28 in the Book of Mormon:

> Have ye walked, keeping yourselves blameless before God? Could ye say, if ye were called to die at this time, within yourselves, that ye have been sufficiently humble? That your garments have been cleansed and made white through the blood of Christ, who will come to redeem his people from their sins? Behold, are ye stripped of pride? I say unto you, if ye are not ye are not prepared to meet God. Behold ye must prepare quickly; for the kingdom of heaven is soon at hand, and such an one hath not eternal life.[55]

According to the LDS Church, as a person gets older, the desire to sin ought to lessen. One teacher's manual says, "Explain that the last step in repentance is striving to keep all the commandments of God (see D&C 1:32). Repentance is a process that we will have to use throughout our lives, but as we become more perfect in keeping the commandments, we will do less for which we need to repent."[56]

Of course, maturity in the faith is important, but the desire to sin is not something that just goes away with time. Consider what the apostle Paul said in Romans 7:15, 18–20:

> For I do not understand my own actions. For I do not do what I want, but I do the very thing I hate. . . . For I know that nothing good dwells in me, that is, in my flesh. For I have the desire to do what is right, but not the ability to carry it out. For I do not do the good I want, but the evil I do not want is what I keep on doing. Now if I do what I do not want, it is no longer I who do it, but sin that dwells within me. (ESV)

Seeking Perfection

Mormon leaders have often made it a point to motivate members to seek after perfection. Apostle Dallin H. Oaks explained, "From modern revelation, unique to the restored gospel, we know that the commandment to seek perfection is part of God the Father's plan for the salvation of His children."[57]

Matthew 5:48 is a verse typically cited, with Mormon leaders giving mixed signals as to whether or not perfection is necessary for exaltation. In a First Presidency message, President Gordon B. Hinckley said:

> Jesus said, "Be ye therefore perfect, even as your Father which is in heaven is perfect" (Matt. 5:48). That is the great crowning example of excellence. May each of us have a rich and wonderful life moving in that direction. We will not become perfect in a day or a month or a year. We will not accomplish it in a lifetime, but we can keep trying, starting with our more obvious weaknesses and gradually converting them to strengths as we go forward with our lives.[58]

Speaking at the spring general conference in 1989, Apostle Marvin J. Ashton stated,

> We need to come to terms with our desire to reach perfection and our frustration when our accomplishments or our behaviors are less than perfect. I feel that one of the great myths we would do well to dispel is that we've come to earth to perfect ourselves, and nothing short of that will do. If I understand the teachings of the prophets of this dispensation correctly, we will not become perfect in this life, though we can make significant strides toward that goal.[59]

Where did this "myth" come from? Perhaps its genesis can be found in the teachings of a number of LDS leaders who have utilized Matthew 5:48 as a rallying cry for personal perfection. For example, Spencer W. Kimball declared:

> This progress toward eternal life is a matter of achieving perfection. Living all the commandments guarantees total forgiveness of sins and assures one of exaltation through that perfection which comes by complying with the formula the Lord gave us. In his Sermon on the Mount he made the command to all men: "Be ye therefore perfect, even as your Father which is in

heaven is perfect" (Matt. 5:48). Being perfect means to triumph over sin. This is a mandate from the Lord. He is just and wise and kind. He would never require anything from his children which was not for their benefit and which was not attainable. Perfection therefore is an achievable goal.[60]

Church writings are replete with command after command to attain perfection. President Lorenzo Snow taught,

> With diligence, patience, and divine aid, we can obey the Lord's command to be perfect. . . . We may think that we cannot live up to the perfect law, that the work of perfecting ourselves is too difficult. This may be true in part, but the fact still remains that it is a command of the Almighty to us and we cannot ignore it.[61]

Harold B. Lee stated,

> Any member of the Church who is learning to live perfectly each of the laws that are in the kingdom is learning the way to become perfect. There is no member of this Church who cannot live the law, every law of the gospel perfectly.[62]

An LDS manual written specifically for women declares,

> Jesus said, "Be ye therefore perfect, even as your Father which is in heaven is perfect" (Matthew 5:48). Because it is very difficult to become perfect, our Father helps us. He has established the Church; called leaders; and given us commandments, principles, and ordinances. In our Church meetings we receive instructions concerning these things. We must obey and live according to God's laws to become perfect.[63]

Much of the confusion the Mormons have on this issue is due to the fact that their leaders have badly misinterpreted this passage. Jesus was not at all addressing the subject of personal or even sinless perfection. The context points to a consistency of behavior toward believers and unbelievers alike. While it is common for some to repay evil deeds done them in a vengeful manner, Jesus was saying that His disciples should take the high road and repay evil with good. As Jesus said, even Gentiles reciprocate good behavior (Matt. 5:44–47). Although it certainly is not easy, Christians should go beyond this expected response and treat favorably even those who treat them badly.[64]

"But I'm Trying!"

The faithful Latter-day Saint is continually admonished to "keep trying" to attain perfection and obey all of the laws of God. If it is impossible to be perfect, then it is wrong for the LDS Church to demand complete obedience to all of the laws of God in order to receive exaltation. It would be better and even more honest for Mormons to merely promise to do their best to keep God's commands. BYU professor Stephen E. Robinson admits that the phrase "keeping the commandments" is a troublesome expression for Mormons, "particularly when they talk to non-Latter-day Saints."[65] In an attempt to clarify what he feels is the LDS position, he writes:

> We generally say "keeping the commandments" when what we really mean is "trying real hard to keep the commandments and succeeding most of the time." Defined in this way, the phrase describes the attempts at obedience that the new covenant requires as our token of "good faith." Defined in this way, "keeping the commandments" is both possible and necessary; that is, trying to keep the commandments, doing the best we can at it, is a requirement of the gospel covenant, even though succeeding right now in keeping all of the commandments all of the time is not.[66]

Apostle Russell M. Nelson said trying *was* good enough. He stated, "Meanwhile, brothers and sisters, let us *do the best we can* and *try* to improve each day."[67] This opinion flatly contradicts Kimball's assessment:

> It is normal for children to try. They fall and get up numerous times before they can be certain of their footing. But adults, who have gone through these learning periods, must determine what they will do, then proceed to do it. To "try" is weak. To "do the best I can" is not strong. We must always do better than we can.[68]

This comment takes on a much stronger meaning when Kimball gives a hypothetical dialogue between an army officer and a soldier to show that trying is "not sufficient":

> An army officer called a soldier to him and ordered him to take a message to another officer. The soldier saluted and said, "I'll try, sir! I'll try!" To this the officer responded: "I don't want you to try, I want you to deliver this message." The soldier, somewhat embarrassed, now replied: "I'll do the best I can, sir." At this the officer, now disgusted, rejoined with some vigor: "I

don't want you to try and I don't want you to 'do the best you can.' I want you to deliver this message." Now the young soldier, straightening to his full height, approached the matter magnificently, as he thought, when he saluted again and said: "I'll do it or die, sir." To this the now irate officer responded: "I don't want you to die, and I don't want you merely to do the best you can, and I don't want you to try. Now, the request is a reasonable one; the message is important; the distance is not far; you are able-bodied; you can do what I have ordered. Now get out of here and accomplish your mission."[69]

Kimball's kick-in-the-tail pep talk hardly allows for failure. When Mormons insist they are trying, it is usually in the context of failing to succeed. Kimball's analogy does not allow for this possibility. There certainly appears to be some theological double-talk among LDS leaders when it comes to this subject. On the one hand, members are told that they must "be ye perfect," but on the other, they are told they can never achieve perfection. Some leaders say complete obedience is the requirement for exaltation, while others declare that partial obedience will suffice. At one point they are told trying is *insufficient,* but then they are taught that trying *is satisfactory.* How are Mormons to decipher the true teaching? And how can they know when they have done enough?

Christianity's Understanding of Salvation

Within the context of salvation, we find three aspects that need to be understood. These are justification, sanctification, and glorification.

Justification

When people accept Jesus Christ as their Lord and Savior, a miraculous event occurs. They become justified before the living God and are thereby declared guiltless, allowing them to be identified with Christ from the point of conversion to eternity future. It comes not by a person's own works but by God's working in that person. Acts 13:39 says, "And by him all that believe are justified from all things, from which ye could not be justified by the law of Moses." In Philippians 3:9, Paul stated that it was possible to "be found in him, not having a righteousness of my own that comes from the law, but that which comes through faith in Christ, the righteousness from God that depends on faith" (ESV). Romans 5:1 adds, "Therefore being justified by faith, we have peace with God through our Lord Jesus Christ." Christian theologian Leon Morris wrote:

> Justification then means the according of the status of being in the right. Sin has put us in the wrong with God and justification is the process whereby we are reckoned as right. In one way or another all religions must face the ultimate question: "How can man, who is a sinner, ever be right with a God who is just?" Most religions answer, in some form, "By human effort." Man committed the sin, so man must do what is required to put things right and undo the effects of his sin. It is the great teaching of the New Testament that we are justified, not by what we do, but by what Christ has done. Paul puts it simply when he says that we are "justified by his blood" (Rom. 5:9). He links our justification directly with the death of Jesus.[70]

Since we are unable to comply with all of God's standards (Rom. 3:23; Gen. 8:21; Ps 51:5, 58:3; Eccles. 9:3; Jer. 17:9), we deserve death because all good works by themselves are like "filthy rags" in the sight of God (Rom. 6:23; Isa. 64:6). But God Himself has provided the way through faith to allow believers to experience the fellowship of God and become righteous in His sight. As Christian theologian B. B. Warfield once said, "The works of a sinful man will, of course, be as sinful as he is, and nothing but condemnation can be built on them."[71]

Belief Equals Salvation

One of the toughest concepts for anyone, especially Mormons, to understand is that faith, not works, justifies a person before God. A good example of justification by faith is the story of the Philippian jailer in Acts 16. Paul and Silas were incarcerated in Philippi when a miraculous earthquake opened their jail cell door. When the jailer saw that all of the prison cells were open as well, he prepared to commit suicide only to be stopped by Paul, who told him not to fear because no one had escaped.

Seeing this to be true, the frightened jailer asked Paul, "What must I do to be saved?" (v. 30). If Paul had been a good Mormon living in modern times, his response might have been, "Believe that Joseph Smith was a prophet of God and that the Book of Mormon is the Word of God. Join the true church, don't drink coffee or tea, pay a full tithe, receive the Melchizedek priesthood, be baptized for your dead relatives, perform your endowments, and make sure you are married for time and eternity. Do these, along with following the whole law, and thou shalt be saved."

Instead, Paul and Silas merely answered, "Believe on the Lord Jesus Christ, and thou shalt be saved, and thy house" (v. 31). It is important to note that Paul made no reference to following any set of rules or rigid standards. Rather, his message was simply, "Believe . . . and thou shalt be saved." As a result of their saving faith, the new believers were immediately baptized.

As stated earlier in this chapter, the word *salvation* has two different meanings according to LDS theology. "Salvation by grace," known as unconditional or general salvation, is a free gift provided by Christ to everyone on this earth. This salvation allows each person the ability to be resurrected. On the other hand, conditional or individual salvation (exaltation) is the right to go to the highest level within the celestial kingdom.

So to which salvation was Paul referring when he spoke to the Philippian jailer? He certainly could not have been speaking of general salvation ("Believe and thou wilt be *resurrected*"), since everyone receives this regardless of belief. On the other hand, Paul could not have been referring to individual exaltation ("Believe and thou wilt be *exalted*"), since perpetual good works and strict adherence to celestial law are the only ways to achieve this, according to Mormonism.

The New Testament contains many examples of how belief alone, not one's works, justifies a person before God. For instance, Jesus said in John 5:24, "Verily, verily, I say unto you, He that heareth my word, and believeth on him that sent me, hath everlasting life." He also said in John 6:47, "Verily, verily, I say unto you, He that believeth on me hath everlasting life."

Paul clearly communicated this truth in Ephesians 2:8–9 when he said faith, not works, justifies a person before God. He also declared in Titus 3:5–6 that Christians are saved, "not because of works done by us in righteousness, but according to his own mercy, by the washing of regeneration and renewal of the Holy Spirit, whom he poured out on us richly through Jesus Christ our Savior" (ESV).

Christian theologian F. F. Bruce expounded on the idea that faith, not one's personal works, brings redemption:

> If there is to be any salvation for either Jews or Gentiles, then, it must be based not on ethical achievement but on the grace of God. What Jews and Gentiles need alike, in fact, is to have their records blotted out by an act of divine amnesty and to have the assurance of acceptance by God for no merit

of their own but by his spontaneous mercy. For this need God has made provision in Christ. Thanks to his redemptive work, men may find themselves "in the clear" before God. . . . The benefits of the atonement thus procured may be appropriated by faith—and only by faith.[72]

Several other terms used by Christians can be easily misunderstood by Mormons. These terms are related to the justification process.

REDEMPTION

Redemption is the deliverance from sin in its guilt, defilement, power, and liability through Christ's sacrifice. Believers can find comfort in the fact that God does not keep track of their sins. Certainly the psalmist knew this when he stated in Psalm 130:3, "If you, O LORD, should mark iniquities, O Lord, who could stand?" (ESV). (See also Isa. 43:25; Jer. 31:34; Heb. 8:12.) Galatians 3:13 states, "Christ hath redeemed us from the curse of the law, being made a curse for us." First Peter 1:18–19 says,

> knowing that you were ransomed from the futile ways inherited from your forefathers, not with perishable things such as silver or gold, but with the precious blood of Christ, like that of a lamb without blemish or spot. (ESV)

Referring to this passage, Leon Morris commented:

> "Your sin," he seems to be saying, "is a very serious matter. It set you in opposition to God and handed you over to eternal condemnation. From that situation there was no escape. You were hopelessly, irrevocably lost. There is no ransom from such a situation. And then, incredibly, unbelievably, a ransom was found. It meant a heavy price, the price of the death of the wonderful Son of God. But that price was paid and you have been redeemed. Never take your redemption for granted. Never count it a common, ordinary thing. It is the most incredible thing that has ever happened. But it did happen. Accept it, then, with gratitude and with awe. Live your life in reverent fear."[73]

GRACE

Grace is unmerited favor from God provided to those who believe (Rom. 12:3, 6). Again there is nothing we can do on our own to achieve this. Romans 5:2 and 20 say:

> Through him we have also obtained access by faith into this grace in which we stand, and we rejoice in hope of the glory of God. . . . Now the law

184

came in to increase the trespass, but where sin increased, grace abounded all the more. (ESV)

Romans 11:5–6 adds:

So too at the present time there is a remnant, chosen by grace. But if it is by grace, it is no longer on the basis of works; otherwise grace would no longer be grace. (ESV)

Morris wrote:

It is not at all unlikely that at first the Christians did not realize the full significance of the cross. But in time they came to see that the crucifixion is rightly understood only when it is seen as God's great saving act. It is the means God used to deal with the problem of human sin. The Christians came to emphasize that the way of salvation is not the way of law, as devout Jews held. It is the way of grace. People do not merit salvation but receive it as a free gift from God on the basis of what Christ's death accomplished.[74]

IMPUTATION

Suppose you received a bank statement informing you that you had ten million dollars in your account, even though you had never deposited this amount. It's more money than most people will earn in a lifetime. Yet imagine if someone had deposited this in your name, even though you did nothing to earn it! In the same way, Christianity has taught that imputation is the righteousness of God credited to a person's account based on belief in Jesus. Since a person's works cannot do this, it was necessary that Christ impute His righteousness to the believer. In Romans 4:6–7 Paul stated that God provides this righteousness apart from works. Paul continued this thought in Romans 4:20–24 when he said that Abraham did not

waver concerning the promise of God, but he grew strong in his faith as he gave glory to God, fully convinced that God was able to do what he had promised. That is why his faith was "counted to him as righteousness." But the words "it was counted to him" were not written for his sake alone, but for ours also. It will be counted to us who believe in him who raised from the dead Jesus our Lord. (ESV)

185

FORGIVENESS

The complete putting away of sin and its consequences with no strings attached summarizes forgiveness. This occurs at the time of belief when a person is redeemed from the penalty of sin. The believer's sins are permanently covered. Ephesians 4:32 reiterates that "God for Christ's sake hath forgiven you." Paul added in Ephesians 1:7, "In whom we have redemption through his blood, the forgiveness of sins, according to the riches of his grace." John declared in 1 John 2:12 that the believer's "sins are forgiven you for his name's sake." Morris commented:

> The blood of animal sacrifices could never cope with the problems of man, made in God's image as he is. But the blood of Christ can and does. Our Day of Atonement was the day of the cross. Jesus "suffered outside the city gate to make the people holy through his own blood" (Heb. 13:12).[75]

Sanctification

While justification—which took place in an instantaneous moment and is good forevermore—is a past event in the Christian's life, sanctification has its roots in conversion and will continue to blossom throughout the rest of the believer's life. Sanctification is synonymous with holiness and means to be set apart for God.

First Corinthians 6:11 says, "And such were some of you: but ye are washed, but ye are sanctified, but ye are justified in the name of the Lord Jesus, and by the Spirit of our God." Hebrews 10:10 says, "And by that will we have been sanctified through the offering of the body of Jesus Christ once for all." Verse 14 adds, "For by a single offering he has perfected for all time those who are being sanctified" (ESV).

On profession of faith, believers are immediately qualified to dwell with the Father. This does not say that believers will always do what is right. They are still human beings fraught with human frailties and defects. However, because God has begun a new work in them, their desires and outlook will be different. Because of the indwelling presence of the Holy Spirit in the believer's life, the fruit of the Spirit as described in Galatians 5:22–23 should become more evident while the "works of the flesh" as described in the previous three verses diminish.

The Christian needs to realize that the sanctification process is what Paul was describing in Philippians 2:12 when he implored the believers to "work out your own salvation with fear and trembling." Although Paul declared in Ephesians 2:10 that the believer was created *unto* good works, he was very clear to also point out in the previous two verses that it is faith and faith alone, not works, that justifies the believer. According to Romans 3:28, "Therefore we conclude that a man is justified by faith without the deeds of the law." Paul says almost the exact same thing in Galatians 2:16 and 21:

> Knowing that a man is not justified by the works of the law, but by the faith of Jesus Christ, even we have believed in Jesus Christ, that we might be justified by the faith of Christ, and not by the works of the law: for by the works of the law shall no flesh be justified. . . . I do not frustrate the grace of God: for if righteousness come by the law, then Christ is dead in vain.

Unfortunately, Mormonism's leaders have a presupposition that Christians don't believe grace and works can fit together. Consider how one church manual focusing on the "life and teaching of Jesus & His Apostles" destroys the context of two verses written by the apostle Paul and creates a classical example of the straw man fallacy:

> **(41–3) Romans 10:9, 10. Can One Achieve Salvation Simply by Confessing with the Mouth?** These two verses of scripture have been quoted very often by those who believe that salvation comes by grace alone and is not dependent in any way upon man's good works. Some groups even go so far as to say that if a man should confess Jesus before he is killed in an accident he will be saved in the kingdom of God, even if he had lived a wicked life prior to that time. Not only does this idea go contrary to the vast weight of Paul's own teachings (some within the Roman epistle itself—for example, 2:5–13; 6:13, 16; all of chapters 12–14), but it is also a gross misinterpretation of what Paul is really saying.[76]

Many Mormons are quick to point to James 2:14–26 in an attempt to show how faith is not enough to justify the believer. If it's just faith that's needed for "salvation," the argument goes, then it would seem reasonable that Christians could do whatever they wished (i.e., murder, commit adultery, steal) and still call themselves Christians. Referring to how he, as a missionary, had conversations with Bible-believing Christians, E. Richard Packham wrote an article in a church magazine titled "My Maturing Views of Grace" using a somewhat sarcastic tone:

187

One verse they commonly used was the Apostle Paul's statement, "For by grace are ye saved through faith; and that not of yourselves: it is the gift of God: Not of works, lest any man should boast" (Eph. 2:8–9). They reasoned with me that grace is a gift of God that freely comes when we accept Christ. For the first time in my life, I realized how easily we can become confused about any doctrine if we focus on a single verse and don't take into account the whole of gospel teachings. I also formed the opinion that people gravitated to the doctrine of unconditional grace because it was so easy to accept. After all, life can appear a whole lot simpler when all one has to do for salvation is "accept Christ."[77]

Never has the Christian church taught that the believer has the license to break God's commands. Paul instructed in Romans 6:15, "What then? shall we sin, because we are not under the law, but under grace? God forbid." As far as James 2:14–26 is concerned, it is important to understand the context of this passage. Written by the half-brother of Jesus to explain how good works *are* important, James never taught that Christians receive salvation through their works. Rather, his point was to show how good works should accompany a valid profession of faith. Like a butterfly that has shed its chrysalis, so, too, do believers begin to be "transformed by the renewing of (their) mind" and display good fruit because of the dramatic life change (Rom. 12:2; 2 Cor. 5:17). Concerning this good fruit, F. F. Bruce wrote, "As an apple-tree does not produce apples by Act of Parliament, but because it is its nature so to do, so the character of Christ cannot be produced in his people by rules and regulations; it must be the fruit of his Spirit within them."[78]

Although it is true that a doctrine can be misapplied, it is a dreadful mistake to suppose that it is false merely because it can be abused. Should good works be minimized merely because groups like the Pharisees took them to a legalistic extreme? Obviously not! Jesus reserved His harshest words for those who felt their good works made them righteous in God's sight, calling the legalistic Pharisees vipers, whitewashed tombs, and hypocrites (Matt. 23:27, 33). These rebukes, however, were not meant to take away the importance of righteous actions. When we accept the love of God as offered through belief in His Son, our response is to obey our Creator and Sustainer. The more we learn about God's love for us, the more we want to reciprocate by demonstrating our love for Him through service. Christian preacher Vance Havner summarized the role works play in the believer's life when he said, "We hear these days about 'cheap grace.' It doesn't mean much to be a Christian. But salvation is the costliest item on earth. It cost our Lord everything to provide it and it costs us everything to possess it."[79]

Glorification

Not only does salvation have a past tense (justification/sanctification) and a present tense (sanctification), but it also implies a future tense as well. The believer has a hope of one day reigning with Christ in glory. This will not be completely fulfilled until heaven.

However, the idea of glorification is such a certainty that it can be counted on. Paul speaks of this as an expected conclusion in Romans 8:30: "Moreover whom he did predestinate, them he also called: and whom he called, them he also justified: and whom he justified, them *he also glorified*" (emphasis added). He also said in 1 Thessalonians 3:13 that this event takes place when the believer sees Christ. Philippians 3:12–14 shows how the believers' work is not complete until they are in the presence of the Redeemer:

> Not that I have already obtained this or am already perfect, but I press on to make it my own, because Christ Jesus has made me his own. Brothers, I do not consider that I have made it my own. But one thing I do: forgetting what lies behind and straining forward to what lies ahead, I press on toward the goal for the prize of the upward call of God in Christ Jesus. (ESV)

As Christians, we can be eternally grateful to God that we "may know that [we] have eternal life" (1 John 5:13). What a glorious promise! What a glorious hope!

Discussion Questions

1. The idea of grace is a difficult topic for many to grasp. After all, how could something of great value not come at great personal cost (i.e., plenty of good works)? What are ways that the evangelical Christian can explain grace without making it appear that good works aren't important?
2. Elaine S. Dalton told a general conference audience, "When you renew your covenants each week by partaking of the sacrament, you covenant

189

that you will always remember the Savior and keep His command-ments."[80] What is the problem in promising to God to keep the com-mandments and then breaking them later in the week?

3. In this chapter, we said that a Christian is a person who has received forgiveness of sins. How would you explain this concept to someone who thinks this sounds too good (and too easy) to be true?

Final Thought

Most Mormons must surely realize their shortcomings and how they lack consistency in keeping God's commandments, no matter how good their intentions. The prospect of having to keep all of the commandments must weigh heavily on thinking Latter-day Saints. Perhaps they understand that they're not doing what they've been commanded to do. Despite the smiles many Mormons may wear, it should not be assumed that all is spiritually well in their personal lives. Strapped with the heavy requirement placed on them by their faith, such a countenance may hide deep-seated feelings of guilt and failure. Because of the unreasonable demand put on them, these people may live their daily lives with the guilt of never being good enough for celestial exaltation. What a shame when the offer of salvation is freely given by Christ.

Notes

1. *Teachings of Presidents of the Church: Heber J. Grant* (Salt Lake City: The Church of Jesus Christ of Latter-day Saints, 2002), 25; brackets in original.

2. McConkie, *Mormon Doctrine,* 669.

3. Ridges, *Mormon Beliefs and Doctrine Made Easier,* 94, 125.

4. *Teachings of Presidents of the Church: Harold B. Lee,* 22.

5. *Ensign* (May 2008): 8.

6. *Old Testament Seminary Teacher Resource Manual,* 15.

7. *Conference Reports* (April 1941): 102–3.

8. *Ensign* (November 2012): 35.

9. *Teachings of Presidents of the Church: Spencer W. Kimball;* italics in original.

10. While verse 15 is specifically spoken to Joseph's wife Emma, verse 16 says "that this is my voice unto all. Amen."

11. *Ensign* (June 2011): 4.

12. *Ensign* (March 2013): 21.

13. *Teachings of Presidents of the Church: Wilford Woodruff,* 212.

14. *Teachings of Presidents of the Church: Joseph F. Smith,* 153.

15. *Teachings of Presidents of the Church: Heber J. Grant*, 38.
16. *Teachings of Presidents of the Church: George Albert Smith*, 53.
17. *Teachings of Presidents of the Church: Joseph Fielding Smith*, 237.
18. *Teachings of Presidents of the Church: Harold B. Lee*, 35.
19. *Teachings of Presidents of the Church: Ezra Taft Benson*, 164.
20. *Ensign* (May 2010): 66.
21. *Ensign* (May 2011): 34; italics in original.
22. *Teachings of Presidents of the Church: Joseph Fielding Smith*, 100.
23. *Ensign* (December 2013): 19.
24. *Ensign* (May 2013): 88.
25. Ibid., 98.
26. *Ensign* (May 2004): 98; italics in original.
27. *Old Testament Student Manual: Genesis–2 Samuel*, 62.
28. *Gospel Principles*, 233.
29. *True to the Faith*, 135.
30. *Building an Eternal Marriage Teacher Manual: Religion 235* (Salt Lake City: The Church of Jesus Christ of Latter-day Saints, 2003), v; italics in original.
31. *Preparing for Exaltation Teacher's Manual* (Salt Lake City: The Church of Jesus Christ of Latter-day Saints, 1998), 123; brackets added.
32. *The Gospel and the Productive Life Student Manual: Religion 150* (Salt Lake City: The Church of Jesus Christ of Latter-day Saints, 2004), 98.
33. *Ensign* (July 2012): 22.
34. David O. McKay, *Gospel Ideals*, comp. G. Homer Durham (Salt Lake City: *Improvement Era*, 1953), 8.
35. *Book of Mormon Teacher Manual: Religion 121–122* (Salt Lake City: The Church of Jesus Christ of Latter-day Saints, 2009), 109. See also Joseph Fielding Smith, *Doctrines of Salvation* 1:69.
36. Hebrews 9:27 and 2 Corinthians 6:2 also deny any possibility of any works being performed after death.
37. *Book of Mormon Student Manual*, 230–31; ellipses in original.
38. Kimball, *The Miracle of Forgiveness* (Salt Lake City: Bookcraft, 1969), 210; italics added. While *The Miracle of Forgiveness* is not an official church publication, it has been treated highly by the LDS leadership. For example, Apostle Richard G. Scott spoke at a general conference saying, "In *The Miracle of Forgiveness*, Spencer W. Kimball gives a superb guide to forgiveness through repentance. It has helped many find their way back," *Ensign* (May 1995): 76. And one teacher's manual states, "If available, hold up a copy of *The Miracle of Forgiveness*, and tell students that reading it has helped many people feel the merciful forgiveness of the Lord," *Presidents of the Church Teacher Manual: Religion 345* (Salt Lake City: The Church of Jesus Christ of Latter-day Saints, 2005), 172. For more information, visit www.themiracleofforgiveness.com.
39. Kimball, *The Miracle of Forgiveness*, 9–10; italics in original. Kimball also taught that this is "why we must make our decisions early in life and why it is imperative that such decisions be right," 244. Quoted in the LDS *Search These Commandments: Melchizedek Priesthood Personal Study Guide* (Salt Lake City: The Church of Jesus Christ of Latter-day Saints, 1984), 82.
40. *True to the Faith*, 134.
41. *Gospel Principles*, 110.
42. Kimball, *Repentance Brings Forgiveness* (Salt Lake City: The Church of Jesus Christ of Latter-Day Saints, 1984).

43. *Ensign* (December 2013): 43. Verses he cited are D&C 1:32, 3 Nephi 9:22; 10:6; 21:22; Moses 6:52; D&C 5:21. For example, when speaking about D&C 1:32, he writes, "He that repents *and* does the commandments of the Lord."

44. *Doctrine and Covenants Student Manual: Religion 324–325* (Salt Lake City: The Church of Jesus Christ of Latter-day Saints, 2001), 122; bold and ellipses in original.

45. *Ensign* (May 2014): 40.

46. *Doctrine and Covenants and Church History Seminary Teacher Resource Manual*, 134; bold in original.

47. *True to the Faith*, 163.

48. *Teachings of Presidents of the Church: Spencer W. Kimball*, 43.

49. Kimball, *The Miracle of Forgiveness*, 170. See also the First Presidency Message, "God Will Forgive," *Ensign* (March 1982).

50. *True to the Faith*, 132.

51. Mark Champneys, ExMormon.net, accessed May 29, 2014, http://home.comcast.net/~champmd/blessing.html. Champneys has shared this summary with a number of Latter-day Saints who have told him his summary is accurate.

52. *Ensign* (December 2013): 43.

53. *Teachings of Presidents of the Church: Heber J. Grant*, 26.

54. Pride, it should be pointed out, is a sin, showing that an individual has violated celestial law. See Proverbs 16:18; 29:23; Obadiah 1:3; Zephaniah 2:10; Mark 7:22; 1 John 2:16.

55. Other Book of Mormon passages, including 2 Nephi 28:12–15 and Jacob 2:13–22, also warn against the dangers of pride.

56. *Preparing for Exaltation Teacher's Manual*, 65.

57. *Ensign* (May 2013): 98.

58. *Ensign* (September 1999): 5.

59. *Ensign* (May 1989): 20–21.

60. Kimball, *The Miracle of Forgiveness*, 208–9.

61. *Teachings of Presidents of the Church: Lorenzo Snow*, 95, 97. The title of the chapter is "Becoming Perfect before the Lord: A Little Better Day by Day."

62. *Teachings of Presidents of the Church: Harold B. Lee*, 33.

63. *The Latter-day Saint Woman: Basic Manual for Women, Part A* (Salt Lake City: The Church of Jesus Christ of Latter-day Saints, 2000), 122.

64. For more on this topic, see pages 162–65 in chapter 20, "Isn't it arrogant to think you already have forgiveness of sins?" in our book *Answering Mormons' Questions*.

65. Stephen E. Robinson, *Believing Christ* (Salt Lake City: Deseret Book Co., 1992), 45.

66. Ibid., 45–46.

67. *Ensign* (November 1995): 88; emphasis added.

68. Kimball, *The Miracle of Forgiveness*, 165. This section was quoted in "Q&A: Questions and Answers" in the church magazine *New Era*, April 1995, 17.

69. Ibid., 164.

70. Morris, *The Atonement*, 196.

71. John E. Meeter, ed., *Selected Shorter Writings of Benjamin B. Warfield*, 2 vol. (Nutley, NJ: Presbyterian and Reformed, 1970), 1.283.

72. F. F. Bruce, *Paul: Apostle of the Heart Set Free* (Grand Rapids: Eerdmans, 1977), 328. Sometimes in an attempt to divert the issue at hand, Mormons ask about those who have never heard the gospel. Our response would be similar to that given by Jesus when the apostle Peter pointed to John and complained "What about him?" when told to feed Jesus's sheep. Jesus answered him, "What is that to thee? Follow thou me" (John 21:20–22). Mormons who have the gospel presented to them are accountable to God. They cannot simply exempt

themselves by pointing to others. While it might be interesting to speculate on what happens to those who never hear the gospel, this is in actuality a moot point. Romans 1:18–20 assures us that all men are "without excuse."

73. Morris, *The Atonement*, 125.

74. Ibid., 11.

75. Ibid., 87.

76. *Life and Teachings of Jesus & His Apostles*, 333; bold in original.

77. *Ensign* (August 2005): 22.

78. Bruce, *Paul: Apostle of the Heart Set Free*, 461.

79. Dennis J. Hester, comp., *The Vance Havner Quote Book* (Grand Rapids: Baker, 1986), 105. For more information on sanctification, see chapter 19, "Doesn't the book of James say that 'faith without works is dead'?" in our book *Answering Mormons' Questions*.

80. *Ensign* (May 2008): 117.

12 | Heaven and Hell

Wives, be faithful to your husbands. I know you have to put up with many unpleasant things, and your husbands have to put up with some things as well. Doubtless you are sometimes tried by your husbands, on account perhaps of the ignorance of your husbands, or perchance at times because of your own ignorance. . . . I do not say but that your husbands are bad—just as bad as you are, and probably some of them are worse; but, never mind: try to endure the unpleasantnesses which arise at times, and when you meet each other in the next life you will feel glad that you put up with those things.

President Lorenzo Snow [1]

age of accountability: Before the age of eight, children are considered innocent. Those who die before the age of eight go to the celestial kingdom.

celestial kingdom: The highest of three degrees of glory where the Mormon hopes to be exalted for eternity.

celestial marriage: In the modern LDS Church, this is synonymous with temple marriage. In earlier days, it referred to plural marriage.

eternal increase: The ability for exalted LDS couples to procreate throughout eternity.

heaven: One of three degrees of glory, comprised of the celestial, terrestrial, and telestial kingdoms.

hell: Depending on the context, it could refer to the temporary state after death known as "spirit prison," Outer Darkness, or anything short of exaltation.

Outer Darkness: A place of torment primarily reserved for those who were not given mortal bodies in the preexistence (Satan and his demons).

paradise: Temporary place in the postmortal spirit world for those Latter-day Saints who were righteous on earth.

spirit prison: Temporary place in the postmortal spirit world where the wicked will be taught the restored gospel.

telestial kingdom: The lowest level of the three degrees of glory where the wicked of the world, including those who rejected the restored gospel in the spirit world, will spend eternity.

terrestrial kingdom: The middle level of three degrees of glory where honorable people will be, including "lukewarm" Mormons.

war in heaven: Conflict in the premortal life started by Lucifer when his plan to become the savior of the world was rejected.

The question "What happens to people when they die?" is probably the foremost topic of every religion in the world. Every faith has its paradise, a "Nirvana" of pleasure and delight. Many religions also have their hells, a place of torture and suffering (whether temporal or eternal) that, as depicted by Dante Alighieri's *The Divine Comedy—Inferno*, is saved for the wicked.

Jesus warned the people of His day about how terrible hell is, yet He also comforted His followers by explaining that He was reserving rooms for them in a great mansion. Historically, the Christian church has asserted that believers will enjoy eternal happiness in the presence of God, while those who don't have faith and reject God will be eternally separated from Him and exposed to the torments of hell. Mormonism has a much different version of these two final states, and it is to this topic that we now turn.

The Temporary States according to Mormonism

Upon death, every person goes to a place called the spirit world. Depending on one's performance during mortality, the deceased will arrive in either paradise or spirit prison. These are temporary states until the final judgment and placement in one of the three degrees of glory. Those who die younger than the age of eight will end up in paradise before being placed in the celestial kingdom. Thus, Mormon children are baptized when they reach this "age of accountability." As President Joseph F. Smith explained,

195

With little children who are taken away in infancy and innocence before they have reached the years of accountability, and are not capable of committing sin, the gospel reveals to us the fact that they are redeemed, and Satan has no power over them. Neither has death any power over them. They are redeemed by the blood of Christ, and they are saved just as surely as death has come into the world through the fall of our first parents.[2]

A student manual states:

At variance with the teachings of many other Christian churches, The Church of Jesus Christ of Latter-day Saints teaches that children are born in a state of innocence (see D&C 93:38). Innocence is defined as the state of being free from guilt or sin, free from blame or censure, spotless or unsullied. During a child's infancy and before the child reaches the age of accountability, Satan is not able to tempt him directly (see D&C 29:47). Children who die before the age of eight years are received into the celestial kingdom (see D&C 137:10). The innocence of a child is, at least in part, what provoked Jesus to say, "Except ye be converted, and become as little children, ye shall not enter into the kingdom of heaven" (Matthew 18:3).[3]

BYU professor Charles R. Harrell commented, "In Mormon thought, not only are little children guaranteed salvation in the celestial kingdom, but they are immediately much better off by being spared the hardships and trials of mortality. . . . unlike those who grow to mortal adulthood, they experience none of the trials while having all of the enjoyments of having a physical body."[4] Most of the other souls will end up in spirit prison, which is a place where those who died without learning about Mormonism or those who rejected the LDS gospel in this life will go. Using 1 Peter 3:18–20 as the proof text, *Gospel Principles* teaches that this place is reserved for "those who have not yet received the gospel of Jesus Christ. These spirits have agency and may be enticed by both good and evil."[5]

The righteous Latter-day Saints will spend their temporary state in paradise where they will be "occupied in doing the work of the Lord" as "the Church is organized in the spirit world, and priesthood holders continue their responsibilities there."[6] Once vicarious work for the dead is performed for a soul by a living Latter-day Saint in one of the many LDS temples located around the world, spirit missionaries will share the LDS gospel with these souls. "If they accept the gospel and the ordinances performed for them in the temples, they may leave the spirit prison and dwell in paradise."[7] Those who reject the gospel in spirit prison "will have to suffer for their own sins but will eventually be resurrected and go to a kingdom of glory."[8]

The Final States according to Mormonism

Depending on a person's actions and attitudes on earth, almost everyone will end up in one of the three kingdom levels. *Gospel Principles* states, "At the Final Judgment we will inherit a place in the kingdom for which we are prepared. The scriptures teach of three kingdoms of glory—the celestial kingdom, the terrestrial kingdom, and the telestial kingdom."[9] The standard works give no definitive description about whether or not it will be possible for a soul to move up to a higher kingdom. According to a 1952 letter written by the Secretary of the First Presidency, "The brethren direct me to say that the Church has never announced a definite doctrine upon this point. Some of the brethren have held the view that it was possible in the course of progression to advance from one glory to another, invoking the principle of eternal progression; others of the brethren have taken the opposite view. But as stated, the Church has never announced a definite doctrine on this point."[10] However, church leaders have held contradictory views about this issue over the years.[11]

A passage often cited to support this view of three kingdoms of glory is 1 Corinthians 15:40, which says, "There are also celestial bodies, and bodies terrestrial: but the glory of the celestial is one, and the glory of the terrestrial is another." In light of verse 41, many scholars believe that Paul was referring to heavenly bodies such as the moon, sun, and stars. The references to terrestrial bodies seem to further explain what he wrote in verse 39 when he spoke of the flesh of men, beasts, fishes, and birds. One thing for sure, there is no mention of "bodies telestial." But this did not stop Joseph Smith from inserting this term into his version of the Bible.[12] Smith's version, however, is the only one to contain the word *telestial,* and there is no ancient Greek manuscript that supports Smith's change to the text. He included this word to bolster what is certainly an erroneous doctrine.

Another Bible passage many Latter-day Saints like to use to support the idea of three degrees of glory is 2 Corinthians 12:2–4:

> I know a man in Christ who fourteen years ago was caught up to the third heaven—whether in the body or out of the body I do not know, God knows.

And I know that this man was caught up into paradise—whether in the body or out of the body I do not know, God knows—and he heard things that cannot be told, which man may not utter. (ESV)

Using these passages to validate the idea of three kingdoms making up heaven ignores the Jewish tradition Paul would have known. According to that tradition, *paradise* was the abode of God, the place of eternal joy for God's people. However, Jewish custom never viewed a first or second heaven as alternative eternal destinations. Rather, these referred to the atmospheric heaven (the sky) and the galactic heaven (the universe).[13]

Outer Darkness: Reserved for the Sons of Perdition

Outer darkness has been depicted a number of ways in LDS theology. In a generic sense it describes the situation of any man or woman who was not qualified to live eternally in the presence of the Father. In a more specific sense, outer darkness is a type of holding tank for the souls of the wicked, who will remain here until the end of the millennium when they will be resurrected and judged. Those with crimes not including murder or apostasy will be allowed entrance into the telestial kingdom, which is the lowest of the kingdoms of glory.[14] Those who fail to prove themselves worthy of a telestial reward will return again to outer darkness, this time for eternity.

> These are they who had testimonies of Jesus through the Holy Ghost and knew the power of the Lord but allowed Satan to overcome them. They denied the truth and defied the power of the Lord. There is no forgiveness for them, for they denied the Holy Spirit after having received it. They will not have a kingdom of glory. They will live in eternal darkness, torment, and misery with Satan and his angels forever.[15]

Ex-Mormons who are deemed "sons of perdition" will be denied one of the three kingdoms. Before he became the church's tenth president, Joseph Fielding Smith, who served as the church historian, wrote, "Before a man can become a son of perdition he must know the power of God and then defy it."[16] He also taught, "The sons of perdition are those who have had a knowledge of the truth, have known that Jesus Christ was the Son of God, have had the testimony of the Spirit of the Lord, the Holy Ghost, and these things have all been revealed so that they know they are true;

and then they turn against them and fight them knowingly. Sons of Perdition are to be cast out with the devil and his angels into outer darkness."[17] Thus, to become a son of perdition, a person must: 1) have full knowledge of Mormonism; 2) have had a personal testimony of Mormonism; 3) fight against Mormonism despite knowing that it is true. Certainly this would disqualify just about every critical ex-Mormon since most, if not all, believe that the LDS Church is *not* true.

While many Mormons do not like the concept of an eternal punishment that includes "hellfire," it is apparent that outer darkness is a place that is anything but pleasant. According to Smith:

> The extent of this punishment none will ever know except those who partake of it. That it is the most severe punishment that can be meted out to man is apparent. Outer darkness is something which cannot be described, except that we know that it is to be placed beyond the benign and comforting influence of the Spirit of God—banished entirely from his presence.[18]

Many Mormons find the Christian view of hell (eternal punishment with no second chances) to be both unfair and offensive. They wonder how a "God of love could send His own children into such punishment." Yet it is taught in Mormonism that the devil and his demons are also God's spirit children, cast out of Elohim's presence following the "war in heaven." If Mormonism is true, then one-third of God's children who were cast out of heaven in the preexistence will automatically end up in hell and eternal torment. How is this any more "fair"?

The Telestial Kingdom: The Lowest Level of Glory

The telestial kingdom is a place where "people did not receive the gospel or the testimony of Jesus either on earth or in the spirit world. They will suffer for their own sins in hell until after the Millennium, when they will be resurrected."[19] This place "will be reserved for individuals who 'received not the gospel of Christ, neither the testimony of Jesus' (D&C 76:82). These individuals will receive their glory after being redeemed from spirit prison, which is sometimes called hell."[20]

Joseph Fielding Smith said those sent here would include the unclean, liars, sorcerers, adulterers, and those who have broken their covenants.[21] We should emphasize that covenant breakers are listed here. All Mormons, upon baptism into the LDS Church, promise to keep all of God's commandments. Naturally, this would mean that breaking God's laws should no longer occur in their lives. Struggling with sin is part of being human. Still, during the sacrament service, all participants must again make this covenant. Since no Mormon can consistently keep all of the commandments, it appears that all of them are covenant breakers to some extent.

Although D&C 76:81–84 describes those residing in this state as being in "hell," it does not compare to the horrors of hell described in the Bible. Seventy B. H. Roberts said:

> But even of the least of the three grand divisions, the telestial kingdom, it is said that it "surpasses all understanding"; and that even its inhabitants, the last to be redeemed, and even then deprived of the personal presence of God and the Christ, shall nevertheless receive the ministration of angels and the Holy Ghost, for they are to be accounted "heirs of salvation." How infinitely more glorious, then, must be the higher kingdoms of God and the Christ![22]

To think that the inhabitants of this state will be "heirs of salvation" is completely foreign to the Bible. In fact, many of the attributes given to those who will be sent to the telestial kingdom are exactly the same as those who will be cast into the lake of fire mentioned in Revelation 21:8: "But the fearful, and unbelieving, and the abominable, and murderers, and whoremongers, and sorcerers, and idolaters, and all liars, shall have their part in the lake which burneth with fire and brimstone: which is the second death."

Note that the unbelieving, sorcerers, liars, and whoremongers (sexually immoral) are together lumped with murderers in the lake of fire. Revelation 20:10 clearly states that the punishment here will be a permanent torment that will last "day and night for ever and ever." It is inconceivable that such a fate could ever be considered having anything to do with "salvation."

The Terrestrial Kingdom: Christ's Presence Reigns

For those whose "righteousness" will enable them to escape both outer darkness and the telestial kingdom, the next level up is a terrestrial kingdom where residents will receive more benefits than their telestial counterparts. Those in the terrestrial kingdom rejected the gospel on earth but afterward received it in the spirit world. These are the honorable people on the earth who were blinded to the gospel of Jesus Christ by the craftiness of men. These are also they who received the gospel and a testimony of Jesus but then were not valiant. They will be visited by Jesus Christ but not by our Heavenly Father.[23]

Spencer W. Kimball stated, "Those who have been decent and upright and who have lived respectable and good lives will go to a terrestrial kingdom whose glory is as the moon."[24] The souls destined for this kingdom are

(1) those who died "without law"—those heathen and pagan people who do not hear the gospel in this life, and who would not accept it with all their hearts should they hear it; (2) those who hear and reject the gospel in this life and then accept it in the spirit world; (3) those "who are honorable men of the earth, who [are] blinded by the craftiness of men"; and (4) those who are lukewarm members of the true church and who have testimonies, but who are not true and faithful in all things.[25]

Since "lukewarm" Mormons are destined here, could it be that the majority of Latter-day Saints are headed for this state? We have spoken to many Mormons who realize they don't follow 2 Nephi 25:23, which says that they are saved by grace "after all they can do." They know they don't do everything they can do. While the terrestrial kingdom is a place of comfort with the presence of Jesus Christ, the presence of Heavenly Father will be missing. In essence, Heavenly Father has no desire to see these spirit children ever again. This glory, which "differs from the celestial glory as the light of the moon differs from the light of the sun," will be inherited by those "who are honorable men of the earth, who were blinded by the craftiness of men . . . (and) who are not valiant in the testimony of Jesus, therefore they obtain not the crown over the kingdom of God."[26]

Celestial Kingdom: The Ultimate Goal

According to a Gospel Topics online essay published on the official LDS website in early 2014, "just as a child can develop the attributes of his or her parents over time, the divine nature that humans inherit can be developed to become like their Heavenly Father's. . . . God's loving parentage and guidance can help each willing, obedient child of God receive of His fulness and of His glory."[27] This can be fully realized by entering the celestial kingdom, with a goal of godhood. As a Mormon educator wrote:

> The scriptures teach that there are many people from other worlds who have already become gods (1 Cor. 8:5; *Teachings of the Prophet Joseph Smith*, pp. 370–71). Many gods will be added to the universe when worthy mortals from this world become gods (D&C 132:20).[28]

According to page 3 of the 2010 *Handbook 2: Administering the Church*, "exaltation in the highest degree of the celestial kingdom can be obtained only by those who have faithfully lived the gospel of Jesus Christ and are sealed as eternal companions." *Gospel Principles* lists these "blessings given to exalted people":

> 1. They will live eternally in the presence of Heavenly Father and Jesus Christ (see D&C 76:62). 2. They will become gods (see D&C 132:20–23). 3. They will be united eternally with their righteous family members and will be able to have eternal increase. 4. They will receive a fulness of joy. 5. They will have everything that our Heavenly Father and Jesus Christ have—all power, glory, dominion, and knowledge (see D&C 132:19–20).[29]

According to an online study guide produced for his Religion 235: Eternal Marriage students, BYU-Idaho religion professor Bruce K. Satterfield stated how "it is imperative that in building an eternal marriage, both partners must always remember what they are trying to become in the end." Satterfield then provides a quote from President Gordon B. Hinckley:

> The whole design of the gospel is to lead us, onward and upward to greater achievement, even, eventually, to godhood. This great possibility was enunciated by the Prophet Joseph Smith in the King Follett sermon (see *Teachings of the Prophet Joseph Smith*, 342–62) and emphasized by President Lorenzo Snow. It is this grand and incomparable concept: As God now is, man may become![30]

Satterfield follows this with a statement given by President Brigham Young that shows how "we are in a process of becoming Gods." Young said,

> The Lord created you and me for the purpose of becoming Gods like himself; when we have been proved in our present capacity, and have been faithful with all things he puts into our possession.[31]

The "Becoming Like God" Gospel Topics essay elaborates further on the teaching of Joseph Smith:

"What kind of a being is God?" he asked. Human beings needed to know, he argued, because "if men do not comprehend the character of God they do not comprehend themselves." In that phrase, the Prophet collapsed the gulf that centuries of confusion had created between God and humanity. Human nature was at its core divine. God "was once as one of us" and "all the spirits that God ever sent into the world" were likewise "susceptible of enlargement." Joseph Smith preached that long before the world was formed, God found "himself in the midst" of these beings and "saw proper to institute laws whereby the rest could have a privilege to advance like himself" and be "exalted" with Him.[32]

According to Mormonism, a person cannot attain godhood based merely on grace and good intentions; rather, it takes lots of work on the part of each person:

The celestial kingdom is the highest of the three kingdoms of glory. Those in this kingdom will dwell forever in the presence of God the Father and His Son Jesus Christ. This should be your goal: to inherit celestial glory and to help others receive that great blessing as well. Such a goal is not achieved in one attempt; it is the result of a lifetime of righteousness and constancy of purpose.[33]

Referring to one of the three Book of Mormon witnesses, a student manual references the Doctrine and Covenants to make this point:

D&C 14:7. Keep the Commandments and Endure to the End. In order for David Whitmer or any of God's children to have eternal life they must endure to the end, that is, remain faithful throughout their mortal probation. The scriptures are replete with this doctrine (see Matt. 10:22; 24:13; Mark 13:13; 1 Cor. 13:7; 1 Nephi 13:37; 2 Nephi 9:24; 31:20; 3 Nephi 15:9; 27:16–17; D&C 10:69; 53:7; Articles of Faith 1:13; see also Topical Guide, "endure," 121)."[34]

It is in the celestial kingdom where a person can truly experience eternal life known as exaltation, or godhood. It has been explained like this:

(40–7) We Can Become like God Because We Have the Seed of Deity Within Us. When Jesus was created after the fashion and in the likeness of the Father, and was therefore in the image of his Father, did he strive also to become like God in every other way? What does the word *equal* mean? And since Jesus thought that it was not robbery for him to become like God, what does Paul say you should strive to do as well? (See Philippians 2:5–8, 12; 3 Nephi 27:27.)[35]

After quoting the Lorenzo Snow couplet (mentioned in chapter 1), President George Albert Smith said,

Being created in the image of God, we believe that it is not improper, that it is not unrighteous, for us to hope that we may be permitted to partake of the attributes of deity and, if we are faithful, to become like unto God; for as we receive and obey the natural laws of our Father that govern this life, we become more like Him; and as we take advantage of the opportunities placed within our reach, we prepare to receive greater opportunities in this life and in the life that is to come.[36]

Joseph Fielding Smith admitted that many Mormons would never see this state:

Those who gain exaltation in the celestial kingdom are those who are members of the Church of the Firstborn; in other words, those who keep *all* the commandments of the Lord. There will be many who are members of the Church of Jesus Christ of Latter-day Saints who shall *never* become members of the Church of the Firstborn.[37]

Theoretically, those who reach the celestial kingdom but were not faithful in all things will be prohibited from enjoying the pleasures of godhood. According to Smith:

Entrance into the kingdom of God, the celestial kingdom, is not the goal which true Latter-day Saints are seeking. There will enter there many who are entitled to be only servants. That kingdom has different degrees in it, and to obtain the highest there are many commandments which have to be kept.[38]

Those prohibited from godhood will include angels, which in LDS theology are ministering servants who were not qualified to become gods and will therefore have a subservient role. Joseph Smith said that some would be "raised to be angels, others are raised to become Gods."[39]

Eternal Increase

Like their Heavenly Father before them, worthy Mormons are taught to hope for celestial exaltation and the reward of godhood. Apostle Russell M. Nelson explained, "Eternal life is to gain exaltation in the highest heaven and live in the family unit."[40] Henry B. Eyring, a counselor in the First Presidency, stated, "Our conviction is that God, our Heavenly Father, wants us to live the life that He does. We learn both the spiritual things and the secular things 'so we may one day create worlds [and] people and govern them.'"[41] *Gospel Principles* reports, "As husbands, wives, and children, we need to learn what the Lord expects us to do to fulfill our purpose as a family. If we all do our part, we will be united eternally."[42] A student manual states, "In the premortal world you were a member of Heavenly Father's family. Now you are a member of an additional family, a mortal family. Because of Heavenly Father's plan of salvation, it is possible for you to become like Him. It is also possible to secure your mortal family in an eternal bond, allowing you to be together as a family after death."[43]

Bruce K. Satterfield explains, "Essential to our progress to becoming God's [*sic*] is marriage. The Lord has declared: 'And again, verily I say unto you, if a man marry a wife by my word, which is my law, and by the new and everlasting covenant' and endure vailiantly [*sic*] in that marriage, 'Then shall they be gods' (D&C 132:19–20)."[44]

Marriage in the temple and having an eternal family are mandated by LDS leaders:

- John Taylor: "Our marriage relations, for instance, are eternal. Go to the sects of the day and you will find that time ends their marriage covenants; they have no idea of continuing their relations hereafter; they do not believe in anything of the kind. It is true there is a kind of natural principle in men that leads them to hope it may be so; but they know nothing about it. Our religion binds men and women for time and all eternity. . . . we expect, in the resurrection, that we shall associate with our wives and have our children sealed to us by the power of the holy priesthood, that they may be united with us worlds without end."[45]
- Joseph F. Smith said: "I have the glorious promise of the association of my loved ones throughout all eternity. In obedience to this work, in the gospel of Jesus Christ, I shall gather around me my family, my

children, my children's children, until they become as numerous as the seed of Abraham, or as countless as the sands upon the seashore. For this is my right and privilege, and the right and privilege of every member of the Church of Jesus Christ of Latter-day Saints who holds the Priesthood and will magnify it in the sight of God."[46]

- Spencer W. Kimball: "Oh, brothers and sisters, *families can be forever*! Do not let the lures of the moment draw you away from them! *Divinity, eternity,* and *family*—they go together, hand in hand, and so must we!"[47]

- *Gospel Principles*: "Those who inherit the highest degree of the celestial kingdom, who become gods, must also have been married for eternity in the temple (see D&C 131:1–4). All who inherit the celestial kingdom will live with Heavenly Father and Jesus Christ forever (see D&C 76:62)."[48]

However, "participating in the ceremony of celestial marriage is not enough. We also have to live a celestial life."[49] By being sealed for eternity, a Mormon husband and his wife will have the ability to populate the world(s). This is called "eternal increase" and includes

> having an unlimited number of spirit children. Spirit children will be born to them as offspring (Acts 17:28–29), just as we were to our heavenly parents (Heb. 12:9). This is also referred to as "a continuation of the seeds forever and ever" (D&C 132:19). As gods, they will create worlds for their spirit children and send them through the same "great plan of happiness" (Alma 42:8) that the Father has in place for us.[50]

Charles R. Harrell questions the use of the Acts and Hebrews passages from the Bible as quoted above. Referring to the Greek legends in Acts 17, he correctly says that "in none of these myths, however, were spirits mentioned as being begotten of God, nor was everyone directly begotten of God in the flesh. It appears that Paul was merely drawing on a source familiar to his Greek audience—to the Greeks, Paul became a Greek (1 Cor. 9:19)—to demonstrate that we are the workmanship of God's hands not vice versa." About Hebrews 12:9, he says that "this passage doesn't say that God is the Father of 'our' spirits, which may be significant given that the same verse refers to the fathers of 'our' flesh. . . . It is also the scholarly consensus that only a figurative fatherhood is implied, with God being the creator and sustainer of these spirits."[51]

Because procreation plays such a vital role in the LDS concept of salvation, it is imperative that marriage relationships formed here on earth be carried on into eternity. To marry and bear children is of the utmost importance to the Latter-day Saint, said Joseph Fielding Smith:

> Those who receive the exaltation in the celestial kingdom will have the "continuation of the seeds forever." They will live in the family relationship. We are taught in the gospel of Jesus Christ that the family organization will be, so far as celestial exaltation is concerned, one that is complete, an organization linked from father and mother and children of one generation to the father and mother and children of the next generation, and thus expanding and spreading out down to the end of time.[52]

Smith also said,

> In order to fulfill the purposes of our Eternal Father, there must be a union, husbands and wives receiving the blessings that are promised to those who are faithful and true that will exalt them to Godhood. A man cannot receive the fullness of the blessings of the kingdom of God alone, nor can the woman, but the two together can receive all the blessings and privileges that pertain to the fullness of the Father's kingdom.[53]

Much of the LDS outlook on true salvation centers on the desires of the Mormon individual and not on Jesus Christ. Rather than the picture portrayed in the book of Revelation, where God's saints pay rightful homage to the One who redeemed them, the Mormon heavenly system is more focused on personal power, gain, and sex.[54]

Heaven on Earth?

What if Mormonism is true and people can become rulers of their own worlds? What will this heavenly state be like? According to Mormonism, exalted LDS couples will be able to rule worlds filled with offspring they will procreate, repeating the process of Heavenly Father and his family.[55]

And while a Mormon might say it is just "speculation," apparently sin will be introduced into this new world as demonstrated by the words of Brigham Young:

Sin is upon every earth that ever was created, and if it was not so, I would like some philosophers to let us know how people can be exalted to become sons of God, and enjoy a fulness of glory with the Redeemer. Consequently every earth has its redeemer, and every earth has its tempter; and every earth, and the people thereof, in their turn and time, receive all that we receive, and pass through all the ordeals that we are passing through.[56]

Exalted humans will "become heavenly parents and have spirit children *just as He does.*" At this council we also learn that "because of our weaknesses, all of us except little children would sin," making it necessary "that a Savior would be provided for us so we could overcome our sins."[57] Why should a Mormon expect his world to be any less polluted by sin and its effects? Young appears to be taking his Mormonism to its logical conclusion. If the people of these worlds need a savior, it makes sense that sin is a problem where they dwell. If Young's scenario is accurate, then every LDS couple that attains an exalted state has no choice but to look forward to the day when one of their own children will serve as a tempter and cause one-third of the other family members to rebel and fall into sin. Thus it will be necessary to sacrifice another one of their sons as a redeemer in order to shed his blood for the sins of the rest of the family. As Young said, "all the ordeals that we are passing through"—such as sorrow, failure, and death—will be experienced again and again.

All of us have seen the effects of a fallen race, and the view is very unpleasant. We hear of terrible tragedies—Auschwitz, Rwanda, Darfur, and the events of 9/11 come to mind—where thousands of people were killed because of mankind's hatred and cruelty to other men, women, and children. Historical figures like Adolf Hitler, Joseph Stalin, Osama bin Laden, and Kim Jong-Il—all of whom supposedly sided with Jesus in premortality—are the epitome of human depravity. This time, however, the Mormon as "God" will be in charge of what we must assume will be a similar mess. This hardly sounds like a blissful, peaceful state!

The Final States according to the Bible

When it comes to heaven, the Bible provides few details. Perhaps with our sin-tainted minds, such a wondrous concept would be difficult to grasp. Probably the greatest description of heaven is found in Revelation 21. The apostle John describes a heavenly city whose walls are adorned with precious stones, gates made of pearl, and streets made of pure gold, transparent like glass. In reality, it is not the description of the walls, the gates, or the streets that places the Christian in awe. Heaven is heaven because it is where Jesus, the Savior and Redeemer, lives. He gives light to all abiding in His presence. Throughout eternity those whose names are written in the Book of Life will dwell with the Lamb who gave His life for them. Their communion with Christ will remain forever constant, unbroken, and unmolested by earthly distractions and satanic deceptions.

Revelation 21:4 says heaven is a place where God Himself will wipe away every tear from the eyes of the believer; death, sorrow, crying, and pain will forever be a thing of the past. Our minds cannot imagine the greatness of this abode. As Paul wrote in 1 Corinthians 2:9, "Eye hath not seen, nor ear heard, neither have entered into the heart of man, the things which God hath prepared for them that love him." All of the redeemed believers represent God's family. Second Corinthians 6:16 says, "As God hath said, I will dwell in them, and walk in them; and I will be their God, and they shall be my people." According to Revelation 19:6, believers will join the angels in praise to their God and King.[58]

Not everyone makes it to this wonderful state. Those who, for whatever reason, reject God's gift of salvation on this earth will exist in a place of endless torment. They will be unable to ever experience the joy of God's eternal presence. This holds true for those who were deluded into thinking that they were not as "bad" as others were. They will forever learn that people were never expected to compare themselves with others of the fallen race but rather see themselves in light of God's holiness and perfection. It is the blindness of sin that keeps a person from crying out, "I am undone!" (see Isa. 6:5). Only a people ignorant of God's righteousness can think that they can establish their own righteousness and thereby meet the standard of God's absolute perfection.

How disappointed they will be to hear the words found in Matthew 25:41: "Depart from me, ye cursed, into everlasting fire, prepared for the devil and his angels." Some like to think that a loving God would never punish unbelievers in such a manner. That conclusion, though, fails to take into account that it was Christ Himself who made such a pronouncement! To assume otherwise is to accuse Jesus of a terrible deception amounting to nothing more than a cruel and dishonest scare tactic.

The fact is that Jesus referred to hell on numerous occasions throughout the Gospels. For instance, Matthew 10:28 says, "And fear not them which kill the body, but are not able to kill the soul: but rather fear him which is able to destroy both soul and body in hell." Jesus said in Matthew 18:9 that "if your eye causes you to sin, tear it out and throw it away. It is better for you to enter life with one eye than with two eyes to be thrown into the hell of fire" (ESV). In addition, He warned His followers in Luke 12:5 to "fear him who, after he has killed, has authority to cast into hell" (ESV).

In all the above passages, the word used to describe hell is *Gehenna*. In using this word, Jesus vividly illustrated the everlasting burnings of hell by comparing it to the perpetual fires in the valley of Hinnom just south of Jerusalem. In this valley was the city garbage dump, a heap of refuse that burned continually; hence His phrase found twice in Mark 9:43–45, "The fire that shall never be quenched."

That all will be judged is a biblical fact. Acts 17:31 declares that God has appointed a day in which He will judge the world in righteousness. On that day no lawyer with beguiling speech will be able to manipulate a jury into an unjust decision. Both believer and unbeliever will have to give an account directly before Christ Himself (John 5:22). Matthew 12:36 tells us that every idle word ever spoken will be carefully scrutinized. While the believer's actions in this life may allow him to either gain or lose unspecified rewards, his ultimate hope lies in knowing he will, with certainty, obtain eternal life (1 John 5:13). Jesus promised in John 5:24 that those who hear His word, and believe on Him, have (right now) eternal life. Those who place their total confidence and trust in the work of Christ will not be condemned, but they have already "passed from death unto life." They need not fear that the final judgment will render them guilty and deserving of eternal damnation.[59]

On the other hand, those who believe that personal merit will vindicate them will be horribly disappointed. According to Christian theologian B. B. Warfield, "The works of a sinful man will, of course, be as sinful as he is, and nothing but condemnation can be built on them."[60] Exposed as insufficient will be sin-tainted deeds performed with the anticipation of individual exaltation. A life dedicated to self-glorification will not be enough to assuage God's demand for perfection.

A horrible end also lies in store for those who pride themselves in their false religion. Many souls will reside in hell because they placed more importance on their membership in a certain religious organization or belief system than in the truth of God's Word, the Bible. How terrible it will be to see that Christ does not grant eternal happiness to those who

210

trusted in false prophets and false messiahs but only to those who trusted in a personal Christ—the One who declared in John 14:6 that He alone was "the way, the truth, and the life." As stated before, not just any Christ will do. Since neither the Jesus of Mormonism nor the Jesus of any other false religion has any power to save, those who trust in such imagined "saviors" will be sorely disappointed. Jesus Himself declared in Matthew 7:22–23:

> On that day many will say to me, "Lord, Lord, did we not prophesy in your name, and cast out demons in your name, and do many mighty works in your name?" And then will I declare to them, "I never knew you; depart from me, you workers of lawlessness" (ESV).

Discussion Questions

1. Exaltation, or eternal life, is the goal that the LDS leaders say every Mormon should have. Based on the information presented in this section on salvation, what is the likelihood that a faithful Latter-day Saint will qualify for this state? How does this view of godhood and eternal increase differ from the Bible's teachings?

2. Many Mormons think that the Christian view of hell is "unfair" and that God loves His children so much He would never send them there for eternity. Using the LDS view of three levels of heaven and the reality that most Mormons will not attain the top level, explain to a Latter-day Saint how this scenario might be perceived as "unfair" by those outside the LDS Church. And how is the LDS view of punishment in outer darkness for one-third of God's spirit offspring another reason to claim Mormonism's view of the afterlife is "unfair"?

3. Why do you think many Mormons bristle at the idea they may have about the biblical view of heaven? If you only had a few minutes to explain the biblical view of heaven, what would you say?

Final Thought

Sooner or later, Judgment Day—that time when every person must give an accounting for their life on earth—is coming. According to Mormonism, humans can expect a resurrection to one of three degrees of glory.

Christianity, on the other hand, says that there will be either a resurrection to heaven or hell. If Mormonism is true, then most people can probably expect eternity in the second heaven called the terrestrial kingdom; if Mormonism is wrong and Christianity is true, the faithful Latter-day Saint who has placed trust in the gospel according to Joseph Smith and the LDS leadership will have eternal consequences. The stakes are no doubt very high. If this is the case, sharing the true gospel (Good News) message with our Mormon friends and family members should never be considered a hobby as it really is the difference between heaven and hell.

Notes

1. *Teachings of Presidents of the Church: Lorenzo Snow*, 131; ellipses in original.

2. *Teachings of Presidents of the Church: Joseph F. Smith*, 129.

3. *Doctrines of the Gospel Student Manual: Religion 430–431* (Salt Lake City: The Church of Jesus Christ of Latter-day Saints, 2004), 63.

4. Harrell, *"This Is My Doctrine,"* 333. Explaining that Apostle Bruce R. McConkie taught how God not only knows but "arranges beforehand" who will die in infancy, Harrell writes, "Since roughly half of the earth's inhabitants who have ever been born have died in infancy, more souls will presumably be exalted in the celestial kingdom than those who inhabit another degree of glory." Harrell speculates that these spirits may have "already proven themselves in premortality" to receive the gift of instant immortality. Even though he admits it's not an official LDS teaching, he says it may "be the best explanation that fits the logic of LDS theology," 334.

5. *Gospel Principles*, 244. For a closer look at 1 Peter 3:18–20, see pages 180–81 in chapter 22, "If there is no baptism for the dead, what about all those who have died without having heard the gospel?" in our book *Answering Mormons' Questions*.

6. Ibid., 243.

7. Ibid., 244.

8. *Preparing for Exaltation Teacher's Manual*, 39.

9. *Gospel Principles*, 271.

10. Secretary to the First Presidency in a 1952 letter, and again in 1965, cited in *Dialogue: A Journal of Mormon Thought*, vol. XV, no. 1 (spring 1982), 181–83.

11. Leaders have fallen into three unofficial camps on this topic: (1) Those who say there can be no further progression. For instance, see Joseph F. Smith, *Improvement Era* (November 1910), 14:87. Saying there will be "no progression between kingdoms," twelfth President Spencer W. Kimball wrote, "After a person has been assigned to his place in the kingdom, either in the telestial, the terrestrial or the celestial, or to his exaltation, he will never advance from his assigned glory to another glory. That is eternal. That is why we must make our decision early in life and why it is imperative that such decisions be right"; see Kimball, *The Miracle of Forgiveness*, 243–44, and *The Teachings of Spencer W. Kimball*, ed. Edward L. Kimball (Salt Lake City: Bookcraft, 1982), 50. This quote is cited in a 1984 church manual, *Search These Commandments: Melchizedek Priesthood Personal Study Guide*, 81–82. (2) Those who say there can be further advancement: Brigham Young, *Journal of Wilford Woodruff*, August 5, 1855 (Salt Lake City: Kraut's Pioneer Press), www.nhfelt .org/doc_other/wilford_wilford.pdf; Woodruff, *Journal of Discourses*, 6:120, December 6,

1857; J. Reuben Clark, *Church News* (April 23, 1960), 3. (3) Those who don't know. For instance, B. H. Roberts said, "The question of advancement within the great divisions of glory celestial, terrestrial, and telestial; as also the question of advancement from one sphere of glory to another remains to be considered," B. H. Roberts, *New Witnesses for God*, (Salt Lake City: George Q. Cannon and Sons, 1895),1:391–92.

12. First Corinthians 15:40 in the Joseph Smith Translation reads, "Also celestial bodies, and bodies terrestrial, and bodies telestial; but the glory of the celestial, one; and the terrestrial, another; and the telestial, another."

13. For more information on the three degrees of glory, see chapter 30, "Didn't the apostle Paul say there were three degrees of glory?" in our book *Answering Mormons' Questions*.

14. McConkie, *Doctrinal New Testament Commentary* (Salt Lake City: Bookcraft, 1966), 3:75. Regarding apostasy, Bruce R. McConkie explained, "Apostates exhibit varying degrees of indifference and of rebellion, and their punishment, in time and in eternity, is based on the type and degree of apostasy which is involved. Those who become indifferent to the Church, who simply drift from the course of righteousness to the way of the world, are not in the same category with traitors who fight the truth, and with those whose open rebellion destines them to eternal damnation as sons of perdition. All apostates are turned over to the buffetings of Satan in one degree or another, with the full wrath of Satan reserved for those who are cast into outer darkness with him in that kingdom devoid of glory."

15. *Gospel Principles*, 273.

16. Joseph Fielding Smith, *Church History and Modern Revelation* (Salt Lake City: Deseret News Press, 1949), 1:278. See also Joseph Fielding Smith, *Conference Reports* (October 1958): 21.

17. Joseph Fielding Smith, *Conference Reports* (April 1942): 27. See also Joseph Fielding Smith, *Conference Reports* (October 1958): 21.

18. Joseph Fielding Smith, *Doctrines of Salvation*, 2:220.

19. *Gospel Principles*, 272.

20. *True to the Faith*, 94.

21. Joseph Fielding Smith, *Answers to Gospel Questions* (Salt Lake City: Deseret Book Co., 1957–63), 2:209.

22. Roberts, comp., *Comprehensive History of the Church*, 1:275.

23. *Gospel Principles*, 272.

24. *Teachings of Presidents of the Church: Spencer W. Kimball*, 8.

25. *Doctrine and Covenants and Church History Gospel Doctrine Teacher's Manual*, (Salt Lake City: Intellectual Resource, Inc., 2003), 112. See also McConkie, *A New Witness for the Articles of Faith* (Salt Lake City: Deseret Book Co., 1985), 146; brackets in original.

26. B. H. Roberts, *New Witnesses for God* (Salt Lake City: Deseret Book Co., 1911, 1950–51), 1:385. See also D&C 76:79.

27. "Becoming Like God," The Church of Jesus Christ of Latter-Day Saints, accessed May 29, 2014, https://www.lds.org/topics/becoming-like-god?lang=eng.

28. Ridges, *Mormon Beliefs and Doctrine Made Easier*, 122.

29. *Gospel Principles*, 277.

30. Bruce K. Satterfield, online study guide, accessed May 29, 2014, http://emp.byui.edu/SatterfieldB/Rel235/Becoming.html. The quote comes from *Teachings of Presidents of the Church: Gordon B. Hinckley*, 179. See also *Ensign* (November 1994): 46.

31. Ibid. The quote comes from *Discourses of Brigham Young* [1954], 57; emphasis added.

32. "Becoming Like God," The Church of Jesus Christ of Latter-Day Saints, accessed May 29, 2014, https://www.lds.org/topics/becoming-like-god?lang=eng.

33. *True to the Faith*, 92.

34. *Doctrine and Covenants Student Manual*, 30; bold in original.

35. *Life and Teachings of Jesus and His Apostles*, 328; bold and italics in original.

36. *Teachings of Presidents of the Church: George Albert Smith*, 70–71.

37. Joseph Fielding Smith, *Doctrines of Salvation*, 2:41; italics in original.

38. Joseph Fielding Smith, quoted in *Selections from Answers to Gospel Questions: Taken from the Writings of Joseph Fielding Smith, Tenth President of the Church* (Salt Lake City: The Church of Jesus Christ of Latter-day Saints, 1972), 125.

39. Joseph Fielding Smith, ed., *Teachings of the Prophet Joseph Smith*, 312.

40. *Ensign*, Special Issue Temples (October 2010): 49.

41. Kimball, *Teachings of Spencer W. Kimball*, 386; quoted by Henry Eyring, *Ensign* (October 2002): 21.

42. *Gospel Principles*, 213.

43. *Introduction to Family History Student Manual: Religion 261* (Salt Lake City: The Church of Jesus Christ of Latter-day Saints, 2012), 3.

44. Bruce K. Satterfield, online study guide, accessed May 29, 2014, http://emp.byui.edu/SatterfieldB/Rel235/Becoming.html. It should be pointed out that, in context, D&C 132 is referring to plural marriage.

45. *Teachings of Presidents of the Church: John Taylor*, 193.

46. *Teachings of Presidents of the Church: Joseph F. Smith*, 386.

47. *Teachings of Presidents of the Church: Spencer W. Kimball*, 212; italics in original.

48. *Gospel Principles*, 272.

49. Seventy Enrique R. Falabella, *Ensign* (May 2013): 102.

50. Ridges, *Mormon Beliefs and Doctrine Made Easier*, 29.

51. Harrell, "*This Is My Doctrine*," 140.

52. *Teachings of Presidents of the Church: Joseph Fielding Smith*, 68.

53. Ibid., 197.

54. For more information on eternal increase, see chapter 14, "If God was once a man, why can't men become gods?" and chapter 23, "Wouldn't you like to have your marriage and family endure for all eternity?" in our book *Answering Mormons' Questions*.

55. According to Mormonism, this earth is a portion of Elohim's inheritance and reward for a life of good works during his mortality. Given this LDS premise, we wonder if the LDS God is overflowing with joy watching his creation stumble through life engaging in behaviors that must surely offend him. When we consider that this earth and the people who live on it are the reward for his faithfulness on another world, does he bubble with pride as he watches his offspring participate in murders, rapes, and other heinous crimes? Or is he pleased seeing them gossip about each other and have petty differences? To watch one's progeny deal with such heart-breaking behaviors is certainly not our idea of a heavenly experience.

56. Brigham Young, *Journal of Discourses*, ed. Watt, 14:71–72.

57. *Gospel Principles*, 11; italics added.

58. While Mormons may disagree with a heaven where the attention is focused on the Godhead (not on ourselves or our families), Mormon 7:7 in the Book of Mormon does state, "And he hath brought to pass the redemption of the world, whereby he that is found guiltless before him at the judgment day hath it given unto him to dwell in the presence of God in his kingdom, to sing ceaseless praises with the choirs above, unto the Father, and unto the Son, and unto the Holy Ghost, which are one God, in a state of happiness which hath no end."

59. For more on the topic of hell, see chapter 18, "How can you believe in a God who would send His children to an eternal hell?" in our book *Answering Mormons' Questions*.

60. John E. Meeter, ed., *Selected Shorter Writings of Benjamin B. Warfield*, 2 vol. (Nutley, NJ: Presbyterian and Reformed Publishing Company, 1970), 1.283–84.

Part V

Examining the LDS Concept of Ordinances

13 | Communion and Baptism

Persons who have been convicted of crimes and seek baptism for the first time or baptism for readmission into the Church are not baptized until they complete their terms of imprisonment, parole, or probation resulting from their convictions (unless the First Presidency has granted an exception). They are encouraged to work closely with local priesthood leaders and to do everything they can to become worthy of baptism. A person who has been convicted of, or who has confessed to, murder (even in private confessions to a priesthood leader) may not be baptized unless the First Presidency gives permission. The request for permission to baptize must include all pertinent details as determined during a personal interview by the mission president (if the person is seeking baptism for the first time) or bishop (if a former member is seeking readmission).

Church Handbook of Instructions, Book I: Stake
Presidencies and Bishoprics (1998) [1]

MORMONESE:

baptism: Required for the remission of sins. Performed by complete immersion in water and valid only if administered by a Mormon male holding priesthood authority.

sacrament: Similar to the Protestant version of communion, or the Lord's Supper. Performed weekly in LDS services, with bread and water as elements.

Although they are not requirements for entrance into heaven, the Lord's Supper and water baptism play important roles in the life of the

Christian. The Latter-day Saints also consider these to be integral to their faith. It is in the purpose and importance of these events, however, that the two faiths differ.

The Sacrament

Similar to the Christian observance known as the Lord's Supper, communion, or the Eucharist (meaning "give thanks"), Mormonism celebrates the "sacrament" each Sunday. Explaining this ordinance, a church reference manual says,

> Today we partake of bread and water in remembrance of Jesus Christ's atoning sacrifice. This ordinance is an essential part of our worship and our spiritual development. The more we ponder its significance, the more sacred it becomes to us.[2]

When Latter-day Saints partake in this ordinance, they promise to keep their covenants, as Henry B. Eyring, a member of the First Presidency, explained in a 1998 general conference talk:

> President J. Reuben Clark Jr., as he pled—as he did many times—for unity in a general conference talk, warned us against being selective in what we will obey. He put it this way: "The Lord has given us nothing that is useless or unnecessary. He has filled the Scriptures with the things which we should do in order that we may gain salvation." President Clark went on: "When we partake of the Sacrament we covenant to obey and keep his commandments. There are no exceptions. There are no distinctions, no differences" (in *Conference Report*, Apr. 1955, 10–11). President Clark taught that just as we repent of all sin, not just a single sin, we pledge to keep all the commandments. Hard as that sounds, it is uncomplicated. We simply submit to the authority of the Savior and promise to be obedient to whatever He commands (see Mosiah 3:19). It is our surrender to the authority of Jesus Christ which will allow us to be bound as families, as a Church, and as the children of our Heavenly Father."[3]

The earliest Mormons used bread and wine for the sacrament. D&C 20:75 says, "It is expedient that the church meet together often to partake of bread and wine in the remembrance of the Lord Jesus." A few months later Smith had a "revelation," recorded in D&C 27, setting forth a new requirement. Verse 3 says that God's people should not "purchase wine neither strong drink of your enemies." Water became the substance used in the LDS sacrament service. Apostle James Talmage explained why:

> In instituting the sacrament among both the Jews and the Nephites, Christ used bread and wine as the emblems of His body and blood; and in this, the dispensation of the fulness of times, He has revealed His will that the saints meet together often to partake of bread and wine in this commemorative ordinance. But He has also shown that other forms of food and drink may be used in place of bread and wine. Soon after the Church had been organized in the present dispensation, the Prophet Joseph Smith was about to purchase wine for sacramental purposes, when a messenger from God met him and delivered the following instructions: "For, behold, I say unto you, that it mattereth not what ye shall eat or what ye shall drink when ye partake of the sacrament, if it so be that ye do it with an eye single to my glory—remembering unto the Father my body which was laid down for you, and my blood which was shed for the remission of your sins. Wherefore, a commandment I give unto you, that you shall not purchase wine neither strong drink of your enemies; Wherefore, you shall partake of none except it is made new among you; yea, in this my Father's kingdom which shall be built up on the earth." Upon this authority, the Latter-day Saints administer water in their sacramental service, in preference to wine.[4]

Almost three years later, Joseph Smith received another revelation recorded in D&C 89:5 where God reversed His mind and once again specifically said wine should be used "in assembling yourselves together to offer up your sacraments before him." Verse 6 adds that it should be "pure wine of the grape of the vine, of your own make."

In the Christian tradition, the Lord's Supper was administered to the disciples on the night before Jesus's death (Luke 22:7–23). Jesus took bread and wine, gave it to His disciples, and instructed them to eat it with Him. It was meant to encourage these men. Whenever they sat down to participate in this ordinance, they were to do so in remembrance of Him. This event was an obvious reference to the Old Testament sacrificial system, whereby the death of the animal sacrifice and the emptying of its blood foreshadowed Christ's sacrifice for the forgiveness of sins; it was the Lamb of God who made all of this possible. First Corinthians 11:26 says Christians should continue to observe the Supper to remember the price paid on behalf of all Christian believers. It is not to be taken lightly.

Matthew 26:29 refers to the "fruit of the vine," so Christians have typically used wine or grape juice to remember the supreme price paid on Calvary. Since water is not a historical element within the universal Christian church, it is curious why this element has been chosen in the LDS tradition to symbolize the blood of Jesus.

Baptism as Practiced in Mormonism

Mormon leaders have maintained that only priesthood members of its church have authority to administer baptism; others performed at non-LDS churches are considered invalid. As Apostle David A. Bednar said, "The saving ordinance of baptism must be administered by one who has proper authority from God."[5]

The procedure of an LDS baptism is very specific:

> Two priests or men who hold the Melchizedek Priesthood witness each baptism to be sure it is performed properly. The baptism must be repeated if the words are not spoken exactly as given in Doctrine and Covenants 20:73 or if part of the person's body or clothing was not immersed completely. The person being baptized and the person performing the ordinance are to wear white clothing that is not transparent when wet.[6]

According to Mormonism, "baptism is essential for salvation"[7] as it is considered "the gateway through which we enter the path to the celestial kingdom."[8] Those who are baptized make promises—also known as covenants—with God. As the February 2013 *Ensign* magazine explained,

> Baptism also includes a sacred covenant, a promise, between Heavenly Father and the individual who is baptized. We covenant to keep His commandments, serve Him and His children, and take upon ourselves the name of Jesus Christ.[9]

Baptism as Practiced in Christianity

While true Christian baptism did not begin until John the Baptist, there have been important Jewish rites that have involved purification through water. For instance, the Jewish high priests made it an important part of their role as mediators between God and people. Jewish ritual immersion baths, called *miqva'ot* (singular, *miqveh*), have been uncovered in archaeological excavations. For example, archaeologist Yigael Yadin discovered two *miqva'ot* at Masada, the large fortress in Israel built by King Herod but occupied by 960 Jews for three years during the Roman destruction of Israel ending in AD 70. Other *miqva'ot* have been found near the Temple Mount in Jerusalem. Purification by water was not necessarily a precursor to baptism, as brought out by Christian scholar G. R. Beasley-Murray:

> If proselyte baptism was a universally accepted institution in Judaism before the Christian era, how are we to explain the fact that there is not one clear testimony to it in pre-Christian writings and its complete absence of mention from the writings of Philo, Josephus and the Bible, particularly the New Testament?[10]

Whatever the influence of Jewish proselyte baptism, it must be admitted that the baptisms performed by John the Baptist were more than ceremonial cleansings. Different from Jewish ritual immersion, Christian baptism is a "one-time ritual that initiates" a person into the group.[11] According to Luke 3:8–14, John the Baptist practiced a baptism of repentance, a confession of sin, and the need to be morally cleansed. Both the cleansed Jew and the sinful Gentile were commanded to repent and be baptized because their sins stained them. This baptism "symbolized preparation to receive the salvation, the kingdom of God which John heralded, and did not imply entrance into that kingdom itself."[12]

Each of the four Gospel accounts records the narrative of Christ's baptism. Though it was Christ's disciples, not Jesus Himself, who baptized individuals, it is clear that Jesus never minimized the need for baptism in the lives of believers.[13] Even the Great Commission found in Matthew 28:19–20 refers to baptizing the new believers in the name of God the Father, Son, and Holy Spirit.

While some may see baptism as being the instrument of salvation, it should be pointed out that Jesus Himself said in Luke 24:46–47: "Thus it is written . . . that repentance and remission of sins should be preached in his name among all nations." No reference is made to water baptism, but consideration of all the Gospel accounts certainly shows that baptism summed up the Christian believer's new attitude as he or she identified with Christ.

During the next step of Christian history, as chronicled in the book of Acts, water baptism continued to play an important role. There can be no argument that the normal procedure for those who had confessed Christ as their Savior was baptism with water. This was a willful act done by the new believer to identify with Jesus Christ and His death, burial, and resurrection.

Referring to Acts 10 and the story of the Roman centurion Cornelius, *Gospel Principles* says that he "did not receive the gift of the Holy Ghost until after he was baptized. The Prophet Joseph Smith taught that if Cornelius had not received baptism and the gift of the Holy Ghost, the Holy Ghost would have left him (see *Teachings of Presidents of the Church: Joseph Smith*, 97)."[14] Actually, Acts 10:44–48 does not support the claim and even reverses the order. Luke reported that

> the Holy Spirit fell on all who heard the word. And the believers from among the circumcised who had come with Peter were amazed, because the gift of the Holy Spirit was poured out even on the Gentiles. For they were hearing them speaking in tongues and extolling God. Then Peter declared, "Can anyone withhold water for baptizing these people, who *have received* the Holy Spirit just as we have?" And he commanded them to be baptized in the name of Jesus Christ. Then they asked him to remain for some days. (ESV)

While different viewpoints later arose about the formula needed to baptize, there is no doubt that Christians considered baptism to be a very important action by those believing in the Gospel message. Referring to baptism in the early church, Beasley-Murray wrote:

> It would have sounded as strange to a first generation Christian as many other queries characteristic of our time such as, "Is it necessary for a Christian to join the Church? Is it necessary to pray? Is corporate worship necessary? Is preaching necessary? Is the Lord's Supper necessary? Is the Bible necessary?" Such matters are self-evident, for they belong to the very structure of the Christian life.[15]

Christian church historian Justo Gonzalez noted that the early church in the first few centuries was cautious as to whom they would allow into the fold, making some converts wait for up to three years before they were allowed to be baptized. He wrote:

In Acts we are told that people were baptized as soon as they were converted. This was feasible in the early Christian community, where most converts came from Judaism or had been influenced by it, and thus had a basic understanding of the meaning of Christian life and proclamation. But, as the Church became increasingly Gentile, it was necessary to require a period of preparation, trial, and instruction prior to baptism. This was the "catechumenate," which, by the beginning of the third century, lasted three years.[16]

Many individual churches believed that baptism was so significant in identifying a person with the Christian community that the major doctrines and catechism were taught and memorized by the convert before this initiation ceremony. If baptism equaled forgiveness, it seems strange that this waiting period would have been enforced.

Misused Bible Passages

Certain Bible proof texts are used in an attempt to show that baptism is a requirement for salvation. The following passages are used to support this erroneous doctrine.

- *Mark 16:16: "He that believeth and is baptized shall be saved; but he that believeth not shall be damned."* Explaining this verse, Walter W. Wessel writes, "Belief and baptism are so closely associated that they are conceived of as virtually a single act. The inward reception (belief) is immediately followed by the external act or witness to that faith (baptism). The result is salvation. Here the word has its eschatological sense. Refusal to believe results in judgment. One of the primary themes of this entire section (vv. 9–20) is the importance of belief and the sinfulness of unbelief."[17] If salvation does not take effect until water baptism, then we must wonder why the second half of the verse does not read "he that believeth not and is baptized not shall be damned." The idea that belief, not baptism—as pointed out by Wessel—is what initiates salvation is supported throughout scripture, including Acts 4:12, Acts 16:31, and Romans 10:9–10.
- *Luke 3:3: "And he came into all the country about Jordan, preaching the baptism of repentance for the remission of sins."* The word *for* (Greek: *eis*) in "for the remission of sins" can mean "with a view

to" or "because of." Those who responded to John's invitation of baptism had already heard his message of coming judgment and of the "Lamb of God, which taketh away the sin of the world" (John 1:29). They responded to baptism based on the convicting message they had already heard. The word *eis* is also translated *at* in Matthew 12:41, where it says the men of Nineveh "repented *at* the preaching of Jonas." Did the men of Nineveh repent in order *to get* the preaching of Jonas? Or did they repent *because of* the preaching of Jonas? The latter, of course, is the proper answer.

- *John 3:5–6: "Jesus answered, Verily, verily, I say unto thee, Except a man be born of water and of the Spirit, he cannot enter into the kingdom of God. That which is born of the flesh is flesh; and that which is born of the Spirit is spirit."* We must ask what being "born of water" would have meant to Nicodemus. He certainly didn't understand Jesus to be referring to water baptism because Nicodemus appears confused as he tried to understand what Jesus meant. In his commentary on John, Leon Morris writes:

  > Nicodemus could not possibly have perceived an allusion to an as yet non-existent sacrament. It is difficult to think that Jesus would have spoken in such a way that His meaning could not possibly be grasped. His purpose was not to mystify but to enlighten. In any case the whole thrust of the passage is to put the emphasis on the activity of the Spirit, not on any rite of the church.[18]

- *Acts 2:38: "Repent, and be baptized every one of you in the name of Jesus Christ for the remission of sins."* Referring to this verse, Bible scholar G. R. Beasley-Murray says that "Peter calls for his hearers to repent and be baptized, with a view to receiving forgiveness and the Spirit."[19] Just as in Luke 3:3, so Peter was encouraging his hearers to be baptized in view of the remission of sins they had received when they were cut to the heart by his message regarding Christ. It is interesting to note that Peter made no reference to baptism in his next recorded sermon. Acts 3:19 ("Repent ye therefore, and be converted, that your sins may be blotted out") refers to forgiveness of sins without mentioning baptism.[20]

- *Acts 22:16: "And now why tarriest thou? arise, and be baptized, and wash away thy sins, calling on the name of the Lord."* Is Ananias

224

stressing the act of water baptism in order to wash away a person's sins? Or is he emphasizing calling on the name of the Lord? In light of the many passages that stress calling on the name of the Lord (see Joel 2:32; Acts 2:21; Rom. 10:13), we must choose the latter interpretation.

- *Romans 6:3–4: "Know ye not, that so many of us as were baptized into Jesus Christ were baptized into his death? Therefore we are buried with him by baptism into death: that like as Christ was raised up from the dead by the glory of the Father, even so we also should walk in newness of life."* There is a strong connection between baptism and the believer's relationship to Christ through His death and resurrection. The use of the aorist (past) tense suggests that, at some specific moment, the believer actually becomes linked to Christ's death and resurrection.

  Again, in New Testament times, faith and baptism were so closely identified because they normally took place so closely together. Paul's main message in this passage was that Christians should consider themselves dead to sin but alive in Christ. If the old nature has been washed away through the death and resurrection of Christ, why should the believer allow sin to reign? Baptism symbolizes a person's new identity with Christ.

- *Colossians 2:12–13: "Buried with him in baptism, wherein also ye are risen with him through the faith of the operation of God, who hath raised him from the dead. And you, being dead in your sins and the uncircumcision of your flesh, hath he quickened together with him, having forgiven you all trespasses."* The context of this passage deals with the physical act of circumcision that took place during the Old Testament times. It is significant that the New Testament tends to depreciate the external act of circumcision. It argues that circumcision is to be replaced, not by another external act (e.g., baptism) but by an internal act of the heart. Paul points out that Old Testament circumcision was an outward formality denoting the Judaic faith, but Romans 2:29 says the true Jew "is one inwardly; and circumcision is that of the heart, in the spirit, and not in the letter; whose praise is not of men, but of God." The New Covenant fulfilled the framework of circumcision and the Law.

- *1 Peter 3:18–20: "For Christ also hath once suffered for sins, the just for the unjust, that he might bring us to God, being put to death in the flesh, but quickened by the Spirit: by which also he went and preached unto the spirits in prison; which sometime were disobedient, when once the longsuffering of God waited in the days of Noah, while the ark was a preparing, wherein few, that is, eight souls were saved by water."* Baptism "saves" only in that it is "an appeal to God," an act of faith acknowledging dependence on Him. Verse 21 says that it comes not by washing of water but by an appeal to God. Christian author Bob L. Ross states that there is a four-step process of how both the ark and the ordinance of baptism symbolize the Christian's salvation in Christ:

1. The ark's occupants were inside *before* the waters came; the believer is likewise "in Christ" *before* water baptism.
2. The ark containing the occupants was surrounded by the waters of the flood, with water beneath and rain above; likewise, those in Christ go into the water.
3. Those in the ark had a resurrection from the waters; similarly, the believer is resurrected out of the water.
4. Those in the ark left behind their former world and started afresh; so also the believer, having risen from the waters of baptism, now goes forth to walk in newness of life.[21]

If these verses are not good proof texts to support the idea that water baptism is necessary for the justification of sins, and if the rest of the Bible supports the idea that faith (not works) is what forgives a person from sin, then we should reject baptism as a necessary addition to belief.

Discussion Questions

1. In what ways is the sacrament in Mormonism similar/different to the communion of Christianity? Suppose you, as a Christian, were invited to attend an LDS service and the elements were passed. Would you participate? Why or why not?
2. Many Christians are not sure what to do when they are invited to a baptismal service for a Latter-day Saint friend or family member. Should a faithful Christian attend the baptism? Provide reasoning for what is obviously a very sensitive issue.

3. Consider the verses that are used by Mormons to support the idea of baptismal regeneration (the idea that water baptism is a requirement for salvation). What approach would you use to show that conclusion to be in error? What are some verses you could share that would be beneficial to explain how salvation comes by grace through faith and not by works?

Final Thought

It needs to be remembered that baptism, like partaking of the Lord's Supper, is a work, and a righteous work at that. Since Titus 3:5 states that our salvation is not based on "works of righteousness which we have done," the act of baptism cannot be considered necessary for salvation. Instead, as Paul stated, the salvation of sinners is an act of mercy given by God. If it is truly mercy, it must always be undeserved. As Christian pastor Charles Spurgeon once observed, "It is undeserved mercy, as indeed all true mercy must be, for deserved mercy is only a misnomer for justice."[22]

Notes

1. *Church Handbook of Instructions, Book I: Stake Presidencies and Bishoprics* (Salt Lake City: The Church of Jesus Christ of Latter-day Saints, 1998), 26.

2. *True to the Faith*, 147.

3. *Ensign* (May 1998): 67–68.

4. Talmage, *Articles of Faith*, 175–76.

5. *Ensign* (May 2006): 29.

6. *Family Guidebook* (Salt Lake City: The Church of Jesus Christ of Latter-day Saints, 2001), 20.

7. Millet et al., *LDS Beliefs*, 63.

8. *Gospel Principles*, 116.

9. *Ensign* (February 2013): 14. See also *Ensign* (July 2012): 23. *True to the Faith* says that the person must "serve Him to the end," 23.

10. G. R. Beasley-Murray, *Baptism in the New Testament* (Grand Rapids: Eerdmans, 1962), 19.

11. *Biblical Archaeology Review* (January/February 1987): 58–59.

12. G. W. Bromiley, ed., *The International Standard Bible Encyclopedia* (Grand Rapids: Eerdmans, 1979), 1:418.

13. If baptism is really the cause of salvation, it seems strange that Jesus and Paul, obviously the two more prominent people in the New Testament, did not regularly perform baptisms. Instead, they left this job to others. See John 4:1–2 and 1 Corinthians 1:10–17.

14. *Gospel Principles*, 122.

15. Beasley-Murray, *Baptism in the New Testament*, 297.

16. Justo L. Gonzalez, *The Early Church to the Dawn of the Reformation*, vol. 1, *The Story of Christianity* (San Francisco: HarperCollins, 1984), 96.

17. Frank E. Gaebelein, ed., *The Expositor's Bible Commentary: Matthew/Mark/Luke*, vol. 8 (Grand Rapids: Zondervan, 1984), 790. Wessel, one of the translators of the New International Version (New Testament), was Eric's professor in seminary.

18. Leon Morris, *The Gospel according to John* (Grand Rapids: Eerdmans, 1995), 215–16.

19. Beasley-Murray, *Baptism in the New Testament*, 105.

20. For a longer commentary on Acts 2:38 as well as more information on this topic, see chapter 21, "Why don't you believe baptism is necessary for salvation when Acts 2:38 teaches this?" in our book *Answering Mormons' Questions*.

21. Bob L. Ross, *Acts 2:38 and Baptismal Remission* (Pasadena, TX: Pilgrim, 1987), 65.

22. Charles Spurgeon, "Morning and Evening—August 17," Teaching the Word Ministries, accessed May 29, 2014, www.teachingtheword.org/apps/articles/web/articleid/60443/default.asp.

14 | The Word of Wisdom

SALVATION AND A CUP OF TEA. You cannot neglect little things. "Oh, a cup of tea is such a little thing. It is so little; surely it doesn't amount to much; surely the Lord will forgive me if I drink a cup of tea." If you drink coffee or tea, or take tobacco, are you letting a cup of tea, or a little tobacco stand in the road and bar you from the celestial kingdom of God, where you might otherwise have received a fullness of glory?

President Joseph Fielding Smith [1]

MORMONESE:

temple recommend: An identification card necessary for Mormons deemed worthy to enter the temple to do work for themselves as well as those who are deceased.

Word of Wisdom: A health code found in Doctrine & Covenants Section 89 instructing Mormons to abstain from things such as hot drinks, tobacco, and alcoholic beverages. It also encourages healthy eating habits.

The introduction to section 89 of the Doctrine and Covenants states:

Revelation given through Joseph Smith the Prophet, at Kirtland, Ohio, February 27, 1833. HC 1:327–329. As a consequence of the early brethren using tobacco in their meetings, the Prophet was led to ponder upon the matter; consequently he inquired of the Lord concerning it. This revelation, known as the Word of Wisdom, was the result.

According to Mormon historians Linda King Newell and Valeen Tippetts Avery, the revelation may have come because of the complaints of Emma, Joseph Smith's wife, as the men who made up the "School of the Elders" were smoking pipes as well as spitting tobacco juice and making a mess of the floor. They write:

> Thus Emma, faced almost daily with "having to clean so filthy a floor" as was left by the men chewing tobacco, spoke to Joseph about the matter. David Whitmer's account supports Brigham Young's description. "Some of the men were excessive chewers of the filthy weed, and their disgusting slobbering and spitting caused Mrs. Smith . . . to make the ironical remark that 'It would be a good thing if a revelation could be had declaring the use of tobacco a sin, and commanding its suppression.'" Emma had support among the women. Whitmer further reports, "The matter was taken up and joked about, one of the brethren suggested that the revelation should also provide for a total abstinence from tea and coffee drinking, intending this as a counter dig at the sisters." Joseph made the issue the subject of prayer, and the "Word of Wisdom" was the result.[2]

Regardless of how it originated, the Word of Wisdom is considered so important to today's Mormons that they cannot be considered faithful by willfully breaking it. Consuming alcohol, coffee, tea, or tobacco will keep Latter-day Saints from getting temple recommends, keeping them from temple work and qualifying for the celestial kingdom. According to Apostle Boyd K. Packer,

> The Word of Wisdom put restrictions on members of the Church. To this day those regulations apply to every member and to everyone who seeks to join the Church. They are so compelling that no one is to be baptized into the Church without first agreeing to live by them. No one will be called to teach or to lead unless they accept them. When you want to go to the temple, you will be asked if you keep the Word of Wisdom. If you do not, you cannot go to the house of the Lord until you are fully worthy.[3]

As President George Albert Smith said, "I sometimes wonder if Latter-day Saints realize that [the Word of Wisdom] has been given to us for our exaltation; not only for our temporal blessing, but to prepare us for spiritual life."[4] D&C 89:2–3 explains that this "revelation" was given as "a principle with a promise" but "not by commandment or constraint."

Though considered more of a suggestion when first given, since the 1930s "under the direction of President Heber J. Grant, the Word of Wisdom became a temple recommend item and thus began to be 'locked in' as being a vital part of being a faithful Saint. It is now become a commandment in the full sense of the word."[5]

According to the *Encyclopedia of Mormonism,*

> There is evidence that Church Presidents John Taylor, Joseph F. Smith, and Heber J. Grant wanted to promote adherence to the Word of Wisdom as a precondition for entering LDS temples or holding office in any Church organization; and indeed, by 1930 abstinence from the use of alcohol, tobacco, coffee, and tea had become an official requirement for those seeking temple recommends. While abstinence from these substances is now required for temple attendance and for holding priesthood offices or other Church callings, no other ecclesiastical sanctions are imposed on those who do not comply with the Word of Wisdom.[6]

Even though the teaching didn't become binding until a century later, Joseph Smith taught that those men in the early Mormon Church who held church offices were "to comply with and obey it."[7] *Gospel Principles* states that "the Lord's Spirit withdraws" from those who disobey this teaching today.[8] And those who decide not to live according to the standards of the Word of Wisdom could even risk economic setbacks in this life, according to President Heber J. Grant:

> Many a professed Latter-day Saint in hard times has lost the home that sheltered his wife and his children, who, if he had observed the Word of Wisdom, would have been able to save it. The violation of the Word of Wisdom has meant the difference between failure and success. By observing the Word of Wisdom, sufficient money to pay the interest on the mortgage would have been forthcoming, with additional help to take care of his family and farm.[9]

A closer look at this doctrine reveals that few (if any) Mormons truly keep the Word of Wisdom as it was said to be given to Smith in 1833. Furthermore, documentation from LDS sources shows that important Mormon leaders who emphasized the adherence to this doctrine broke it themselves.

The Specifics of the Word of Wisdom

Let's consider D&C 89 and the items it banned.

Beverages

After the introductory verses explain the purpose of the command, verse 5 reads: "That inasmuch as any man drinketh wine or strong drink among you, behold it is not good, neither meet in the sight of your Father, only in assembling yourselves together *to offer up your sacraments* before him." As mentioned in the last chapter, although wine was to be used "to offer up your sacraments" when the early church members gathered together, today the LDS Church advocates the use of water in its celebration of what is called the sacrament. Verses 7 and 9 of the Word of Wisdom say:

> And again, strong drinks are not for the belly, but for the washing of your bodies. . . . And again, hot drinks are not for the body or belly.

While coffee and tea are not specifically mentioned in the LDS scripture, it has been interpreted as being what God meant. According to President Brigham Young:

> I have heard it argued that tea and coffee are not mentioned therein; that is very true; but what were the people in the habit of taking as hot drinks when that revelation was given? Tea and coffee. We were not in the habit of drinking water very hot, but tea and coffee—the beverages in common use.[10]

Gospel Principles states,

> The Lord also counsels us against the use of "hot drinks" (D&C 89:9). Church leaders have said that this means coffee and tea, which contain harmful substances. We should avoid all drinks that contain harmful substances.[11]

Notice the stress on how Mormons should "avoid all drinks that contain harmful substances," disregarding what appears to be the intent of the Word of Wisdom. It specifically mentions *hot* drinks, not *all* drinks that are bad for human consumption.

Over the years, different Mormons have interpreted the Word of Wisdom in their own postmodern ways. It has even been a point of confusion.

232

For example, when it comes to hot drinks, one LDS apologetic website explains that caffeine "is not the only reason the Lord may have invoked a prohibition against these substances" such as coffee and tea. It explains:

> A study printed in the *International Journal of Cancer* recently reported these startling findings: Drinking very hot beverages appears to raise the risk of esophageal cancer by as much as four times. The researchers analyzed results from five studies involving nearly three thousand people. The study found that hot beverages did increase the cancer risk. The study provided evidence of a link between esophageal cancer induced by the consumption of very hot drinks.[12]

Mormons who drink hot chocolate or even soups seem to be at the same risk, yet that doesn't stop many from imbibing in these types of beverages and liquid foods. Strangely enough, nineteenth century general authority George Q. Cannon said these too should be prohibited.[13]

Some have claimed that coffee and tea are harmful because they contain caffeine. Hence, many Mormons over the years have been unclear about whether or not drinking caffeinated sodas was prohibited by the Word of Wisdom. In September 2012, the church finally decided to clear up this matter. An article in *The Salt Lake Tribune* reported that the LDS Church had posted "a statement on its website saying that 'the church does not prohibit the use of caffeine' and that the faith's health-code reference to 'hot drinks' 'does not go beyond [tea and coffee].'" The article continued,

> This week's clarification on caffeine "is long overdue," said Matthew Jorgensen, a Mormon and longtime Mountain Dew drinker. Jorgensen, who is doing a two-year research fellowship in Germany, grew up "in a devout Mormon household, in a small, devout Mormon town," where his neighbors and church leaders viewed "drinking a Coca-Cola as so close to drinking coffee that it made your worthiness . . . questionable."[14]

Concerning the idea many Mormons have regarding the harm that the caffeine in coffee and tea can do to a human body, this assumption is not supported by scientific studies. For instance,

> coffee may also protect against Type 2 diabetes, Parkinson's disease, dementia, liver cancer and cirrhosis. It has been linked to lower risks of abnormal

233

heart rhythms and strokes among women. A recent National Institutes of Health study found older adults who drank coffee—caffeinated or decaf—had lower risk of death overall compared with nondrinkers. Coffee drinkers were also less likely to die from heart disease, respiratory disease, stroke, injuries and accidents, diabetes and infections. It is unclear, however, if coffee provides the benefit or if coffee drinkers have better diets or exercise more. And since coffee has more than 1,000 compounds, it's unclear what in coffee could be beneficial. For the general population "coffee is one of the good, healthy beverage choices," Rob van Dam, a Harvard School of Public Health professor, said on the school's website. According to the National Institutes of Health MedlinePlus database, green tea may help prevent cancers, including ovarian and pancreatic, reduce the risk of Parkinson's, and decrease cholesterol levels and protect against heart disease. It may also help prevent Type 2 diabetes and strokes. A recent symposium on tea and health, backed by the tea industry, along with the likes of the American Cancer Society and the American Society for Nutrition, extolled the virtues of the second-most-consumed beverage in the world. It presented research linking tea consumption with weight loss, bone and muscle strength and healthier hearts.[15]

While every Christian needs to make a personal decision about alcohol usage, it appears that wine can be beneficial if it isn't abused. According to one article,

Is wine good for you? In moderation and as part of an overall healthy diet, the short answer is yes! Thanks to its alcohol content and non-alcoholic phytochemicals (natural occurring plant compounds), wine has been shown to reduce the risk of heart disease, certain cancers and slow the progression of neurological degenerative disorders like Alzheimer's and Parkinson's Disease.[16]

An LDS student manual oddly explains how alcohol can be used as a "cleansing agent for wounds and abrasions" as well as bathing "an injured part of the body," for which it "performs a service for which it was intended."[17] Typically rubbing alcohol or hydrogen peroxide are good cleansing agents, but this is different from alcohol that is meant to be imbibed. If the Word of Wisdom statement is true, then we wonder how many Latter-day Saints keep bottles of "strong drinks," such as whiskey or vodka, around their homes for cleansing purposes.

234

Tobacco

D&C 89:8 reads, "And again, tobacco is not for the body, neither for the belly, and is not good for man, but is an herb for bruises and all sick cattle, to be used with judgment and skill." Concerning the odd commandment on tobacco being used for sick cattle, church leaders explain,

> Tobacco, like alcohol, possesses medicinal properties for use on sick animals. When applied with skill, a tobacco poultice can be useful in healing the cuts and bruises of cattle. Alcohol and tobacco have place when used as the Lord intended.[18]

If it is true that tobacco provides "medicinal properties" for animals with cuts and bruises, why wouldn't these properties be beneficial for humans as well? Yet the verse specifically excludes its usage for humans. And we have to wonder how many sick cattle around the world today are benefitting from tobacco?

Meat

Continuing, D&C 89:12–13 says:

> Yea, flesh also of beasts and of the fowls of the air, I, the Lord, have ordained for the use of man with thanksgiving; nevertheless they are to be used sparingly; And it is pleasing unto me that they should not be used, only in times of winter, or of cold, or famine.

A student manual states,

> This verse has caused some to ask if meat should be eaten in the summer. Meat has more calories than fruits and vegetables, which some individuals may need fewer of in summer than winter. Also, before fruits and vegetables could be preserved, people often did not have enough other food to eat in winter. Spoiled meat can be fatal if eaten, and in former times meat spoiled more readily in summer than winter. Modern methods of refrigeration now make it possible to preserve meat in any season. The key word with respect to the use of meat is *sparingly* (D&C 89:12).[19]

Mormons are taught that "the flesh of birds and animals is also provided for our food. However, we should eat meat sparingly (see D&C 49:18;

89:12). Fish is also good for us to eat. Grains are good for us. Wheat is especially good for us."[20] And, "Fruits, vegetables, grains, and wholesome herbs are good for us. We should eat meat sparingly. (See D&C 89:10–17)."[21] But notice how the word *sparingly* is used when this wasn't the emphasis on the original passage; instead, the Word of Wisdom suggests that it is good to eat meat *only* in winter during times of cold and famine. We wonder:

- Should those who live in tropical or moderate climates never partake of meat?
- Does a season of the year really define when meat should be eaten?
- If regular consumption of meat is so wrong, why did God provide the children of Israel with quail on a daily basis during their wilderness journey to Canaan (Num. 11:31)? In fact, why were they told to eat as much meat as their hearts desired (Deut. 12:15, 20)?

It appears that many Mormons might not be living up to the original standards that God provided, if the Word of Wisdom really came from God. Mormon writer John J. Stewart admitted in 1966, "The admonition to eat little meat is largely ignored, as are some other points of the revelation."[22]

While we don't believe the Word of Wisdom plays a role in a person's salvation, we do believe that healthy habits ought to be very important to Christians. Paul taught in 1 Corinthians 6:19 that our bodies are "temple(s) of the Holy Ghost." This is why many Christians abstain from tobacco as well as other destructive substances.[23] While they are not requirements for a person's salvation, exercise, a proper diet, and getting sufficient rest are disciplines that the Christian should consider in order to be fully fit and available to do the work of God.

The Destroying Angel

Doctrine and Covenants section 89 ends with a pledge that states, "And I, the Lord, give unto them a promise, that the destroying angel shall pass by them, as the children of Israel, and not slay them. Amen." This is an obvious reference to the original Passover as described in Exodus 12. Whether the destroying angel is something that should seriously concern a Latter-day Saint could be debated since angels sent specifically for the purpose of destruction are extremely rare in the Bible (e.g., Num. 22:21–35; 1 Chron. 21:15–30; Isa. 37:36–37). Some Mormon leaders have stated that verse 21 in section 89 of the D&C is not implying that Latter-day Saints shall never die. They insist that while many faithful LDS people have passed away, it should not be assumed that a "destroying angel" was responsible, since destroying angels only strike the disobedient and unrighteous.

Hypocrisy in the LDS Leadership

If the principle known as the Word of Wisdom was delivered by God, then why have Mormonism's leaders not always been faithful to it? For instance, Joseph Smith did at times use tobacco and liquor. He stated:

> We then partook of some refreshments, and our *hearts were made glad* by the fruit of the vine. . . . Elders Orson Hyde, Luke S. Johnson, and Warren Parrish, then presented the Presidency with three servers of glasses filled with wine, to bless. . . . It was then passed round in order, the cake in the same order; and suffice it to say, our *hearts were made glad* while partaking of the bounty of earth which was presented, until we had taken our fill.[24]

According to the January 22, 1935 *Saint's Herald*, a newspaper owned by the Independence, Missouri–based Reorganized Church of Jesus Christ of Latter Day Saints, Smith ran a tavern from his home. His wife, Emma, disapproved and ordered him to get rid of it, which he did. Mormon Oliver B. Huntington told of one story concerning Smith and a man named Robert Thompson. Smith told Thompson that he should "get drunk and have a good spree. If you don't you will die." Robert did not do it. He was a very pious exemplary man and never guilty of such an impropriety as he thought that to be. In less than two weeks he was dead and buried.[25] Mormon Church leaders and historians have sanitized some things in LDS publications to protect the reputation of their founding prophet. For instance, Joseph Smith is quoted as saying: "It was reported to me that some of the brethren had been drinking whisky that day in violation of the Word of Wisdom. I called the brethren in and investigated the case, and was satisfied that no evil had been done."[26] The original account found in the *Millennial Star* adds these words: "and gave them a couple of dollars, with directions to replenish the bottle to stimulate them in the fatigues of their sleepless journey."[27]

Apparently, keeping the Word of Wisdom was difficult for many early Latter-day Saints. In 1873 Brigham Young reported that the cooperative store in Utah "was doing a great business in tea, coffee and tobacco."[28] On March 10, 1860, Young rebuked the LDS men for chewing tobacco in the semiannual conference and spitting it on the floor but came short of calling their habit "sin." He said:

> Many of the brethren chew tobacco, and I have advised them to be modest about it. . . . If you must use tobacco, put a small portion in your mouth when no person sees you, and be careful that no one sees you chew it. I do not charge you with sin. You have the "Word of Wisdom." Read it.[29]

Young's hesitancy to call this act a sin is noteworthy. Even though Smith revealed the Word of Wisdom in 1833, as noted above, its observance did not become a requirement for entrance into a temple until almost a century later.

While he did discourage the use of tobacco, Young seemed to be more concerned about the amount of money being spent on these substances. On October 9, 1865, he said:

> What I am now about to say is on the subject of the use of tobacco. Let us raise our own tobacco, or quit using it. In the years [18]'49, '50, '51, '52, and '53, and so long as I kept myself posted respecting the amount expended yearly by this people at the stores for articles of merchandise, we spend upwards of 100,000 dollars a year for tobacco alone! We now spend considerably more than we did then.[30]

Some Mormons have argued that because the Word of Wisdom was originally given "without constraint," early members were living under different standards that were more lenient than they are today. This begs the question as to why God would give a revelation in 1833 that was only meant to be a suggestion just to have humans (the LDS leaders themselves) later decide that these rules would become mandatory.

Another popular myth is the idea that the Word of Wisdom affirms Smith's position as a true prophet who recognized the dangers of tobacco, alcohol, and caffeine many years before the medical profession understood their effects. Dr. James Mason, a Mormon who was the director of the Centers for Disease Control in Atlanta, Georgia, said, "Few revelations have come under more scrutiny than this 'word of wisdom,' and few have served as well to vindicate Joseph Smith's calling as a prophet."[31]

While this may sound reasonable, it is far from the truth. What is not mentioned by those who boast about Smith's "revelation" is that the Word of Wisdom ideas were being advocated by others during the time of Joseph Smith. According to Dean D. McBrien, one group called the American Temperance Society was successful in "eliminating a distillery in Kirtland [OH] on February 1, 1833, just twenty-seven days before the Latter-day Saint revelation counseling abstinence was announced, and that the distillery at Mentor, near Kirtland, was also closed at the same time."[32] Three years before the Word of Wisdom revelation, the November 6, 1829 edition of the *Wayne Sentinel,* which was published in the neighborhood where Smith grew up, talked about tobacco as being "an absolute poison." Regarding alcoholic drinks, warnings had been given years before by the temperance movement. It is extremely possible that Smith picked up his ideas from these other sources.

Discussion Questions

1. According to Mormonism, keeping the Word of Wisdom is tied to one's salvation, as a person cannot receive a temple recommend without foregoing coffee, tea, alcohol, and tobacco. Without this recommend, a person cannot do the work necessary to attain the celestial kingdom. Is there any biblical precedent that one's intake of certain foods or even the use of alcohol and drugs could put one's spiritual destiny in jeopardy? What does the Bible have to say about this?

2. Suppose a Mormon says that the Word of Wisdom proves how Joseph Smith truly was a prophet of God, such as his ability to know the dangers of tobacco. How would you respond?

3. Sometimes situations arise that the Bible does not provide specifics about. Suppose, for instance, that you were having dinner with a fellow believer who was once an alcoholic. The waiter asks at the beginning of your meal if you would like something to drink. If you normally felt comfortable in public ordering a glass of wine with your meal, what would be your course of action? In another situation, suppose the dinner partner was a Latter-day Saint co-worker to whom you have been sharing your faith. Would you order the glass of wine with dinner or perhaps a cup of coffee after dinner? What biblical precedence would you cite for your decision(s)?

Final Thought

If Mormons wish, they are free to abstain from anything they want, including alcohol, tobacco, and, yes, even hot drinks. It is unfortunate, however, that these hardworking people are made to think that keeping commands such as the Word of Wisdom somehow makes them more "worthy" in God's sight. A person who refuses to follow these health codes cannot be considered a member in good standing, as breaking these rules will lead to a banishment from the temple, which is where important ordinances take place. In effect, this rule has diverted people from those things that are really important. As Jesus said in Matthew 15:11, "it is not what goes into the mouth that defiles a person, but what comes out of the mouth" that "defiles a person" (ESV). Regardless of how much effort the Latter-day Saint exerts in successfully abstaining from coffee, tobacco, and alcoholic beverages, it must be understood that God is much more concerned with the spiritual condition of a person's heart rather than what they consume.

Notes

1. *Doctrines of Salvation*, 2:16.
2. Linda King Newell and Valeen Tippetts Avery, *Mormon Enigma: Emma Hale Smith*, 2nd ed. (Urbana: University of Illinois Press, 1994), 47; ellipses in original.
3. *Ensign* (May 1996): 17.
4. *Teachings of Presidents of the Church: George Albert Smith*, 207; brackets in original.
5. Ridges, *Mormon Beliefs and Doctrines Made Easier*, 335.
6. Ludlow, ed., *Encyclopedia of Mormonism*, s.v. "Word of Wisdom," 4:1584.
7. Joseph Fielding Smith, ed., *Teachings of the Prophet Joseph Smith*, 117.
8. *Gospel Principles*, 167.
9. *Teachings of Presidents of the Church: Heber J. Grant*, 193.
10. *Teachings of Presidents of the Church: Brigham Young*, 212.
11. *Gospel Principles*, 169.
12. "Response to Claims Made in Chapter 14: The Word of Wisdom," *FairMormon*, accessed May 29, 2014, http://en.fairmormon.org/Criticism_of_Mormonism/Books/Mormonism_101/Index/Chapter_14.
13. Watt, ed., *Journal of Discourses*, 12:221–23. However, a May 5, 1962, editorial in the church section of the *Deseret News* said those who, like Cannon, believe that hot chocolate and soup are implied in the Word of Wisdom do "not state the truth."
14. Peggy Fletcher Stack, "OK, Mormons, Drink Up—Coke and Pepsi Are OK," *Salt Lake Tribune*, September 5, 2012, www.sltrib.com/sltrib/news/54797595-78/church-drinks-caffeine-lds.html.csp, accessed May 29, 2014.
15. Heather May, "What Science Says about Mormonism's Health Code," *Salt Lake Tribune*, October 6, 2012, www.sltrib.com/sltrib/news/54897327-78/health-coffee-disease-tea.html.csp, accessed May 29, 2014.

16. Joy Bauer, "Is Wine Good for You?," *Today* Health, accessed May 29, 2014, www .today.com/id/21478144/#.UpZ0gMRDvng.

17. *Doctrine and Covenants Student Manual*, 208.

18. Ibid., 209.

19. Ibid., 210; italics in original.

20. *Gospel Principles*, 170.

21. *Gospel and the Productive Life Student Manual*, 85.

22. John Stewart, *Joseph Smith, the Mormon Prophet* (Salt Lake City: Hawkes Publishing, 1966), 90.

23. Some issues are areas of freedom. For instance, Paul dealt with the problem of meat offered to idols in 1 Corinthians 8 and 10. In issues such as this, Paul indicated that we are free to partake as long as we use discretion and don't cause fellow believers in Christ to stumble. Romans 14:15 says, "For if your brother is grieved by what you eat, you are no longer walking in love. By what you eat, do not destroy the one for whom Christ died." Verses 20–21 add, "Do not, for the sake of food, destroy the work of God. Everything is indeed clean, but it is wrong for anyone to make another stumble by what he eats. It is good not to eat meat or drink wine or do anything that causes your brother to stumble" (ESV).

24. *History of the Church*, 2:369, 378. In his book *Hearts Made Glad: The Charges of Intemperance against Joseph Smith the Mormon Prophet* (Salt Lake City: LaMar Petersen, 1975), LaMar Petersen documented "the statements and testimonies of scores of witnesses and redactors regarding Smith's interest in 'the fruit of the vine.'"

25. *Life of Oliver B. Huntington*, typed copy at the Special Collections Department, Marriott Library, University of Utah.

26. *History of the Church*, 5:450.

27. *Millennial Star* 21, April 30, 1859, 283.

28. Brigham Young, *Journal of Discourses*, ed. Watt, 16:238. Young explained that the Church-owned store was selling tobacco for the purpose of killing ticks on sheep. However, some Saints were buying it for personal use, for which he offered a sharp rebuke.

29. Ibid., 8:361.

30. Brigham Young, *Journal of Discourses*, ed. Watt, 11:140.

31. *A Sure Foundation*, 85.

32. *BYU Studies* (winter 1959): 39–40.

15 | The Temple

If Satan and his hosts can persuade you to take the broad highway of worldly marriage that ends with death, he has defeated you in your opportunity for the highest degree of eternal happiness through marriage and increase throughout eternity. . . . Those who make themselves worthy and enter into the new and everlasting covenant of marriage in the temple for time and all eternity will be laying the first cornerstone for an eternal family home in the celestial kingdom that will last forever. Their reward is to have "glory added upon their heads forever and forever" (see Abraham 3:26).

President Harold B. Lee[1]

MORMONESE:

born in the covenant: The children born to Latter-day Saint parents who were married in a Mormon temple are automatically sealed to them for eternity.

endowment: Course of instruction performed in a Mormon temple.

patron: A person who participates in the temple ceremony.

sealing: Temple ceremony binding a husband and wife together, not just for this life but throughout eternity. Children who are not born in the covenant also can be sealed to parents.

temple: A special building where Latter-day Saints in good standing do important works on behalf of themselves as well as for those already deceased.

Unlike the chapels where Mormons regularly meet to conduct worship services, LDS temples are places where worthy Mormons—known as patrons—go to perform "sacred" works for both themselves and those who have already died, including deceased relatives. In fact, most temple work is done on behalf of the dead. As President Thomas S. Monson stated, "Our job is to search out our dead and then go to the temple and perform the sacred ordinances that will bring to those beyond the veil the same opportunities we have."[2]

Mormons are taught that God presides over the ceremonies in each of these temples scattered throughout the world and are accessible to most LDS members, as 85 percent live within 200 miles of a temple.[3] These buildings

> are literally houses of the Lord. They are holy places of worship where the Lord may visit. Only the home can compare with temples in sacredness. Throughout history, the Lord has commanded His people to build temples. Today the Church is heeding the Lord's call to build temples all over the world, making temple blessings more available for a great number of our Heavenly Father's children.[4]

Among the rites are the endowment ceremony, baptisms for the dead, eternal marriages, and "sealings" of families for time and eternity. Temple patrons "learn more about Heavenly Father and His Son, Jesus Christ. We gain a better understanding of our purpose in life and our relationship with Heavenly Father and Jesus Christ. We are taught about our premortal existence, the meaning of earth life, and life after death."[5]

As President Brigham Young put it, "It is absolutely necessary that the Saints should receive the further ordinances of the house of God before this short existence shall come to a close, that they may be prepared and fully able to pass all the sentinels leading into the celestial kingdom and into the presence of God."[6] President Joseph Fielding Smith stated,

> If you want salvation in the fullest, that is exaltation in the kingdom of God, . . . you have got to go into the temple of the Lord and receive these holy ordinances which belong to that house, which cannot be had elsewhere. No man shall receive the fullness of eternity, of exaltation alone; no woman shall receive that blessing alone; but man and wife, when they receive the sealing power in the temple of the Lord, shall pass on to exaltation, and shall

continue and become like the Lord. And that is the destiny of men, that is what the Lord desires for His children.[7]

Only the Worthy

When they are first built, Mormon temples are opened to the general public in an "open house" format for a short time. After this, the temple is then dedicated by LDS general authorities and reopened only to worthy members. A member is considered worthy if he or she holds a "temple recommend." As it has been explained,

> To enter the temple, you must be worthy. You certify your worthiness in two interviews—one with a member of your bishopric or your branch president and another with a member of your stake presidency or the mission president. Your priesthood leaders will keep these interviews private and confidential. In each of the interviews, the priesthood leader will ask you about your personal conduct and worthiness. You will be asked about your testimony of Heavenly Father and the Atonement of Jesus Christ, and you will be asked whether you support the general and local leaders of the Church. You will be asked to confirm that you are morally clean and that you keep the Word of Wisdom, pay a full tithe, live in harmony with the teachings of the Church, and do not maintain any affiliation or sympathy with apostate groups. If you give acceptable answers to the questions in the interviews and if you and your priesthood leaders are satisfied that you are worthy to enter the temple, you will receive a temple recommend. You and your priesthood leaders will sign the recommend, which will allow you to enter the temple for the next two years, as long as you remain worthy.[8]

In the temple members can do works on behalf of themselves as well as for the deceased for whom they have done genealogical research. Temple-worthy Mormons are also allowed to attend the marriage ceremonies of those relatives or friends who invite them; those without temple recommends—even the parents of the bride and groom—are not allowed to watch the ceremony. Doctrine and Covenants 101:1 in the 1835 edition reads, "According to the custom of all civilized nations, marriage is regulated by laws and ceremonies: therefore we believe, that all marriages in this church of Christ of Latter Day Saints, should be solemnized in a public meeting, or feast, prepared for that purpose."[9]

The Inside Works of the LDS Temple

In the temple Mormons are encouraged to perform ceremonies for themselves as well as on behalf of dead relatives whom they believe will be offered a chance to improve their eternal standing while awaiting the judgment in "spirit prison." Henry B. Eyring, the first counselor in the First Presidency, explained,

> There is no greater opportunity for that invitation than in the temples of the Church. There the Lord can offer the ordinances of salvation to our ancestors who could not receive them in life. They look down upon you with love and hope. The Lord has promised that they will have the opportunity to come into His kingdom (see D&C 137:7–8), and He has planted a love for them in your heart.[10]

There are six major parts to these works: washing and anointing, new names and temple garments, pre-endowment instructions, the endowment ceremony, baptism for the dead, and marriage for time and eternity. A person must be a member for "at least one full year after baptism and confirmation" to participate in the temple endowment ceremony.[11]

Washing and Anointing

First-time patrons go through an ordinance called "washing and anointing." They begin by entering the men's or women's locker room, where street clothes are replaced with poncho-like "shields." Wearing nothing but the shield, patrons enter an area of the temple that contains the washing and anointing rooms. Here a temple worker ceremonially washes and blesses them, making reference to various parts of the body. Men are separated from the women during this ceremony. Two temple workers lay hands on the member's head, and one of the workers prayerfully "confirms" the washing. The member is ceremonially anointed with olive oil, and then the anointing is confirmed.

Temple Garments and New Names

After the washing and anointing, the patron is taken into a small curtained room. At this point, a temple worker actually puts the temple garment on the patron. Sewn into this "garment of the holy priesthood" are

245

markings similar to those used in Freemasonry. Over the right breast is a mark that resembles a backward *L*, and over the left breast is a mark that resembles a capital *V.* Sewn over the abdomen and over the knee area is another marking that looks like an ordinary buttonhole.

As part of the ceremony, the patron receives a new name that is considered sacred and is supposed to never be revealed, except at a certain time later in the ceremony. All men entering the temple on that particular day are given the same name, usually taken from either the Bible or the Book of Mormon; the same is true for women. Historically, Mormon leaders have taught that the husband has the ability to raise his wife on resurrection day. Every Mormon husband who has been through the temple is told his wife's "new name," though she is not permitted to know his. According to Charles W. Penrose, who later became a First Counselor to Heber J. Grant:

> In the resurrection, they stand side by side and hold dominion together. Every man who overcomes all things and is thereby entitled to inherit all things, receives power to bring up his wife to join him in the possession and enjoyment thereof.[12]

In 1857 Apostle Erastus Snow proclaimed:

> Do you uphold your husband before God as your lord? "What!—my husband to be my lord?" I ask, Can you get into the celestial kingdom without him? Have any of you been there? You will remember that you never got into the celestial kingdom without the aid of your husband. If you did, it was because your husband was away, and some one had to act proxy for him. No woman will get into the celestial kingdom, except her husband receives her, if she is worthy to have a husband; and if not, somebody will receive her as a servant.[13]

President Spencer W. Kimball told members at a Manchester, England area conference on June 21, 1976:

> Today you or I could not stand here and call to life a dead person, but the day will come when I can take my wife by the hand and raise her out of the grave in the resurrection. The day will come when you can bring each of your family who has preceded you in death back into a resurrected being to live forever.[14]

Pre-Endowment Instructions

After returning to the locker room and putting on white temple clothing over their garments, patrons are then welcomed to the temple and reminded to be "alert, attentive, and reverent during the presentation of the endowment." Patrons are told that if they are "true and faithful," the day will come when they will be called up and anointed "kings and queens, priests and priestesses."

During this time, further explanations of their temple garments are given. Patrons are told:

> You have had a Garment placed upon you, which you were informed represents the garment given to Adam and Eve when they were found naked in the Garden of Eden, and which is called the "Garment of the Holy Priesthood." This you were instructed to wear throughout your life. You were informed that it will be a shield and a protection to you inasmuch as you do not defile it and if you are true and faithful to your covenants.[15]

The church administrative *Handbook 2* explains:

> When properly worn, it provides protection against temptation and evil. Wearing the garment is also an outward expression of an inward commitment to follow the Savior. Endowed members should wear the temple garment both day and night. They should not remove it, either entirely or partially, to work in the yard or for other activities that can reasonably be done with the garment worn properly beneath the clothing. Nor should they remove it to lounge around the home in swimwear or immodest clothing. When they must remove the garment, such as for swimming, they should put it back on as soon as possible. Members should not adjust the garment or wear it contrary to instructions in order to accommodate different styles of clothing nor should they alter the garment from its authorized design. When two-piece garments are used, both pieces should always be worn. The garment is sacred and should be treated with respect at all times. Garments should be kept off the floor. They should also be kept clean and mended. After garments are washed, they should not be hung in public areas to dry. Nor should they be displayed or exposed to the view of people who do not understand its significance.[16]

While this handbook says that a person wearing the garments is protected from "temptation and evil," President Spencer W. Kimball said that he was "convinced that there could be and undoubtedly have been many cases where there has been, through faith, an actual physical protection, so we must not minimize that possibility."[17] In the Old Testament, only priests from the line of Levi and not the common Jew wore the linen undergarments.[18] Indeed, there is no biblical support for the notion that the priestly garments offered any special protection as described by various LDS authorities. In the New Testament, the Christian is told to have his "loins girt about with truth" and to put on the "breastplate of righteousness." However, such metaphorical language never implies that we should trust in actual physical objects. It appears that the idea of protective undergarments falls into the same category as the proverbial rabbit's foot or talisman.

The Endowment Ceremony

This ceremony is performed for both the living and the dead where "certain special, spiritual blessings [are] given [to] worthy and faithful saints in the temples . . . because in and through them the recipients are endowed with power from on high."[19] The ceremony includes a type of melodrama to explain the LDS view of the creation and fall of humanity. These dramas were originally performed by Mormon temple workers playing such parts as that of Elohim (God the Father), Jehovah (Jesus), and Lucifer. Video is utilized today in most temples.

The ceremony is made up of different sections. These include the following: the creation and fall, where the Mormon God sends "Jehovah" and "Michael" to organize unorganized matter into a world "like unto the other worlds" that have previously been formed; the law of obedience, when patrons vow to live up to the full law of God; the law of the gospel and the law of chastity, when additional vows are made; the law of consecration, when patrons consecrate themselves, their time, talents, and "everything with which the Lord has blessed them." As the vows are made, the patrons learn special handshakes, called "tokens," along with secret "signs" and "words" that they are told will be needed in the afterlife for admittance into heaven.

Numerous changes have been made to the ceremony over the years. For instance, in April 1990, a scene where Lucifer hired a Christian minister to preach false doctrine was eliminated. In the pre-1990 ceremony, Lucifer himself interviewed the pastor to see if he had "been to college and received training for the ministry." If this pastor would covenant to convert people to his "orthodox religion," Lucifer promised, "I will pay you well." Adam and Eve were introduced to the pastor as those who "desire religion." The preacher then attempted to convince Adam to believe in a God surrounded by a myriad of beings who had been "saved by grace," in a God who filled the universe but was still so small that He could dwell in a person's heart.

Adam, the "good guy" in the scenario, rejected the pastor's teachings on God, salvation by grace alone, and the reality of hell. The entire scene was intended to make Christian pastors look like they were in the employ of Satan. All mention of this scene was entirely dropped, and Mormons who did not enter the temple before 1990 may know nothing about it.

Baptism for the Dead

The most often practiced ordinance in the Mormon temple is vicarious baptism for the dead. Apostle Boyd K. Packer told a general conference audience, "One of the characteristics that sets us apart from the rest of the

Baptism for the dead is commonly practiced in the dozens of Mormon temples located around the world. This replica found in an LDS visitor's center in Salt Lake City gives an idea of what a typical font (positioned on the back of twelve oxen) looks like.

world and identifies us as the Lord's Church is that we provide baptism and other ordinances for our deceased ancestors."[20] Brigham Young declared,

Our fathers cannot be made perfect without us; we cannot be made perfect without them. They have done their work and now sleep. We are now called upon to do ours; which is to be the greatest work man ever performed on the earth. Millions of our fellow creatures who have lived upon the earth and died without a knowledge of the Gospel must be officiated for in order that they may inherit eternal life (that is, all that would have received the Gospel). And we are called upon to enter into this work.[21]

President Wilford Woodruff said,

If we do not do what is required of us in this thing, we are under condemnation. If we do attend to this, then when we come to meet our friends in the celestial kingdom, they will say, "You have been our saviors, because you had power to do it. You have attended to these ordinances that God has required."[22]

Woodruff also said,

Our forefathers are looking to us to attend to this work. They are watching over us with great anxiety, and are desirous that we should finish these temples and attend to certain ordinances for them, so that in the morning of the resurrection they can come forth and enjoy the same blessings that we enjoy.[23]

Since Christianity was said to be dead in apostasy from the time after the apostles until the early nineteenth century, members as young as twelve "can visit the temple to be baptized for their ancestors who have died without being baptized."[24] This doctrine of baptism for the dead teaches that a Mormon can "become a savior on Mount Zion" and that his or her "effort approaches the spirit of the Savior's atoning sacrifice" because they are performing "a saving work for others that they cannot do for themselves."[25] These "people in the spirit world can exercise faith and accept the gospel message, but they cannot receive the ordinances of the gospel, such as baptism, the endowment, and sealings, for themselves."[26] These souls "do not automatically become members of the Church when someone is baptized as proxy for them. Rather, they are free to accept it or reject it."[27] All of this work takes place in a font resembling the description of King Solomon's "brazen sea."[28]

Normally located in the lower part of the temple, the font is situated on top of twelve life-size oxen, which are said to symbolize the twelve tribes of Israel. According to LDS Church resources, there are certain rules to how this work can be done.

> You must provide at least the given name or the surname of your ancestor, the person's gender, a locality for a qualifying event (such as birth, christening, marriage, death, or burial), and enough additional information to uniquely identify the person. Additional information may include dates, localities, and relationships of other family members. Remember that in order for temple ordinances to be performed, individuals must be deceased for at least one year, and if that individual was born within the last 95 years, permission from the closest living relative must be obtained before temple ordinances are to be performed.[29]

In addition,

> Persons who are presumed dead because they are missing in action (for example, in times of war), lost at sea, declared legally dead, or who disappeared under circumstances where death is apparent but no body was ever recovered may have their temple ordinances performed after 10 years have passed since the time of presumed death. In all other cases of missing persons, the temple ordinances may not be performed until after 110 years have passed from the time of a person's *birth* (an assumption that if the person was missing but alive, he or she would have died within 110 years).[30]

Despite the emphasis on this doctrine, Christianity teaches that salvation is offered to the living. The Bible is very clear in Hebrews 9:27 that judgment follows this life. Further hope of attaining favor with God is lost at death. In fact, Paul wrote in 2 Corinthians 6:2 that "now is the accepted time; behold, now is the day of salvation."

Although Mormons like to reference 1 Corinthians 15:29 to support baptism for the dead, there is no evidence that Christians actually participated in a rite that is similar to that practiced by Mormons. While biblical scholars have noted that heretical groups such as the Cerinthians and Marcionites practiced a form of baptism for the dead, Paul separated himself from such as these when he said, "Else what shall *they* do which are baptized for the dead, if the dead rise not at all? why are *they* then baptized for the dead?" If baptism for the dead was, as D&C 128:17 puts it, the "most glorious of all subjects belonging to the everlasting gospel," it seems odd that Paul would not include himself as a participant; Paul neither condones nor condemns the practice, referring to it as nothing more than an illustration to support his point of resurrection of the body. Another interesting point comes from D. A. Carson, a research professor of New Testament at Trinity Evangelical Divinity School in Deerfield, Illinois. He wrote:

> When something is mentioned only once, it cannot be given the same weight of importance as the central themes of Scripture. . . . When something is mentioned only once, there is more likelihood of misinterpreting it, whereas matters repeatedly discussed are clarified by their repetition in various contexts.[31]

BYU professor Charles R. Harrell makes an interesting observation about this teaching:

> There is no indication in the Book of Mormon that Christ introduced the doctrine of salvation for the dead during his visit to the Nephites—even though, according to LDS doctrine, he had just visited the spirits in prison and opened the door for their salvation. On the contrary, the Book of Mormon people were taught not to worry about those who die without having heard the gospel in this life since they are redeemed automatically through the Atonement. The whole notion of vicarious work for the dead seems incongruous with Book of Mormon theology.[32]

Marriage for Time and Eternity

"Celestial marriages" of LDS couples for "time and eternity" take place in the temples.[33] This is an important teaching, since "only in the temple can we be sealed together forever as families."[34] At the October 2008 general conference, Apostle Russell M. Nelson said, "To qualify for eternal life, we must make an eternal and everlasting covenant with our Heavenly Father. This means that a temple marriage is not only between husband and wife; it embraces a partnership with God."[35]

Marriages performed outside of the temple are considered binding only "until death." *Gospel Principles* states,

> Only in the temple can we be sealed together forever as families. Marriage in the temple joins a man and woman as husband and wife eternally if

they honor their covenants. Baptism and all other ordinances prepare us for this sacred event. When a man and woman are married in the temple, their children who are born thereafter also become part of their eternal family.[36]

Children born to a couple married in the temple are automatically "sealed" (known as "born in the covenant") to their parents for eternity. Those couples not married in the temple will not only lose the right to be together after death, but they have no "claim upon their children, for they have not been born under the covenant of eternal marriage."[37]

Those not born "under the covenant" of celestial marriage must have their families sealed in a separate temple ceremony. President Howard W. Hunter wrote: "If children are born before the wife is sealed to her husband, there is a temple sealing ordinance that can seal these children to their parents for eternity, and so it is that children can be sealed vicariously to parents who have passed away."[38] Although continued good works are essential, Mormonism teaches that a person must be married in the temple to have a chance at exaltation. Nelson said,

> On occasion, I read in a newspaper obituary of an expectation that a recent death has reunited that person with a deceased spouse, when, in fact, they did *not* choose the eternal option. Instead, they opted for a marriage that was valid only as long as they both should live. Heavenly Father has offered them a supernatural gift, but they refused it. And in rejecting the gift, they rejected the Giver of the gift.[39]

Apostle Dallin H. Oaks agreed, saying, "Under the great plan of the living Creator, the mission of His Church is to help us achieve exaltation in the celestial kingdom, and that can be accomplished only through an eternal marriage between a man and a woman."[40] It is believed that there is a danger in "delaying marriage" since "all normal people should plan their lives to include a proper temple marriage in their early life and to multiply and have their families in the years of their early maturity."[41]

Jesus and the Sadducees

In an account given in the Synoptic Gospels, Jesus was approached by members of the Sadducees, the Jewish religious party that did not believe in a bodily resurrection from the dead (Matt. 22:23–33; Mark 12:18–27; Luke 20:27–38). Trying to trick Him, these leaders presented what appears to be a hypothetical situation involving seven brothers. When the oldest brother died, he left a wife and no children. According to the Mosaic law, the next oldest unmarried brother took the woman for his wife. However, the second brother died, as did the third through seventh brothers. Before they died, each of them had married the oldest brother's wife, making her a widow seven times over.

In Mark 12:23 they asked, "In the resurrection, when they rise again, whose wife will she be? For the seven had her as wife." Jesus chastised His inquisitors in verse 24, saying they did not know the Scriptures. Verse 25 reads, "For when they rise from the dead, they neither marry nor are given in marriage, but are like angels in heaven" (ESV).

At face value and as it has been historically interpreted, Jesus appears to be saying that heaven will be much different from life as it is known on earth. While the gifts of sex and procreation are important parts of the earthly life, these will not be a part of the afterlife. The joys in store for the believer are incredibly more magnificent than the temporary pleasure of sexual or familial fulfillment.

In addition, there will be no need to procreate in heaven. Thus, while it appears we will be able to recognize fellow believers in heaven, there is no indication from the Bible that we will be eternally paired with a particular mate. Historically, Christians view all believers as part of God's great family rather than millions of smaller groups. However, Mormon leaders have interpreted this passage quite differently than the historic Christian view. Apostle Bruce R. McConkie wrote:

> What then is the Master Teacher affirming by saying, "in the resurrection they neither marry, nor are given in marriage, but are as the angels of God in heaven"? He is not denying but limiting the prevailing concept that there will be marrying and giving in marriage in heaven. He is saying that as far as "they" (the Sadducees) are concerned, that as far as "they" ("the children of this world") are concerned, the family unit does not and will not continue in the resurrection. Because he does not choose to cast his pearls before swine, and because the point at issue is not marriage but resurrection anyway, Jesus does not here amplify his teaching to explain that there is marrying and giving of marriage in heaven only for those who live the fulness of gospel law—a requirement which excludes worldly people.[42]

Saying that this was not "the Lord's final word on the subject," David H. Yarn Jr., a former BYU professor of philosophy and religion, said, "The Lord did not say there would be no people in the married state in the resurrection but that there would be no marriages made in the resurrection."[43] Some Mormon leaders have read their own interpretations into this passage, explaining that the fictional wife in the parable had been eternally sealed to the first husband. For instance, Apostle James E. Talmage wrote:

> The Lord's meaning was clear, that in the resurrected state there can be no question among the seven brothers as to whose wife for eternity the woman shall be, since all except the first had married her for the duration of mortal life only, and primarily for the purpose of perpetuating in mortality the name and family of the brother who first died.[44]

While these explanations may sound good to a Mormon audience that cherishes the institution of marriage, the ability to read between the lines of Jesus's teaching does not make a doctrine true.[45] How many people would, on reading this Synoptic Gospel account alone in conjunction with the teachings of the Bible, exclaim, "Here's evidence for the biblical principle of eternal marriage!"? Rather than supporting the view of eternal marriage, Jesus explained that the institution of marriage was for this life only and not the life to come. To assume anything more is biblically and exegetically unsound.

The Masonic and Occultic Background of the Ceremony

Because those who have participated in the LDS temple endowment ceremony make a covenant to not talk about what goes on inside LDS temples, it is often asserted that this is a "secret ceremony." However, many Mormons become offended by this description, claiming that the ceremony is not "secret" but rather "sacred." Apostle Boyd K. Packer wrote:

> A careful reading of the scriptures reveals that the Lord did not tell all things to all people. There were some qualifications set that were prerequisite to receiving sacred information. Temple ceremonies fall within this category. We do not discuss the temple ordinances outside the temples. . . . The ordinances and ceremonies of the temple are simple. They are beautiful. They are sacred. They are kept confidential lest they be given to those who are unprepared.[46]

255

Why would categorizing the ceremony in such a manner make this subject off-limits? Latter-day Saints deem many areas *sacred*, yet they seem to have no problem discussing them. For instance, the Book of Mormon is a sacred book, yet few Mormons or missionaries would hesitate to tell their testimony about this book and the gospel contained within its pages. If what goes on inside the temple is supposed to be kept from public knowledge, this would certainly fit the definition of *secret*.

Mormons are told that the endowment is representative of the ancient ceremony mentioned in the Bible, there is no evidence to suggest that Jewish worshipers in Bible times were threatened for revealing what went on inside the Jerusalem temple. For a person who wants to understand the biblical temple, a look at the Old Testament not only reveals its furnishings but also the ceremonies that took place there. Animal sacrifice by the Levite priests was the priority, which is discussed in both biblical as well as ancient outside source accounts.[47] With what we know about biblical temple rituals and practices, there is no biblical evidence to suggest that these were similar to those enjoined by Mormons in their temples today.

Although D&C 124:41 says that the LDS temple ordinances were "kept hid from before the foundation of the earth," they are suspiciously close to those used in Freemasonry. A person need only look closely at the outside structure of the Salt Lake City temple to see many designs peculiar to Freemasonry. These include the All-Seeing Eye, the inverted five-pointed star (known as the eastern star), and the clasped hands or grip. All of these were a part of Freemasonry long before Smith incorporated them. Markings in the priesthood garments also bear resemblance to the compass, square, and level of Freemasonry. Signs, grips, oaths, and tokens used in the ceremony are so similar that one can't escape the suspicion that Smith "borrowed" these Masonic practices, especially since he became a Mason on March 15, 1842.[48] Apostle Heber C. Kimball, who was a Mason (as were the first three presidents of the LDS Church), saw a parallel between the endowment and Masonry. In 1842 he wrote: "thare is a similarity of preast Hood in masonary. Br Joseph ses masonry was taken from preasthood but has become degenerated. but menny things are perfect."[49]

Mormon historian Reed C. Durham Jr. insists Joseph Smith did, in fact, use the Masonic ritual as a springboard for the Mormon ceremony. He wrote:

> There is absolutely no question in my mind that the Mormon ceremony which came to be known as the Endowment, introduced by Joseph Smith

to Mormon Masons initially, just a little over one month after he became a Mason, had an immediate inspiration from Masonry.[50]

Charles R. Harrell also notices the similarity with Masonry: "LDS teachings on temple worship, preexistence, and the cosmos during the Nauvoo era seem to resonate with ideas in contemporary Masonry and hermetic traditions which were publicized in Joseph Smith's day."[51]

There are other practices in Mormonism that are occultic in nature, such as contact with the dead. Wilford Woodruff reported the following:

> The dead will be after you, they will seek after you as they have after us in St. George. . . . I will here say, before closing, that two weeks before I left St. George, the spirits of the dead gathered around me, wanting to know why we did not redeem them. . . . These were the signers of the Declaration of Independence, and they waited on me for two days and two nights.[52]

Mormon Joseph Heinerman reported matter-of-factly about numerous spirit sightings by Mormons at and around LDS temples. For instance, at the same St. George temple where the deceased signers of the Declaration of Independence allegedly appeared to President Woodruff, temple worker M. F. Farnsworth said "persons have told me of seeing their dead friends for whom they have officiated, manifesting themselves to them."[53] Horatio Pickett, another St. George temple worker, had the following vision on March 19, 1914:

> Do those people for whom this work is being done, know that it is being done for them, and, if they do, do they appreciate it? While this thought was running through my mind I happened to turn my eyes toward the southeast corner of the font room and there I saw a large group of women. The whole southeast part of the room was filled; they seemed to be standing a foot or more above the floor and were all intently watching the baptizing that was being done.[54]

Still another temple worker, John Mickleson Lang, said that in 1928 he "distinctly heard a voice at the east end of the font, very close to the ceiling, calling the names of the dead to witness their own baptism, allowing a moment for each spirit to present itself."[55] Meanwhile, at the Manti temple, spirits of early LDS Church leaders appeared at the 1888 dedication ceremony, including the deceased Joseph Smith and Brigham Young.

The apostles were said to look like they had halos of light on top of their heads.[56] Apostle Anthon H. Lund told a chilling story:

> I remember one day in the Temple at Manti, a brother from Mount Pleasant rode down to the Temple to take part in the work, and as he passed the cemetery in Ephraim, he looked ahead (it was early in the morning), and there was a large multitude all dressed in white, and he wondered how that could be. Why should there be so many up here; it was too early for a funeral, he thought; but he drove up and several of them stepped out in front of him and they talked to him. They said, "Are you going to the Temple?" "Yes." "Well, these that you see here are your relatives and they want you to do work for them." "Yes," he said, "but I am going down today to finish my work. I have no more names and I do not know the names of those who you say are related to me." "But when you go down to the Temple today you will find there are records to give our names." He was surprised. He looked until they all disappeared, and drove on. As he came into the Temple, Recorder Farnsworth came up to him and said, "I have just received records from England and they all belong to you." And there were hundreds of names that had just arrived, and what was told him by these persons that he saw was fulfilled. You can imagine what joy came to his heart, and what a testimony it was to him, that the Lord wants this work done.[57]

A number of other manifestations are said to have taken place in temples such as Kirtland, Nauvoo, Salt Lake, San Diego, and Hawaii. It seems curious that Mormons would find contact with the dead as a positive experience when the Old Testament adamantly warns against necromancy and having contact with "familiar spirits."[58] If God was not the creator of the ceremony, then could it be possible that Smith—using his imaginative creativity and pagan practices—created an atmosphere that would be a conduit for evil spirits? It appears that this has taken place, and for this reason Christians should have nothing to do with such a practice.

Temples: The Christian Perspective

The Old Testament temple was a place where sacrifices were made on behalf of the sins of pious Jews. The blood of the slain animal symbolized propitiation (appeasement for God's anger) and expiation (cancellation of sin). Blood sacrifices included burnt, sin, trespass, and fellowship offerings of several kinds of animals; bloodless sacrifices involved grain offerings and libations. Forgiveness was received through the faith of those who offered these sacrifices.

The temple and its priesthood foreshadowed the coming Great High Priest, Jesus Christ, to whom Hebrews 4:16 says Christians can now go to obtain mercy. Because Jesus is alive forevermore, there is no need for a human high priest. This office has been filled. The blood that was shed in the temple ceremonies foreshadowed the work that would be performed by Christ Himself. Hebrews 9:26 says "he has appeared once for all at the end of the ages to put away sin by the sacrifice of himself" (ESV). Hebrews 10:14 vividly depicts how Christ "has perfected for all time those who are being sanctified" (ESV).[59]

Discussion Questions

1. Describe the temple of Bible times and then contrast its characteristics with those of the Mormon temples. Do you see more similarities or differences? Give three examples to support your case.

2. Mormons typically see nothing wrong with having encounters with those who are dead, especially in the temple. How would you explain your views on such a practice?

3. Certain people holding temple recommends have gone into the temple and secretly recorded the endowment ceremony, even putting the information on the Internet.[60] What are your thoughts on this? What role could your knowledge of what goes on inside the temple play in your evangelistic efforts with your Latter-day Saint friend or family member?

Final Thought

When it comes to evangelism, the issue of the temple is not likely to be a priority since Mormons promise not to divulge the details of what takes place there. While there is not a mystery to us about what goes on inside the temple, we don't want to make our LDS friends and family feel uncomfortable. Still, many questions arise when this topic is introduced, such as why is there a need for the temple when Jesus has already done the work once required there? Why should we do work on behalf of the dead since every person is accountable to God based on the time they were living? Why should we get married for "eternity" when marriage was meant for this life only? If temples are supposed to be similar to what took place in biblical times, why don't animal sacrifices take place there? And why should we want to have contact with dead spirits when God has made it clear to have nothing to do with the deeds of darkness? The more we study Mormonism's version of the temple, the more we see a vast contrast between the biblical message and Mormon practice.

Notes

1. *Teachings of Presidents of the Church: Harold B. Lee*, 111.
2. *Ensign* (June 2014): 4.
3. *Ensign* (May 2014):46.
4. *True to the Faith*, 170.
5. *Gospel Principles*, 233, 235.
6. *Teachings of Presidents of the Church: Brigham Young*, 303.
7. *Teachings of Presidents of the Church: Joseph Fielding Smith*, 221.
8. *True to the Faith*, 172. A teacher's manual adds, "As you live worthily, the recommend will allow you to enter any temple of the Church as often as you wish during the next two years." *Endowed from on High*, 28.
9. See Joseph Smith, "Statement on Marriage, circa August 1835," *The Joseph Smith Papers*, accessed May 29, 2014, http://josephsmithpapers.org/paperSummary/statement-on-marriage-circa-august-1835#!/paperSummary/statement-on-marriage-circa-august-1835 &p=1. This was later changed.
10. *Ensign* (December 2013): 5.
11. *Church Handbook of Instructions*, 65.
12. Charles Penrose, *Mormon Doctrine, Plain and Simple* (Salt Lake City: Juvenile Instructor, 1888), 51.
13. Erastus Snow, *Journal of Discourses*, ed. Watt, 5:291.
14. David J. Ridges, *Doctrinal Details of the Plan of Salvation* (Springville, UT: Cedar Fort, 2005), 115. For many other quotes on husbands raising wives from the grave, see Lane A. Thuet, response to Benjamin McGuire, "Mormonism 201: Chapter 15—The Temple," Mormonism Research Ministry, www.mrm.org/topics/rebuttals-rejoinders/mormonism-201/temple-mcguire.
15. Jerald Tanner and Sandra Tanner, *Evolution of the Mormon Temple Ceremony 1842–1990* (Salt Lake City: Utah Lighthouse Ministry, 2005), 110.
16. *Handbook 2: Administering the Church 2010* (Salt Lake City: The Church of Jesus Christ of Latter-day Saints, 2010), 191.
17. Kimball, *Teachings of Spencer W. Kimball*, 539. While we are not insinuating that Mormons believe the garments will protect the wearer in all circumstances, certainly Kimball thought that there are "many cases" where there has been "an actual physical protection." For instance, Bill Marriott of the Marriott hotel chain told CBS *60 Minutes* interviewer Mike Wallace in 1996 that his garment had protected him in a boat fire. Despite the testimonies of Mormons who believe their garment has protected them from physical harm, it should

be pointed out that there are seemingly faithful Mormons who wear their garment on a regular basis yet are killed or injured.

18. While some might argue that garment-wearing Mormon males also hold the priesthood, this does not account for the many LDS women who also wear temple garments, even though they are not priests.

19. McConkie, *Mormon Doctrine*, 226–27.

20. *Ensign* (October 2007): 22.

21. *Teachings of Presidents of the Church: Brigham Young*, 311.

22. *Teachings of Presidents of the Church: Wilford Woodruff*, 192.

23. Ibid., 190.

24. *Ensign*, Special Issue Temples (October 2010): 77.

25. *True to the Faith*, 63.

26. *Introduction to Family History Teacher Manual: Religion 261* (Salt Lake City: The Church of Jesus Christ of Latter-day Saints, 2005), 7.

27. Ridges, *Mormon Beliefs and Doctrine Made Easier*, 29.

28. We're unsure why the font resembles Solomon's brazen sea. Joseph Fielding Smith admitted that "this font, or brazen sea, was not used for baptisms for the dead, for there were no baptisms for the dead until after the resurrection of the Lord," Joseph Fielding Smith, *Answers to Gospel Questions*, 5:13. Solomon's brazen sea was destroyed centuries earlier when Babylon captured Judah and did not exist during the time of Christ or after His resurrection.

29. *Introduction to Family History Student Manual*, 30.

30. Ibid., 62; italics in original.

31. D. A. Carson, "Did Paul Baptize for the Dead?" *Christianity Today*, August 10, 1998, 63.

32. Harrell, *"This Is My Doctrine,"* 361. On the previous page, Harrell refers to Moroni 8:22–23 ("baptism availeth nothing") and says that "in the Book of Mormon baptism is a covenant intended to be received only while in morality." For more information on baptism for the dead, see chapter 22, "If there is no baptism for the dead, what about all those who have died without having heard the gospel?" in our book *Answering Mormons' Questions*.

33. It should be noted that celestial marriage was once synonymous with plural marriage or polygamy. See Orson Pratt's talk on polygamy in *Journal of Discourses*, ed. Watt, 6:361–62, as well as John A. Widtsoe, *Evidences and Reconciliations*, comp. G. Homer Durham (Salt Lake City: Bookcraft, 1960), 340. According to Harrell, "It was firmly held and fervently taught through much of the latter-half of the nineteenth century that plural marriage, at least when in force, was essential to exaltation," Harrell, *"This Is My Doctrine,"* 319–20. Although Harrell points out that "LDS commentators today generally refrain from speculating on the future practice of polygamy," Apostle Bruce R. McConkie taught that it would one day be restored, *Mormon Doctrine*, 578. For more information on this topic, see chapter 16.

34. *Gospel Principles*, 235.

35. *Ensign* (November 2008): 93.

36. *Gospel Principles*, 235.

37. Le Grand Richards, *A Marvelous Work and a Wonder* (Salt Lake City: Deseret Book Co., 1976), 193. See also Talmage, *The Vitality of Mormonism*, 229. For more information about eternal increase, see chapter 12 (Heaven and Hell).

38. Howard W. Hunter, *Ensign* (February 1995): 2.

39. *Ensign* (November 2008): 93; italics in original.

40. *Ensign* (January 2011): 25–26.

41. *Teachings of Presidents of the Church: Spencer W. Kimball*, 195.

42. McConkie, *Doctrinal New Testament Commentary*, 1:605–6.

43. *A Sure Foundation*, 115.

44. James E. Talmage, *Jesus the Christ* (Salt Lake City: Deseret Book Co., 1981), 548.

45. In its chapter on "eternal marriage," *Gospel Principles* lists only three biblical passages as support for this teaching (listed as "additional scriptures" on page 223): Genesis 1:26–28, 2:21–24; and Matthew 19:3–8. The first passage deals with the command for Adam and Eve to procreate and fill the earth. The second describes the creation of Eve and how she and Adam were to become "one flesh." The third talks about divorce and for man not to undo what God intended to be a lifelong relationship. All three deal with situations in this life; none of these references has anything to do with eternal marriage. A person would have to presuppose that these passages were meant for eternity; the context of each passage, however, prevents this conclusion.

46. *Ensign* (February 1995): 32.

47. Some have implied that there is little evidence for the rituals and practices from the biblical temple. This is not true. Although it takes some research, the temple rituals—including sacrifices, the different holidays, and vows and purifications—are readily available from both biblical and outside sources. In the Old Testament, Exodus chapters 24–31 give details about both the tabernacle as well as the future temple. And the book of Leviticus provides plenty of description about the different rites. Outside sources are also a help in understanding the temple. As Alfred Edersheim explained, "Abundant materials . . . though scattered far and wide, are within our reach. Not to speak of contemporary writings, as those of Josephus and Philo, and references in the New Testament itself, we have in the *Mishnah* a body of authoritative traditions, reaching up, not only to Temple-times, but even to the days of Jesus Christ," Alfred Edersheim, *The Temple: Its Ministry and Services* (Peabody, MA: Hendrickson Publishers, 1994), ix.

48. *History of the Church*, 4:550–51.

49. As cited in Quinn, *Early Mormonism*, 185. Spelling is in original.

50. Reed C. Durham Jr., *Is There No Help for the Widow's Son?* (Nauvoo, IL: Martin Publishing, 1980).

51. Harrell, *"This Is My Doctrine,"* 22.

52. Woodruff, *Journal of Discourses*, ed. Watt, 19:229.

53. Heinerman, *Temple Manifestations* (Salt Lake City: Magazine Printing and Publishing, 1974), 64–66. Before it went out of print, this book was distributed at LDS-owned Deseret Bookstores.

54. Ibid., 68.

55. Ibid., 70.

56. Ibid., 96–97.

57. Ibid.

58. These passages include Leviticus 19:31; 20:6; Deuteronomy 18:10–12; 1 Samuel 28:3–20 (where Saul is reprimanded for dealing with the witch of Endor); 2 Kings 21:6; 23:24 (where familiar spirits are called "abominations" and equated with idols); Isaiah 8:19; 19:3. Even the Book of Mormon warns against familiar spirits in 2 Nephi 18:19.

59. For more information on temples, see chapter 29, "Why doesn't your church build temples?" in our book *Answering Mormons' Questions*.

60. For instance, see " Mormon Temple Endowment Ceremony (With Movie)," YouTube video, 1:18:47, accessed May 29, 2014, https://www.youtube.com/watch?v=5VrsFEiTpsQ.

Part VI

Examining
the LDS Concept
of Revelation

16 | Lamanites, the Seed of Cain, and Plural Marriage

I would not want you to believe that we bear any animosity toward the Negro. "Darkies" are wonderful people, and they have their place in our church.

President Joseph Fielding Smith [1]

MORMONESE:

plural marriage: Also called polygamy or polygny, one man who is married to two (or more) women simultaneously.
polyandry: One woman who is married to two (or more) men simultaneously.

Since LDS leaders claim that their church has a "latter-day" authority once possessed by the Christian church of the New Testament apostles, Mormons often like to refer to the authenticity of their scriptures and leadership. These leaders are said to have been picked by God to guide His people in these days. Are these men receiving true revelations from God?

The Lamanites

The Book of Mormon opens with the story of a Jewish man by the name of Lehi who was warned by God to leave Jerusalem just prior to its capture by the Babylonians in 587 BC. Lehi had a wife, Sariah, and four sons named Laman, Lemuel, Nephi, and Sam. They, along with some others, traveled across the ocean to the Western Hemisphere. A great portion of the Book of Mormon narrative revolves around the story of Laman and Nephi and their respective followers and descendants, the Lamanites and Nephites. Apparently Laman was always a problem child; once they arrived in America, both Laman and Lemuel proved to be quite wicked. At one point they even plotted to kill their father and brother Nephi. God punished them for their wickedness, and in order to identify them and their followers, they were given a "skin of blackness." Second Nephi 5:21–23 says:

> And he [God] had caused the cursing to come upon them, yea, even a sore cursing, because of their iniquity. For behold, they had hardened their hearts against him, that they had become like unto a flint; wherefore, as they were white, and exceedingly fair and delightsome, that they might not be enticing unto my people the Lord God did cause a skin of blackness to come upon them. And thus saith the Lord God: I will cause that they shall be loathsome unto thy people, save they shall repent of their iniquities. And cursed shall be the seed of him that mixeth with their seed; for they shall be cursed even with the same cursing. And the Lord spake it, and it was done.

Throughout much of the Book of Mormon, the dark-skinned Lamanites plagued the light-skinned Nephites. Eventually the Lamanites succeeded in annihilating their light-skinned counterparts at the battle of Hill Cumorah. According to LDS belief, American Indians are descendants of these Lamanite people and are therefore Semitic in heritage. Despite the curse placed on them, the Book of Mormon did predict that it could, and would, be lifted. Prior to 1981, 2 Nephi 30:6 explains how "their scales of darkness shall begin to fall from their eyes; and many generations shall not pass away among them, save they shall be a white and a delightsome people." In 1981 the LDS Church made some textual revisions to the Book of Mormon and in doing so changed the word *white* in 2 Nephi 30:6 (page 117 in the original 1830 edition) to the word *pure*.

Some have insisted that the word *pure* is the correct rendering, which is used in the 1840 edition of the Book of Mormon. Those who argue this point insist that skin color was not the issue at all. Rather, the passage was speaking more of a spiritual purity. While it is true that the 1840 edition did use the word *pure,* for some reason later editions of the Book of Mormon went back to using the word *white*. Insisting that the word *pure* is the correct rendering does not explain why so many LDS leaders ignored the 1840 correction.[2]

Perhaps this is explained by the fact that 3 Nephi 2:15 in the Book of Mormon also states that the Lamanites' skin color would change after conversion, saying, "And their [the Lamanites] curse was taken from them, and their skin became white like unto the Nephites." A number of Latter-day Saints have verified that the context refers to skin color. For instance, Joseph Smith was given a revelation foretelling of a day when intermarriage with the Lamanites would produce a white and delightsome posterity. To say Smith corrected the word *white* in 1840 is odd, since he himself used the expressions "white" and "delightsome" in 1831. Mormon writer George Smith wrote:

> This unpublished 17 July 1831 revelation was described three decades later in an 1861 letter from W. W. Phelps to Brigham Young quoting Joseph Smith: "It is my will, that in time, ye should take unto you wives of the Lamanites and Nephites, that their posterity, may become white, delightsome and just." In the 8 December 1831 Ohio Star, Ezra Booth wrote of a revelation directing Mormon elders to marry with the natives.[3]

Brigham Young saw the Lamanites' skin color as a divine punishment but looked to a day when they would become "white," not pure. Citing 2 Nephi 30:6 in an 1859 address, he stated:

> You may inquire of the intelligent of the world whether they can tell why the aborigines of this country are dark, loathsome, ignorant, and sunken into the depths of degradation; and they cannot tell. I can tell you in a few words: They are the seed of Joseph and belong to the household of God; and he will afflict them in this world, and save every one of them hereafter, even though they previously go into hell. When the Lord has a people, he makes covenants with them and gives unto them promises: then, if they transgress his law, change his ordinances, and break the covenants he has made with them, he will put a mark upon them, as in the case of the Lamanites and other portions of the house of Israel; but by-and-by they will become a white and delightsome people.[4]

President Spencer W. Kimball utilized the language of 2 Nephi 30:6 at the October 1960 LDS general conference when he stated how the Indians "are fast becoming a white and delightsome people." He said:

> The day of the Lamanites is nigh. For years they have been growing delight-some, and they are now becoming white and delightsome, as they were

promised. In this picture of the twenty Lamanite missionaries, fifteen of the twenty were as light as Anglos; five were darker but equally delightsome. The children in the home placement program in Utah are often lighter than their brothers and sisters in the hogans on the reservation. At one meeting a father and mother and their sixteen-year-old daughter were present, the little member girl—sixteen—sitting between the dark father and mother, and it was evident she was several shades lighter than her parents—on the same reservation, in the same hogan, subject to the same sun and wind and weather. There was the doctor in a Utah city who for two years had had an Indian boy in his home who stated that he was some shades lighter than the younger brother just coming into the program from the reservation. These young members of the Church are changing to whiteness and to delightsomeness. One white elder jokingly said that he and his companion were donating blood regularly to the hospital in the hope that the process might be accelerated.[5]

Mormon writer George Edward Clark gave a similar account in his 1952 book *Why I Believe:*

The writer has been privileged to sit at table with several members of the Catawba tribe of Indians, whose reservation is near the north border of South Carolina. That tribe, or most of its people, are members of the Church of Jesus Christ of Latter-day Saints (Mormon). Those Indians, at least as many as I have observed, were *white and delightsome;* as white and fair as any group of citizens of our country. I know of no prophecy, ancient or modern, that has had a more literal fulfillment.[6]

The 1978 "Revelation" and the Seed of Cain

For much of the LDS Church's history, those of African heritage were banned from holding any priesthood authority. Prior to 1978 when the ban was removed, many LDS leaders publically explained why the prohibition was necessary. On February 29, 2012, the church posted the following on its official website:

For a time in the Church there was a restriction on the priesthood for male members of African descent. It is not known precisely why, how, or when this restriction began in the Church but what is clear is that it ended decades ago. Some have attempted to explain the reason for this restriction but

268

these attempts should be viewed as speculation and opinion, not doctrine. The Church is not bound by speculation or opinions given with limited understanding.[7]

To say that explanations regarding the ban are either based in "speculation and opinion, not doctrine," is misleading. To understand the ban at all, one needs to take into account the LDS doctrine of preexistence (first estate). According to LDS teaching, behavior in the preexistence determines where people are born and their status in mortality (second estate). According to President George Albert Smith,

> We believe that we are here because we kept our first estate and earned the privilege of coming to earth. We believe that our very existence is a reward for our faithfulness before we came here, and that we are enjoying the fruits of our efforts in the spirit world.[8]

Prior to 1978, LDS leaders connected race with performance in the preexistence. President Joseph Fielding Smith taught:

> *There is a reason why one man is born black* and with other disadvantages, while *another is born white* with great advantages. The reason is that we once had an estate before we came here, and were obedient, more or less, to the laws that were given us there. *Those who were faithful in all things there received greater blessings here, and those who were not faithful received less.*[9]

Before the foundation of the world, "a council of the Gods" was called to decide who was to become the savior of humanity.[10] Lucifer and the preincarnate Jesus (Jehovah) presented plans for the salvation of those who would inhabit earth. When Lucifer's plan was rejected, he rebelled and convinced one-third of God's spirit children to join him. Joseph Fielding Smith explained:

> When the plan of redemption was presented and Jesus was chosen to be the Redeemer of the world, some rebelled. They were not willing to accept him as "the Lamb slain from the foundation of the world." . . . In this great rebellion in heaven, Lucifer, or Satan, a son of the morning, and one-third of the hosts thereof were cast out into the earth because Lucifer sought to destroy the free agency of man and the one-third of the spirits sided with him. . . . There were no neutrals in the war in heaven. *All took sides either with Christ or with Satan.* Every man had his agency there, and men receive

269

rewards here based upon their actions there, just as they will receive rewards hereafter for deeds done in the body. The Negro, evidently, is receiving the reward he merits.[11]

The less valiant spirits who did not perform adequately in the pre-existence would be known by their black skin. In a 1939 general conference talk, Apostle George F. Richards taught:

The Negro is an unfortunate man. He has been given a black skin. But that is as nothing compared with that greater handicap that he is not permitted to receive the Priesthood and the ordinances of the temple, necessary to prepare men and women to enter into and enjoy a fulness of glory in the celestial kingdom.[12]

President John Taylor felt the existence of the black race served to be the devil's representative:

And after the flood we are told that the curse that had been pronounced upon Cain was continued through Ham's wife, as he had married a wife of that seed. And why did it pass through the flood? Because it was necessary that the devil should have a representative upon the earth as well as God.[13]

He later added:

Why is it, in fact, that we should have a devil? Why did the Lord not kill him long ago? Because he could not do without him. He needed the devil and a great many of those who do his bidding to keep men straight, that we may learn to place our dependence upon God, and trust in Him, and to observe his laws and keep his commandments. When he destroyed the inhabitants of the antediluvian world, he suffered a descendant of Cain to come through the flood in order that he might be properly represented upon the earth.[14]

On August 17, 1951, the LDS First Presidency issued a statement regarding the "Negro Question," saying "the conduct of spirits in the premortal existence has some determining effect upon the conditions and circumstances under which these spirits take on mortality." Because they apparently were not as valiant, those preexistent spirits were "willing to come to earth and take on bodies no matter what the handicap may be as to the kind of bodies they are to secure." The handicap was "failure of the right to enjoy in mortality the blessings of the priesthood." John Lund, who at the time was the assistant LDS Church historian, claimed this was a result of a lack of preparation in the preexistence:

> It is vitally important to re-emphasize at this point that Cain's descendants are not being denied the Priesthood because of the sins of Cain. The fact that they are required to wait this great length of time in order to receive the Priesthood is not because of Cain's slaying of Abel, but because of their own individual preparation and worthiness in the pre-existence.[15]

Since it is taught that a loss of memory about the preexistence accompanies mortality, it would appear that those with black skin were being punished for something they could not remember doing. Saying that his God knew what he was doing when he sent some preexistent spirits to black homes and others to white homes, John J. Stewart admitted that he believed the white race is born with important spiritual advantages:

> The circumstances of our birth in this world are dependent upon our performance in the spirit world, just as the circumstances of our existence in the next world will depend upon what use we make of the blessings and opportunities we enjoy in this world. According to LDS doctrine, Dr. George Washington Carver—who, incidentally, was a mulatto rather than a Negro—will be far ahead of many of us born under more favorable circumstances in this life, for he made the most of his opportunities, while many of us are forfeiting our birthright. We were ahead of him in the first lap of the race, but he has gone far ahead of many of us in the second. . . . There were those in the spirit world whose performance caused them to forfeit the right to bear the Priesthood of God and enjoy its attendant blessings in this world.[16]

Because of these priesthood restrictions, many outside of the LDS Church have assumed blacks were not welcomed as members. This is not true. However, their spiritual status was looked on as second-rate:

> Negroes in this life are denied the priesthood; under no circumstances can they hold this delegation of authority from the Almighty. (Abra. 1:20–27.) The gospel message of salvation is not carried affirmatively to them. . . . The Negroes are not equal with other races where the receipt of certain spiritual blessings are concerned, particularly the priesthood and the temple blessings that flow therefrom, but this inequality is not of man's origin. It is the Lord's doing, is based on his eternal laws of justice, and grows out of the lack of spiritual valiance of those concerned in their first estate.[17]

271

In a speech given at BYU in 1954, Apostle Mark E. Petersen taught that those with black skin could become "servants" in the celestial kingdom: "If that Negro is faithful all his days, he can and will enter the celestial kingdom. He will go there as a servant, but he will get a celestial resurrection."[18] Petersen believed in complete segregation, although he claimed to have no animosity toward blacks:

> Now we are generous with the Negro. We are willing that the Negro have the highest kind of education. I would be willing to let every Negro drive a Cadillac if they could afford it. I would be willing that they have all the advantages they can get out of life in the world. But let them enjoy these things among themselves. I think the Lord segregated the Negro and who is man to change that segregation?[19]

What would prevent someone from achieving the priesthood? According to Petersen, even one drop of proverbial "Negro blood" would disqualify a person.

> If I were to marry a Negro woman and have children by her, my children would all be cursed as to the priesthood. Do I want my children cursed as to the priesthood? If there is one drop of Negro blood in my children, as I have read to you, they receive the curse. There isn't any argument, therefore, as to inter-marriage with the Negro, is there? There are 50 million Negroes in the United States. If they were to achieve complete absorption with the white race, think what that would do. With 50 million Negroes inter-married with us, where would the priesthood be? Who could hold it, in all America? Think what that would do to the work of the church![20]

John Lund affirmed that "the mark of a black skin deals specifically with the problems of intermarriage. The Lord did not want the seed of Cain to intermingle with the rest of Adam's children."[21] To even have relations with a black woman would warrant death, according to Brigham Young: "Shall I tell you the law of God in regard to the African race? If the white man who belongs to the chosen seed mixes his blood with the seed of Cain, the penalty, under the law of God, is death on the spot. This will always be so."[22]

On December 3, 1854, Brigham Young insisted that blacks would not be able to gain the priesthood until after the resurrection:

When all the other children of Adam have had the privilege of receiving the Priesthood, and of coming into the kingdom of God, and of being redeemed from the four quarters of the earth, and have received their resurrection from the dead, then it will be time enough to remove the curse from Cain and his posterity.[23]

Who Originated the Priesthood Ban?

In December 2013 the LDS Church posted a Gospel Topics essay on its website titled "Race and the Priesthood" where Joseph Smith's involvement in this teaching was exonerated; instead, blame for the introduction of this teaching was laid at the feet of Brigham Young. The article says:

> In 1852, President Brigham Young publicly announced that men of black African descent could no longer be ordained to the priesthood, though thereafter blacks continued to join the Church through baptism and receiving the gift of the Holy Ghost. Following the death of Brigham Young, subsequent Church presidents restricted blacks from receiving the temple endowment or being married in the temple. Over time, Church leaders and members advanced many theories to explain the priesthood and temple restrictions. None of these explanations is accepted today as the official doctrine of the Church.[24]

While the church wants to blame Young for originating the teaching, Seventy Milton R. Hunter denied this idea sixty-five years earlier, saying it could be traced back to Mormonism's founder:

> Brigham Young did not originate the doctrine that Negroes could not hold the Priesthood in this life but some day some of them may be granted that privilege, but he was taught it by the Prophet Joseph. The minutes of a meeting of the general authorities of the Church which was held on August 22, 1895, read as follows: "President George Q. Cannon remarked that the Prophet taught this doctrine: That the seed of Cain could not receive the Priesthood nor act in any of the offices of the Priesthood until the seed of Abel should come forward and take precedence over Cain's offspring."[25]

Joseph Fielding Smith also pointed to the minutes of this meeting and, like Hunter, called it a doctrine.[26] Regardless of how the *doctrine* originated, LDS leaders tenaciously held to this position, even during the Civil

Rights movement of the 1960s, claiming it was to continue "while time endures."[27] When a reporter asked Prophet David O. McKay in 1964 if blacks would receive the priesthood, he was told, "Not in my lifetime, young man, nor yours."[28] In 1967 Lund placed this teaching in the realm of "doctrine" and said it would always remain, explaining that "those who believe that the Church 'gave in' on the polygamy issue and subsequently should give in on the Negro question are not only misinformed about Church History, but are apparently unaware of Church doctrine." He added, "Therefore, those who hope that pressure will bring about a revelation need to take a closer look at Mormon history and the order of heaven."[29] The First Presidency made a statement on December 15, 1969, saying in part, "Our living prophet, President David O. McKay, has said, 'The seeming discrimination by the Church toward the Negro is not something which originated with man; but goes back into the beginning with God. . . . Revelation assures us that this plan antedates man's mortal existence, extending back to man's pre-existent state.'"

In light of the previous teachings, no doubt many Mormons were surprised to learn that President Kimball supposedly received a revelation that would officially take away the restrictions barring those of black heritage from priesthood blessings. On June 8, 1978 a statement given by the LDS church included the following words:

> Aware of the promises made by the prophets and presidents of the Church who have preceded us that at some time, in God's eternal plan, all of our brethren who are worthy may receive the priesthood. . . . He has heard our prayers, and by revelation has confirmed that the long-promised day has come when every faithful, worthy man in the Church may receive the holy priesthood.[30]

To which "promises" is Kimball referring? Prior to 1978 it was generally understood that the promise of priesthood for the "seed of Cain" would only come to pass *after* the resurrection and not before. The October 1978 opening of a temple in São Paulo, Brazil, may have been a contributing factor. Brazil has been a hotbed for Mormon growth but it is also a country comprised of people of mixed descent. Because many Brazilians are descendants of former slaves, it would be impossible to tell who was "unqualified" to participate in the priesthood under the old standard. The church website explains:

Brazil in particular presented many challenges. Unlike the United States and South Africa where legal and de facto racism led to deeply segregated societies, Brazil prided itself on its open, integrated, and mixed racial heritage. In 1975, the Church announced that a temple would be built in São Paulo, Brazil. As the temple construction proceeded, Church authorities encountered faithful black and mixed-ancestry Mormons who had contributed financially and in other ways to the building of the São Paulo temple, a sanctuary they realized they would not be allowed to enter once it was completed. Their sacrifices, as well as the conversions of thousands of Nigerians and Ghanaians in the 1960s and early 1970s, moved Church leaders.[31]

Mormons often make an issue that the written standard works are to be the measuring rod for truth and that revelation cannot contradict them. President Harold B. Lee stated, "If it is not in the standard works, we may well assume that it is speculation, man's own personal opinion; and if it contradicts what is in the scriptures, it is not true."[32] Given the fact that Abraham 1:26 in the Pearl of Great Price was used as a proof text to ban blacks from the priesthood, the 1978 reversal appears to violate Lee's admonition.[33]

All of this information raises other questions. If the Mormon God has removed the curse that was once on the black race, why has he not also removed the physical mark? If the sole purpose of the black skin was merely to identify those who should not receive priesthood blessings, and that no longer applies, why are people still being born with this mark?

Today the official position of the Mormon Church allows all worthy male members, regardless of race, to hold the position of priest. Meanwhile, the church wants to cut ties to its racist past; in doing so, the leadership must rewrite their church's history by making it appear that this teaching was never considered a doctrine. As the church website states, "Today, the Church disavows the *theories* advanced in the past that black skin is a sign of divine disfavor or curse, or that it reflects actions in a premortal life; that mixed-race marriages are a sin; or that blacks or people of any other race or ethnicity are inferior in any way to anyone else."[34]

The claim that Young could create a doctrine based on racist tendencies of his culture only opens up a slippery slope that could swallow up any other "revelation" given by other LDS leaders. Quoting LDS historian Richard L. Bushman, *The Salt Lake Tribune* reported:

By depicting the exclusion as fitting with the common practices of the day, says Bushman, who wrote "Rough Stone Rolling," a critically acclaimed biography of Smith, "it drains the ban of revelatory significance, makes it something that just grew up and, in time, had to be eliminated." But accepting that, Bushman says, "requires a deep reorientation of Mormon thinking." Mormons believe that their leaders are in regular communication with God, so if you say Young could make a serious error, he says, "it brings into question all of the prophet's inspiration."[35]

While Mormon apologists certainly acknowledge the racist comments made by their past leaders, they try to excuse them by pointing to offensive comments made by non-LDS religious leaders during the same time period. This would make the LDS leaders nothing more than products of their time who are quite capable of ignoring God's true will on this subject. If a leader like Young was capable of creating a racist doctrine that would be echoed by later LDS leaders for more than a century, then common sense would dictate that the other unique doctrines espoused by the church quite possibly are creations of men rather than God.[36]

Plural Marriage: One Man, Many Wives

Another controversial issue of Mormonism involves the teaching of plural marriage, also known as polygamy, which is one man marrying more than one woman simultaneously. According to Mormon historian Todd Compton, the practice can be traced directly to Joseph Smith:

> Thus the doctrine of plural marriage was of central importance to Smith for religious, doctrinal, ecclesiastical, and emotional reasons. William Clayton, his scribe and companion in Nauvoo, wrote that the Mormon prophet spoke of little else in private in the last year of his life. As he developed the principle of sealing ordinances that connected families for eternity, this doctrine was inextricably bound up with plural marriage. Later nineteenth century Mormons taught that a monogamist could not gain complete salvation, a belief that was clearly based on Smith's teachings.[37]

One of the main arguments used to support this practice was the example of Old Testament patriarchs and kings. Compton writes, "The example of Abraham and the Abrahamic promise are prominently mentioned in the LDS Church's Doctrine and Covenants (D&C 132), the officially canonized revelation on polygamy and exaltation."[38] However, polygamy according to the Bible was never commanded and instead merely tolerated by God. The mere fact that God created Eve alone for the companionship of Adam points to the monogamous relationship between a man and a woman as the ideal. This is confirmed by 1 Corinthians 7:2, in which the apostle Paul stated that "every man have his own *wife*," not *wives*. According to Titus 1:6 and 1 Timothy 3:2, monogamy was a qualification for church office, and in Matthew 19:5 even Jesus affirmed monogamy when He stated "and they twain [two] shall be one flesh."

Although many members of the LDS Church knew polygamy was being practiced,[39] the doctrine was not officially announced until 1852.[40] For years Mormon leaders taught that the practice of polygamy was necessary for a man to receive exaltation, yet the majority of the membership remained monogamous.[41] According to *The Encyclopedia of Mormonism*:

> Although polygamy had been practiced privately prior to the exodus, Church leaders delayed public acknowledgment of its practice until 1852. In August of that year, at a special conference of the Church at Salt Lake City, Elder Orson Pratt, an apostle, officially announced plural marriage as a doctrine and practice of the Church. A lengthy revelation on marriage for eternity and on the plurality of wives, dictated by Joseph Smith on July 12, 1843, was published following this announcement (D&C 132).[42]

No doubt this practice came as a surprise to many of the converts who came to Utah from Europe. As far as they knew, polygamy was merely a vicious rumor propounded by enemies of the church. Why should they have thought otherwise? After all, the idea that Mormons were practicing polygamy was denied outright in the European edition of the Doctrine and Covenants. For example, D&C section CIX:4, printed in Liverpool, England, in 1866, read:

> Inasmuch as this Church of Christ has been reproached with the crime of fornication and polygamy: we declare that we believe that one man should have one wife: and one woman but one husband, except in case of death, when either is at liberty to marry again.[43]

In Utah the message was quite different. The same year that the above-mentioned Liverpool edition came out, Brigham Young proclaimed, "The only men who become Gods, even the Sons of God, are those who enter into polygamy."[44]

When this practice came under severe criticism, it was evident church leaders would not easily abandon this teaching. The defense of this doctrine by LDS leaders can be easily documented, including the following examples:

You might as well deny "Mormonism," and turn away from it, as to oppose the plurality of wives.[45]

Where did this commandment come from in relation to polygamy? It also came from God. . . . When this commandment was given, it was so far religious, and so far binding upon the Elders of this Church, that it was told them if they were not prepared to enter into it, and to stem the torrent of opposition that would come in consequence of it, the keys of the kingdom would be taken from them. When I see any of our people, men or women, opposing a principle of this kind, I have years ago set them down as on the high road to apostasy, and I do today; I consider them apostates, and not interested in this Church and kingdom.[46]

If we were to do away with polygamy, it would only be one feather in the bird, one ordinance in the Church and kingdom. Do away with that, then we must do away with prophets and Apostles, with revelation and the gifts and graces of the Gospel, and finally give up our religion altogether and turn sectarians and do as the world does, then all would be right. We just can't do that, for God has commanded us to build up His kingdom and to bear our testimony to the nations of the earth, and we are going to do it, come life or come death. He has told us to do thus, and we shall obey Him in days to come as we have in days past.[47]

This doctrine of eternal union of husband and wife, and of plural marriage, is one of the most important doctrines ever revealed to man in any age of the world. Without it man would come to a full stop; without it we never could be exalted to associate with and become gods.[48]

If plurality of marriage is not true or in other words, if a man has no divine right to marry two wives or more in this world, then marriage for eternity is not true, and your faith is all vain, and all the sealing ordinances and powers, pertaining to marriages for eternity are vain, worthless, good for nothing; for as sure as one is true the other also must be true.[49]

Despite the rhetoric, the federal government began its efforts to force the abandonment of polygamy on July 1, 1862. The Anti-Bigamy Act defined the illegality of polygamy, but it was not really enforced for another twenty years. In 1882 the government enacted what was known as the Edmunds Law. This provision

> made the "cohabiting" with more than one woman a crime, punishable by a fine not to exceed three hundred dollars, and by imprisonment not to exceed six months. This law also rendered persons who were living in polygamy, or who believed in its rightfulness, incompetent to act as grand or petit jurors; and also disqualified all polygamists for voting or holding office.[50]

Five years later the Edmunds-Tucker Act became law. Its effects on the LDS Church proved to be most devastating. In 1890 President Wilford Woodruff signed what has come to be known as the Manifesto, or Declaration 1.[51] This document was basically a promise to the United States stating that the LDS Church would submit to the laws of the land and desist from solemnizing plural marriages while denying any accusations that the church was encouraging or performing any such marriages.

The signing of the Manifesto was certainly a major blow to the "prophetic insight" of Mormonism's leaders. Perhaps Woodruff forgot that it was he himself who said his church would continue to practice polygamy "come life or come death." In light of the many statements supporting polygamy made by nineteenth century Mormon leaders, it is surprising that Woodruff claimed he acted according to the will of God. In saying this, he would have to admit that either God has a very short memory or that the previous declarations from LDS leaders were outside of God's will.

It would also appear that the signing of the Manifesto was merely a ploy to get the federal government to relax its sanctions against the LDS Church and to allow Utah to become a state in 1896. History shows that the promise to abolish plural marriage was really disingenuous. Except for Lorenzo Snow, who lived with his youngest wife, "not a single apostle or member of the First Presidency discontinued connubial relationships with plural wives."[52]

For instance, Heber J. Grant, who later became the LDS Church's seventh president, was arrested, tried, and convicted for unlawful cohabitation in 1899 and fined $100. He fathered 76 children by 27 plural wives during the years 1890–1905. On November 25, 1906, *The Salt Lake Tribune* reported that Joseph F. Smith "pleaded guilty before Judge M. L. Ritchie in the

District Court Friday to the charge of cohabitating with four women in addition to his lawful wife." He was fined $300.[53]

In the Gospel Topics essay "Plural Marriage and Families in Early Utah," LDS leaders officially acknowledged that plural marriages continued to be performed through 1904. According to the article,

> After the Manifesto, monogamy was advocated in the Church both over the pulpit and through the press. On an exceptional basis, some new plural marriages were performed between 1890 and 1904, especially in Mexico and Canada, outside the jurisdiction of U.S. law; a small number of plural marriages were performed within the United States during those years.[54]

In today's world of Mormonism, Joseph Smith, Brigham Young, Orson Pratt, John Taylor, and many other well-known heroes of the LDS faith would be promptly excommunicated for their participation in practicing their view of celestial marriage. Apostle Bruce R. McConkie declared, "All who pretend or assume to engage in plural marriage in this day, when the one holding the keys has withdrawn the power by which they are performed, are guilty of gross wickedness."[55] While McConkie denounced the practice of polygamy in this life, he did say, "Obviously the holy practice will commence again after the Second Coming of the Son of Man and the ushering in of the millennium."[56]

Many Mormons insist that the reason plural marriage is no longer practiced is because it violates the law. Such an argument begs the following questions: Does God really care what American law says? And if it were truly God's will, wouldn't He expect plural marriages among His people, despite the law?

Today, there are dozens of polygamous groups not affiliated with the Mormon Church that claim to be the true followers of Joseph Smith and the other early leaders. Besides retaining a ban on those with black skin from holding the priesthood, these "fundamentalists" continue to practice plural marriage. Estimates range from thirty thousand to as many as one hundred thousand in the United States, though the practice is so secretive nobody will ever know for sure. Television shows such as *Big Love*, *Sister Wives*, *Polygamy USA*, and *My Five Wives* have depicted polygamy as a possible alternative lifestyle while glamorizing the practice in a modern-day setting.

President Spencer W. Kimball warned his people to keep their distance from those who belong to such "cults." In a 1974 general conference address, he said:

We warn you against the so-called polygamy cults which would lead you astray. Remember the Lord brought an end to this program many decades ago through a prophet who proclaimed the revelation to the world. People are abroad who will deceive you and bring you much sorrow and remorse. Have nothing to do with those who would lead you astray. It is wrong and sinful to ignore the Lord when he speaks. He has spoken—strongly and conclusively.[57]

Warren Jeffs, who was married to approximately eighty wives, is probably best known for leading a modern polygamist church; he was sentenced to life in prison in 2011 for marrying two teenaged girls. However, he is just one of many American fundamentalist leaders—some family names include the Allreds, Kingstons, and LeBarons—who claim to follow early Mormon teachings. Meanwhile, thousands of women and their young children—especially in the United States, Canada, and Mexico—are entrapped in the cycle of poverty and abuse; many of them believe that nobody from the outside world cares for them. Young teenaged boys—labeled "Lost Boys" by some—also suffer, as they are often kicked out of polygamist groups because the older men consider them as competition for the younger girls. This slavery without physical chains is a direct result of the teaching delivered by the early leaders of Mormonism.[58]

Discussion Questions

1. Regarding the priesthood ban for those of African heritage, the Mormon website lds.org claims, "It is not known precisely why, how or when this restriction began in the Church, but it has ended." What are your thoughts on this assessment?

2. When the issue of plural marriage is brought up, many like to point to the Old Testament patriarchs and kings who had married multiple wives. It is argued that if these people practiced plural marriage, it should not be considered sinful or immoral. How would you respond to this argumentation?

3. Some sects not officially aligned with the Salt Lake City–based Mormon Church believe this organization entered apostasy by eliminating important teachings such as polygamy and the ban on blacks holding the priesthood. Given the statements of LDS leaders prior to 1890

and 1978, who do you think has a stronger case as true followers of Joseph Smith and Brigham Young?

Final Thought

Before the Manifesto was given in 1890, it would have been impossible to find any Latter-day Saints who held that polygamy and banning blacks from the priesthood would ever be changed by God. Their leaders drilled these teachings into the membership, saying that they would always be. Anyone who would have publically held to the version of Mormonism depicted by the twenty-first century LDS Church would have been excommunicated. In the same way, if these doctrines were not set in stone and later were changed due to political correctness, isn't it possible that other LDS doctrines could also fall? Some possibilities include the ordination of women to the LDS priesthood, homosexual marriage unions in Mormon temples, or the encouragement of praying to "Heavenly Mother." We can only wonder what other doctrinal changes will someday be made due to a shift in the cultural or political winds.

Notes

1. *Look* magazine, October 22, 1963, 79.
2. Some Mormons claim that the words *white* and *pure* in the Book of Mormon are interchangeable. However, Alma 32:42; Mormon 9:6; and Moroni 7:47 show this is not true. The word *white* was used in the printer's manuscript, so this was not a typographical error as some LDS apologists want people to believe. For further details, see the *Salt Lake Messenger*, no. 46 (October 1981), available here: www.utlm.org/newsletters/no46.htm.
3. George Smith, *Sunstone* (November 1993): 52n5. While we can understand the possibility of Mormon men taking wives from among the Lamanites, why did Smith also include Nephites, since they were said to have been completely wiped out? LDS Apostle James Talmage notes that Moroni was the "last Nephite representative," Talmage, *Articles of Faith*, 260.
4. Brigham Young, *Journal of Discourses*, ed. Watt, 7:336.
5. Spencer W. Kimball, *Improvement Era* (December 1960): 922–23.
6. George Edward Clark, *Why I Believe* (Salt Lake City: Publisher's Press, 1989), 129; italics in original.
7. "Church Statement Regarding 'Washington Post' Article on Race and the Church," www.mormonnewsroom.org/article/racial-remarks-in-washington-post-article, accessed May 29, 2014. According to "The Church and New Media: Clarity, Context and an Official Voice Newsroom LDS.org," June 29, 2007, Newsroom, http://newsroom.lds.org/article/the-church-and-new-media:-clarity,-context-and-an-official-voice-newsroom-lds.org-full-story,

"information on official Church Web sites is reliable and consistent with the doctrines and policies of the Church. All materials on Newsroom and other Church Web sites are carefully reviewed and approved before they are posted. . . . In a complementary way, Newsroom, LDS.org and other Church Web sites provide an official voice from the Church."

8. *Teachings of Presidents of the Church: George Albert Smith*, 70–71. For more on premortality, see chapter 4.

9. Joseph Fielding Smith, *Doctrines of Salvation*, 1:61; italics in original.

10. Joseph Fielding Smith, ed., *Teachings of the Prophet Joseph Smith*, 349.

11. Joseph Fielding Smith, *Doctrines of Salvation*, 1:64–66; italics in original.

12. George F. Richards, *Conference Report* (April 1939): 58.

13. John Taylor, *Journal of Discourses*, ed. Watt, 22:304.

14. Ibid., 23:336.

15. John Lewis Lund, *The Church and the Negro: A Discussion of Mormons, Negroes and the Priesthood* (Paramount Publishers, 1967), 49.

16. John J. Stewart, *Mormonism and the Negro* (Orem, UT: Bookmark, 1960), 33, 38.

17. McConkie, *Mormon Doctrine*, 527–28.

18. Mark E. Petersen, "Race Problems—As They Affect the Church," Convention of Teachers of Religion on the College Level, Brigham Young University, Provo, Utah, August 27, 1954.

19. Ibid.

20. Ibid.

21. Lund, *The Church and the Negro*, 15.

22. Brigham Young, *Journal of Discourses*, ed. Watt, 10:110.

23. Ibid., 2:143. Joseph Fielding Smith also quoted Young's statement in *The Way to Perfection* (Salt Lake City: Deseret Book Co., 1975), 106.

24. "Race and the Priesthood," The Church of Jesus Christ of Latter-Day Saints, accessed May 29, 2014, www.lds.org/topics/race-and-the-priesthood.

25. Milton R. Hunter, *Pearl of Great Price Commentary* (Salt Lake City: Stephens and Wallis, 1948), 142.

26. Joseph Fielding Smith, *The Way to Perfection*, 110.

27. Ibid., 101.

28. Lund, *The Church and the Negro*, 45.

29. Ibid., 47, 104–5.

30. This portion is included in what is known as Declaration 2 found at the end of the *Doctrine and Covenants*.

31. "Race and the Priesthood," The Church of Jesus Christ of Latter-Day Saints, accessed December 9, 2013, www.lds.org/topics/race-and-the-priesthood.

32. *Improvement Era* (January 1969): 13.

33. According to Lund, President David O. McKay wrote a letter on November 3, 1947, in which he said, "I know of no scriptural basis for denying the Priesthood to Negroes other than one verse in the Book of Abraham (1:26)." Lund, *The Church and the Negro*, 91.

34. "Race and the Priesthood," The Church of Jesus Christ of Latter-Day Saints, accessed May 29, 2014, www.lds.org/topics/race-and-the-priesthood; italics added.

35. "Mormon Church Traces Black Priesthood Ban to Brigham Young," *Salt Lake Tribune*, December 10, 2013, A5.

36. This issue will be discussed further in chapter 18.

37. Compton, *In Sacred Loneliness*, 10. We will deal more with Smith's polygamous and polyandrous ways in the next chapter.

38. Ibid., 10.

39. This was especially true among the leaders. Joseph Smith himself claimed in 1844 that he had only one wife (*History of the Church*, 6:411), but the *Historical Record*, 5:114 published in 1886 shows that he had at least twenty-seven wives at the time he said this!

40. *Comprehensive History of the Church*, 4:57–58. This is also supported by President Joseph F. Smith, *Journal of Discourses*, ed. Watt, 20:29. Section 132 did not become a part of the *Doctrine and Covenants* until 1876.

41. Richard S. Van Wagoner, *Mormon Polygamy: A History* (Salt Lake City: Signature Books, 1989), 91.

42. Ludlow, ed., *Encyclopedia of Mormonism*, s.v. "History of the Church," 2:617.

43. Bear in mind that this denial was a part of the *Doctrine and Covenants* until 1876—twenty-four years after polygamy became an official LDS doctrine.

44. Brigham Young, *Journal of Discourses*, ed. Watt, 11:269. Young also said, "Now if any of you will deny the plurality of wives and continue to do so, I promise that you will be damned," *Deseret News*, November 14, 1885.

45. Heber C. Kimball, *Journal of Discourses*, ed. Watt, 5:203.

46. John Taylor, *Journal of Discourses*, ed. Watt, 11:221.

47. Wilford Woodruff, *Journal of Discourses*, ed. Watt, 13:166.

48. Joseph F. Smith, *Journal of Discourses*, ed. Watt, 21:10.

49. Orson Pratt, *Journal of Discourses*, ed. Watt, 21:296.

50. B. H. Roberts, *Outlines of Ecclesiastical History*, (Salt Lake City: George Q. Cannon and Sons Co., 1893), 437.

51. The Manifesto can be found following section 138 in the *Doctrine and Covenants*. It would be incorrect to think polygamy is a dead issue within Mormonism. Section 132 of the Doctrine and Covenants, the portion of LDS scripture that established its validity, is still included in the LDS canon.

52. Van Wagoner, *Mormon Polygamy*, 155.

53. Ibid.

54. "Plural Marriage and Families in Early Utah," The Church of Jesus Christ of Latter-Day Saints, accessed May 29, 2014, https://www.lds.org/topics/plural-marriage-and-families-in-early-utah?lang=eng. It should be added that no justification for the authorization of these *exceptional* plural marriages that were performed after 1890 was ever given!

55. McConkie, *Mormon Doctrine*, 579.

56. Ibid., 578.

57. Kimball, *The Teachings of Spencer W. Kimball*, 447–48. This quote is provided on www.mormon.org/faq/practice-of-polygamy, accessed May 29, 2014. More about Joseph Smith's polygamous ways will be discussed in the next chapter. For additional information on the issue of polygamy/polyandry, see chapter 6, "Why do so many equate our church to splinter groups when we no longer practice polygamy?" in our book *Answering Mormons' Questions*.

58. To read more about the consequences of polygamy today, see www.polygamy.org. We highly recommend A Shield and Refuge Ministry, which is led by former polygamist Doris Hanson (www.shieldandrefuge.org), as well as the online video *Lifting the Veil of Polygamy* that is produced by Sourceflix, http://sourceflix.com/lifting-the-veil-of-polygamy.

17 | Joseph Smith

Many of the benefits and blessings that have come to me have come through that man who gave his life for the gospel of Jesus Christ. There have been some who have belittled him, but I would like to say that those who have done so will be forgotten and their remains will go back to mother earth, if they have not already gone, and the odor of their infamy will never die, while the glory and honor and majesty and courage and fidelity manifested by the Prophet Joseph Smith will attach to his name forever.

President George Albert Smith [1]

Joseph Smith was born on December 23, 1805, in Sharon, Vermont, the fifth of eleven children born to Joseph and Lucy Mack Smith. There is no doubt that the Mormon religion centers around this charismatic individual who claimed to have restored the Christian faith to the world after an apostate hiatus of many centuries. President Harold B. Lee said:

> We must accept the divine mission of the Prophet Joseph Smith as the instrumentality through which the restoration of the gospel and the organization of the Church of Jesus Christ was accomplished. Each member of the Church, to be prepared for the millennial reign, must receive a testimony, each for himself, of the divinity of the work established by Joseph Smith.[2]

Since 1998, every manual from the *Teachings of Presidents of the Church* series has dedicated at least one chapter to Joseph Smith.[3] In fact, more chapters in this series of manuals have been devoted to Smith than any other topic, including the celestial kingdom, the temple, or Jesus Christ! Consider some of the flattery given to Smith by the LDS presidents, as included in this series:

- Brigham Young: "I honor and revere the name of Joseph Smith. I delight to hear it; I love it. I love his doctrine."[4]
- Joseph F. Smith: "Where shall we go to find another man who has accomplished a one-thousandth part of the good that Joseph Smith accomplished?"[5]
- Heber J. Grant: "The whole foundation of this Church rests firmly upon the inspiration of the living God through Joseph Smith the Prophet."[6]
- George Albert Smith: "To my mind one of the strongest testimonies of the divinity of the life of our Savior is the testimony of Joseph Smith who laid down his life as a witness of the truth of the gospel of Jesus Christ."[7]

Mormonism cannot stand without acceptance of the church's founder. As President Gordon B. Hinckley put it,

An acquaintance said to me one day: "I admire your church very much. I think I could accept everything about it—except Joseph Smith." To which I responded: "That statement is a contradiction. If you accept the revelation, you must accept the revelator."[8]

A student manual explains Smith's contribution to humankind:

While Joseph Smith lived only thirty-eight and a half years, his accomplishments in the service of mankind are incalculable. In addition to translating the Book of Mormon, he received hundreds of revelations, many of which are published in the Doctrine and Covenants and the Pearl of Great Price. He unfolded eternal principles in a legacy of letters, sermons, poetry, and other inspired writings that fills volumes. He established the restored Church of Jesus Christ on the earth, founded a city, and superintended the building of two temples. He introduced vicarious ordinance work for the dead and restored temple ordinances by which worthy families could be sealed by the priesthood for eternity. He ran for the presidency of the United States, served as a judge, mayor of Nauvoo, and lieutenant general of the Nauvoo Legion.[9]

It is an honor for many Latter-day Saints to associate themselves with their church's founder. As Seventy Emeritus Cecil O. Samuelson put it, "How grateful we are to Joseph for his worthiness to witness what he did for us. How grateful we should be that we are allowed to stand by Joseph with our own actions and testimonies of the Father and the Son."[10]

Joseph Smith as Prophet

Joseph Smith wore many hats. However, he was also a walking contradiction, as illustrated by former Mormon historian D. Michael Quinn:

> Few Mormons today can grasp the polarizing charisma of their founding prophet. Some may feel uncomfortable when confronted with the full scope of Joseph Smith's activities as youthful mystic, treasure-seeker, visionary, a loving husband who deceived his wife regarding about forty of his polygamous marriages, a man for whom friendship and loyalty meant everything but who provoked disaffection by "testing" the loyalty of his devoted associates, an anti-Mason who became a Master Mason, church president who

The gravesites of Joseph Smith, his wife Emma, and his brother Hyrum are located in Nauvoo, Illinois, which is the city where the Mormon Church was based in the early 1840s.

physically assaulted both Mormons and non-Mormons for insulting him, a devoted father who loved to care for his own children and those of others, temperance leader and social drinker, Bible revisionist and esoteric philosopher, city planner, pacifist and commander-in-chief, student of Hebrew and Egyptology, bank president, jail escapee, healer, land speculator, mayor, judge and fugitive from justice, guarantor of religious freedom but limiter of freedom of speech and press, preacher and street-wrestler, polygamist and advocate of women's rights, husband of other men's wives, a declared bankrupt who was the trustee-in-trust of church finances, political horse-trader, U.S. presidential candidate, abolitionist, theocratic king, inciter to riot, and unwilling martyr.[11]

Latter-day Saints are taught that their founder was called by God to restore true Christianity, which was said to have been corrupted soon after the death of the biblical apostles. President Spencer W. Kimball said:

> Joseph knew, as no other soul living, these absolutes: He knew that God lives, that He is a [glorified] person with flesh and bones and personality, like us or we like Him, in His image. He knew that the long-heralded trinity of three Gods in one was a myth, a deception. He knew that the Father and the Son were two distinct beings with form, voices, and . . . personalities. He knew that the gospel was not on the earth, for by the Deities he had learned it, and the true Church was absent from the earth, for the God of heaven and earth had so informed him.[12]

Looking back into history, one can't help but be amazed at the trust Smith's followers had in him and their belief that he had the ability to change the historic Christian faith in a number of ways. Early LDS history is replete with accounts of faithful Mormons who left friends and loved ones to respond to the prophet's latest revelation. A classic example of this type of obedience can be traced to the early 1830s when hundreds of Latter-day Saints left for Missouri on the hope that God was going to establish Zion. Smith proclaimed that cities would be established in the area and prophesied that three temples would be built in the following areas: Independence, Far West, and Adam-ondi-Ahman. None of the predicted temples were ever built, and by 1838, the Mormons had been driven out of Missouri.

To this day the Mormons cite cases of persecution in Missouri as a fulfillment of Bible verses such as 2 Timothy 3:12. The problem with this assumption is that persecution is only one of many signs following true faith. If persecution was the only determinate of truth, the Mormons would have to recognize that those whom they claim are apostate must also be true, since Christians are persecuted on a daily basis throughout the world and even die because of their faith.[13]

Those Latter-day Saints who rely on those writing faith-promoting history fail to see that there are two sides to the persecution story. Many have been led to believe that the trouble early Mormons faced in Missouri was based solely on their religious convictions. Quinn denies this conclusion:

Fear of being overwhelmed politically, socially, culturally, economically by Mormon immigration was what fueled anti-Mormonism wherever the Latter-day Saints settled during Joseph Smith's lifetime. Religious belief, as non-Mormons understood it, had little to do with anti-Mormonism. On the other hand, by the mid–1830s Mormons embraced a religion that shaped their politics, economics, and society. Conflict was inevitable.[14]

Historian Stephen C. LeSueur explained,

Non-Mormon land speculators could not hope to compete with the Mormons, who were purchasing large tracts of land with Church funds, and the huge immigration of Mormons to the area also threatened to displace older towns as the political and commercial centers for their counties. The Missouri settlers saw their status and security threatened by the burgeoning Mormon population.[15]

Many Mormons believe that the early Saints were merely innocent victims of religious bigotry. Historians James B. Allen and Glen M. Leonard state,

The Saints themselves may not have been totally without blame in the matter. The feelings of the Missourians, even though misplaced, were undoubtedly intensified by the rhetoric of the gathering itself. They were quick to listen to the boasting of a few overzealous Saints who too-loudly declared a divine right to the land. As enthusiastic millennialists, they proclaimed that the time of the gentiles was short, and they were perhaps too quick to quote the revelation that said that "the Lord willeth that the disciples and the children of men should open their hearts, even to purchase this whole region of country, as soon as time will permit." Even though the Saints were

289

specifically and repeatedly commanded to be peaceful and never to shed blood, some seemed to unwisely threaten warfare if they could not fulfill the commandment peacefully.[16]

Continued disagreements and violence resulted in Smith's arrest in 1838. Shortly thereafter, his followers were forced to leave Missouri. They eventually settled in a swampland in western Illinois and founded the city of Nauvoo, which at its peak rivaled the city of Chicago in population. It should come as no surprise that among the many excuses Mormons have raised for the failure of Smith's Missouri predictions, few admit it was due to his lack of prophetical insight. When the state of Missouri failed to "redress the wrongs" against the Saints, Smith declared:

> I prophesy in the name of the Lord God of Israel, unless the United States redress the wrongs committed upon the Saints in the state of Missouri and punish the crimes committed by her officers that in a few years the government will be utterly overthrown and wasted, and there will not be so much as a potsherd left.[17]

Mormon leaders want to make it appear that their prophet is a victim who was unjustly persecuted:

> Throughout his life the Prophet Joseph Smith was falsely accused of many evils. Men appeared in courts and gave false testimony against the Prophet, and the courts accepted this testimony while refusing to hear testimony in the Prophet's favor. Officers of the court would invite the Church to produce the names of witnesses who could testify on the Prophet's behalf, and then would arrest them, drive them from the country, or threaten them to keep them from testifying.[18]

The Prophet and His Philandering Practices

Describing Smith's temperament and behavior, Richard S. Van Wagoner wrote:

> His backwoods savoir-faire sometimes impressed visitors whom he lavished with food, wine, and tall tales, but his frequent misuse of Latin, Hebrew, and German were plainly pedantic. His relish for competition in sports, matched by his ambition in commerce and politics, was not what people

expected from a divine. Nor could Smith resist the flourishes of military dress and parade, or dramatic staging of ritual and ceremony of all kinds. Embracing friends and lashing out verbally and physically at enemies, he was no Buddah [*sic*]. But perhaps the most scandalous manifestation of Smith's lust for manly achievement was his inclination toward extra-marital romantic liaisons, which he believed were licensed by the Old Testament and countenanced by God's modern revelation.[19]

Smith's polygamous practices are even documented in a church history manual:

His first recorded plural marriage in Nauvoo was to Louisa Beaman; it was performed by Bishop Joseph B. Noble on 5 April 1841. During the next three years Joseph took additional plural wives in accordance with the Lord's commands. As members of the Council of the Twelve Apostles returned from their missions to the British Isles in 1841, Joseph Smith taught them one by one the doctrine of plurality of wives, and each experienced some difficulty in understanding and accepting this doctrine. . . . After their initial hesitancy and frustration, Brigham Young and others of the Twelve received individual confirmations from the Holy Spirit and accepted the new doctrine of plural marriage. They knew that Joseph Smith was a prophet of God in all things. At first the practice was kept secret and was very limited. Rumors began to circulate about authorities of the Church having additional wives, which greatly distorted the truth and contributed to increased persecution from apostates and outsiders. Part of the difficulty, of course, was the natural aversion Americans held against "polygamy." This new system appeared to threaten the strongly entrenched tradition of monogamy and the solidarity of the family structure. Later, in Utah, the Saints openly practiced "the principle," but never without persecution.[20]

According to LDS Church historian Marlin K. Jensen, who served as a Seventy, Joseph Smith was both polygamous and polyandrous. In a Q&A session in Stockholm, Sweden, he explained, "Polygamy is when a man has multiple wives. Polyandry is when a man marries another man's wife. Joseph Smith did both."[21] Assistant LDS Church historian Richard E. Turley, Jr. agreed, adding, "Did Joseph Smith practice plural marriage? Yes. Many church members don't know it but the answer is yes. Did Joseph Smith practice polyandry? The answer is yes."

A Mormon who knows about Smith's polygamy may say this is common knowledge, but notice how Turley said "many church members don't know it." Our experience proves Turley's conclusion correct.[22] While most Mormons seem to be aware that Brigham Young was a practicing polygamist, many have no idea that Smith was one as well. Even if they do know this fact, they may not have heard that one-third of Smith's thirty-three plural wives were teenagers when they were married to Smith. According to Todd Compton,

> Eleven (33 percent) were 14 to 20 years old when they married him. Nine wives (27 percent) were twenty-one to thirty years old. Eight wives (24 percent) were in Smith's own peer group, ages thirty-one to forty. In the group aged forty to fifty, there is a substantial drop off: two wives, or 6 percent, and three (9 percent) in the group fifty-one to sixty. The teenage representation is the largest, though the twenty-year and thirty-year-groups are comparable, which contradicts the Mormon folk-wisdom that sees the beginnings of polygamy as an attempt to care for older, unattached women.[23]

Smith did not limit his secret marriages to single women, as one-third of his wives were already married to other men. Compton explains:

> A common misconception concerning Joseph Smith's polyandry is that he participated in only one or two such unusual unions. In fact, fully one-third of his plural wives, eleven of them, were married civilly to other men when he married them. If one superimposes a chronological perspective, one sees that of Smith's first twelve wives, nine were polyandrous. . . . none of these women divorced their "first husbands" while Smith was alive and all of them continued to live with their civil spouses while married to Smith.[24]

Some might argue that these relationships were strictly platonic. Compton disagrees:

> Because Reorganized Latter-Day Saints claimed that Joseph Smith was not really married polygamously in the full (i.e., sexual) sense of the term, Utah Mormons (including Smith's wives) affirmed repeatedly that he had physical sexual relations with them—despite the Victorian conventions in nineteenth-century American culture which ordinarily would have prevented any mention of sexuality. . . . Some, like Emma Smith, conclude that Joseph's marriages were for eternity only, not for time (thus without earthly sexuality). But many of Joseph's wives affirmed that they were married to him for eternity *and* time, with sexuality included.[25]

Compton concluded that

> though it is possible that Joseph had some marriages in which there were no sexual relations, there is not explicit or convincing evidence for this (except, perhaps, in the cases of the older wives, judging from later Mormon polygamy). And in a significant number of marriages, there is evidence for sexual relations.[26]

While there is no DNA evidence to prove that Smith had children with these plural wives, "persistent oral and family traditions insist that Joseph fathered children by at least four of his plural wives."[27] Regardless, Jacob 2:30 provides what appears to be the only legitimate reason in the Book of Mormon for the allowance of polygamy: to "raise up seed" (or have children). As a Gospel Topics essay ("Race and the Priesthood") explains,

> Latter-day Saints do not understand all of God's purposes for instituting, through His prophets, the practice of plural marriage during the 19th century. The Book of Mormon identifies one reason for God to command it: to increase the number of children born in the gospel covenant in order to "raise up seed unto [the Lord]" (Jacob 2:30). Plural marriage did result in the birth of large numbers of children within faithful Latter-day Saint homes.[28]

Yet if Smith had several dozen wives whom he married in order to produce more children, then why aren't these offspring known? And why would he marry other men's wives who already had husbands to father children by them?

Indeed, it is difficult to justify Smith's behavior of marrying other men's wives. Leviticus 20:10 declares that an adulterous act was punishable by death: "And the man that committeth adultery with another man's wife, even he that committeth adultery with his neighbour's wife, the adulterer and the adulteress shall surely be put to death." Besides teenagers and women who were married to living husbands, Smith married a mother and her daughter (Patty Bartlett [Sessions] and Sylvia Porter Sessions Lyons) as well as pairs of sisters (Huntington, Partridge, and Lawrence). This certainly seems in conflict with Leviticus 18:17–18 and 20:14.

Smith also targeted the young daughters of two of his closest associates. For instance, he attempted to make nineteen-year-old Nancy Rigdon one of his secret plural wives but was soundly rebuffed by her. When her father, Sidney, heard of the incident, he confronted Smith. Van Wagoner noted that Smith at first denied the story but recanted when Nancy failed to back off from her accusation. Shortly thereafter Smith had a letter sent to Nancy justifying his proposal when he said, "That which is wrong under one circumstance, may be, and often is, right under another."[29]

In May 1843 the thirty-seven-year-old prophet of Mormonism convinced fourteen-year-old Helen Mar Kimball to be sealed to him as his plural wife. The daughter of Heber C. Kimball stated how Smith promised that if she would "take this step," it would ensure the eternal salvation and exaltation of her father's household and kindred. Helen was led to believe that the relationship was more of a spiritual nature and claimed she would have never gone through with it had she known otherwise.[30]

Except for a brief period of time, Emma, Joseph's wife, was never in favor of polygamy. For instance, when Joseph's brother Hyrum took the revelation on plural marriage to Emma in the summer of 1843 to get her approval, he returned with his head down, saying, "I have never received a more severe talking to in my life. Emma is very bitter and full of resentment and anger," he said.[31] Newell and Avery write, "Emma would eventually know about some of Joseph's plural wives, her knowledge of seven can be documented conclusively, and some evidence hints that she may have known of others."[32] However, she was deceived by Smith on a number of occasions, and when she found out that certain women—including some of her best friends—were married to her husband, she became angry and even defiant. For instance, "when the full realization of the relationship between her friend Eliza [Snow] and her husband Joseph came to her, Emma was stunned. . . . Although no contemporary account of the incident between Emma and Eliza remains extant, evidence leads to the conclusion that some sort of physical confrontation occurred between the two women."[33]

When Joseph finally convinced his wife to accept plural marriage in May 1843, Emma told him that she would allow him to marry other women as long as she got to choose the new brides. As reported by Newell and Avery:

> Emma chose the two sets of sisters then living in her house, Emily and Eliza Partridge and Sarah and Maria Lawrence. Joseph had finally converted Emma to plural marriage, but not so fully that he dared tell her he had married the Partridge sisters two months earlier. Emily said that "to save family trouble Brother Joseph thought it best to have another ceremony performed. . . . [Emma] had her feelings, and so we thought there was no use in saying anything about it so long as she had chosen us herself."[34]

The authors added that it didn't take long before "Emma began to talk as firmly and urgently to Joseph about abandoning plural marriage as he had formerly talked to her about accepting it." And even if it had been commanded by God, "she opposed the doctrine" and even "threatened divorce."[35] The fact that Emma married a nonmember after the death of Joseph tends to prove that she did not believe plural marriage (or marriage at all) had anything to do with true salvation, as was taught in the LDS Church.

Scholars acknowledge that most of Joseph's marriages took place behind Emma's back and that it was common for him to rendevous with these other wives in clandestine locations.[36] While many Mormons remain naïve about the polygamous ways of their church's founding prophet, how could a modern Mormon in good conscience revere someone who lied to his wife about his affairs with other women and secretly married women already married to his friends (often without their knowledge)? Any man who is willing to deceive his wife and his friends is certainly capable of lying to others.

Speaking at a general conference, Apostle M. Russell Ballard stated that one of the characteristics of a false prophet was someone who attempted "to change the God-given and spiritually based doctrines that protect the sanctity of marriage, the divine nature of the family, and the essential doctrine of personal morality."[37] Ballard said such false prophets tend to redefine morality to justify, among other things, adultery and fornication. On such issues Mormons tend to turn a blind eye to Smith's egregious behavior. Why don't the standards given by Ballard apply to Joseph Smith?

The Proud Prophet

In the Joseph Smith Translation of the Bible, a whole section was added by Smith to Genesis chapter 50. Verses 24–38 include a missing prophecy about a certain seer named Joseph who had a father named Joseph. Mormons believe this speaks about Joseph Smith, the founder of the LDS Church. One teacher's manual says,

> **The great latter-day Joseph.** The Joseph Smith Translation of Genesis 50:24–38 contains prophecies that Joseph made about one of his descendants who would become a "choice seer." The Book of Mormon prophet Lehi restated

these prophecies in 2 Nephi 3:5–15. The descendant referred to in these prophecies is the Prophet Joseph Smith.[38]

To be able to add a prophecy about oneself—in the Bible, no less—and then pass it off as if Moses had originally written it is, no doubt, audacious, especially when there is not even one ancient Old Testament manuscript to support this addition. Smith thought very highly about himself, as his grandnephew Joseph Fielding Smith explained:

> No one else, but Joseph Smith, has ever made the claim that this restoration and setting up of the kingdom (i.e., Church of Jesus Christ) has ever been revealed. Joseph Smith has proclaimed to the world that power, keys, and authority were bestowed upon him. No one else has arisen to make such a claim; yet, this was revealed preparatory to these momentous and final restorations.[39]

According to D&C 135:3, "Joseph Smith, the Prophet and Seer of the Lord, has done more, save Jesus only, for the salvation of men in this world, than any other man that ever lived in it." Smith's role was said to be so important that God allowed him to be visited by a number of heavenly messengers, more than double any other individual as recorded in the Bible.[40] In addition, there were a number of times when Smith was supposedly visited by God, as taught by Apostle Russell M. Nelson at a general conference: "Our Eternal Father and Jesus Christ made multiple appearances to the Prophet Joseph Smith."[41]

Brigham Young said Smith's character was on the same level as that of Jesus and others of both the Old and New Testament. He stated in 1871:

> Well, now, examine the character of the Savior, and examine the characters of those who have written the Old and New Testaments; and then compare them with the character of Joseph Smith, the founder of this work . . . and you will find that his character stands as fair as that of any man's mentioned in the Bible. We can find no person who presents a better character to the world when the facts are known.[42]

Listen to several boasts made by Smith in the sixth volume of the *History of the Church*:

I combat the errors of ages; I meet the violence of mobs; I cope with illegal proceedings from executive authority; I cut the gordian knot of powers, and I solve mathematical problems of universities, with truth—diamond truth; and God is my "right hand man."[43]

God made Aaron to be the mouthpiece for the children of Israel, and He will make me to be god to you in His stead, and the Elders to be mouth for me; and if you don't like it, you must lump it.[44]

Come on! ye prosecutors! ye false swearers! All hell, boil over! Ye burning mountains, roll down your lava! for I will come out on the top at last. I have more to boast of than ever any man had. I am the only man that has ever been able to keep a whole church together since the days of Adam. A large majority of the whole have stood by me. Neither Paul, John, Peter, nor Jesus ever did it. I boast that no man ever did such a work as I. The followers of Jesus ran away from Him; but the Latter-day Saints never ran away from me yet.[45]

The Bible indicates that pride is a dangerous trait. Proverbs 16:5 explains, "Every one that is proud in heart is an abomination to the Lord." Verse 18 adds, "Pride goeth before destruction, and an haughty spirit before a fall." Some Mormons insist that Smith's words should be taken no differently than Paul's "boast" in 2 Corinthians 11. However, the two accounts are different. Citing Philippians 3:3 and Galatians 6:14, commentator Philip E. Hughes explains that Paul's "object is not to draw attention to himself but to safeguard the gospel of which he is a ministry by God's appointment. . . . Thus Paul is not really succumbing to the foolishness and vanity of self-esteem. Any appearance to the contrary remains only as an appearance—he speaks 'as in foolishness', not actually in it."[46]

No Salvation without Joseph Smith

According to a student manual, Joseph Smith is guaranteed the celestial kingdom and eternal life. Referring to a temple ceremony that certain members can receive, it states:

D&C 132:49–50. Exaltation Assured to Joseph Smith. The Prophet Joseph Smith received the promise of eternal life—he had his calling and election made sure. God will extend the same promise to all of his children if they will obey him. Verse 49 explains why the Prophet Joseph received this promise.

297

He was willing to lay all he had on the altar. He was hunted and persecuted, sued in courts of law, torn from family and loved ones, and all because he had testified that the heavens were not closed and that God speaks to His children. The Prophet Joseph is an example in this dispensation of how children of God should act.[47]

Despite the fact that Christians throughout the centuries have pointed to Jesus Christ as the only way to eternal life, early Mormon leaders taught that Joseph Smith will apparently be a deciding factor as well. Brigham Young said:

If I can pass brother Joseph, I shall stand a good chance for passing Peter, Jesus, the Prophets, Moses, Abraham, and all back to Father Adam, and be pretty sure of receiving his approbation. . . . If we can pass the sentinel Joseph the Prophet, we shall go into the celestial kingdom, and not a man can injure us. If he says, "God bless you, come along here"; if we will live so that Joseph will justify us, and say, "Here am I, brethren," we shall pass every sentinel.[48]

Concerning Judgment Day, Young stated that entrance into the celestial kingdom was conditional on Smith's consent:

No man or woman in this dispensation will ever enter into the celestial kingdom of God without the consent of Joseph Smith. From the day that the Priesthood was taken from the earth to the winding-up scene of all things, every man and woman must have the certificate of Joseph Smith, junior, as a passport to their entrance into the mansion where God and Christ are—I with you and you with me. I cannot go there without his consent. He holds the keys of that kingdom for the last dispensation—the keys to rule in the spirit world.[49]

George Q. Cannon agreed that Smith holds the keys to everyone's salvation when he wrote:

He stands, therefore, at the head of this dispensation and will throughout all eternity, and no man can take that power away from him. If any man holds these keys, he holds them subordinate to Joseph Smith. . . . If we get our salvation, we shall have to pass by him; if we enter into our glory, it will be through the authority that he has received. We cannot get around him.[50]

President Joseph Fielding Smith affirmed this, saying that nobody could reject this "testimony without incurring the most dreadful consequences, for he cannot enter the kingdom of God."[51]

Either Smith was called of God or he wasn't. Mormon Church historian Andrew Jenson wrote:

> If Joseph Smith is what he professed to be: A true Prophet of God, no one can reject his testimony without being condemned, while on the other hand, if he was an impostor, or a false prophet, we can reject him without fear of Divine punishment, and the condemnation will rest upon the man who assumes to speak in the name of the Lord presumptuously.[52]

This veneration for Smith even extends to the point of modifying Scripture to accommodate the Mormon prophet. For instance, on September 9, 1860, Brigham Young referred to 1 John 5:1 and proclaimed:

> For unbelievers we will quote from the Scriptures—"Whosoever believeth that Jesus is the Christ is born of God." Again—"Hereby know ye the Spirit of God: Every spirit that confesseth that Jesus Christ is come in the flesh, is of God." I will now give my scripture—"Whosoever confesseth that Joseph Smith was sent of God to reveal the holy Gospel to the children of men, and lay the foundation for gathering Israel, and building up the kingdom of God on the earth, that spirit of God; and every spirit that does not confess that God has sent Joseph Smith, and revealed the everlasting Gospel to and through him, is of Antichrist, no matter whether it is found in a pulpit or on a throne, nor how much divinity it may profess, nor what it professes with regard to revealed religion and the account that is given of the Saviour and his Father in the Bible."[53]

The Bible states that Jesus, not Joseph, will be the final judge. Jesus said in John 5:22–23a, "The Father judges no one, but has given all judgment to the Son, that all may honor the Son, just as they honor the Father" (ESV). Both believer and nonbeliever alike will someday acknowledge that Jesus is Lord (Phil. 2:9–11). Unfortunately, those who refuse to submit themselves to the lordship of Christ in this life will only have Him to be their judge in the next.[54]

Discussion Questions

1. There is no doubt that Joseph Smith has captured the imagination of the Latter-day Saint people. What is it about this man that you

think appeals to the faithful? If it was discovered that Smith was not the man he's been made out to be, what could that possibly do to someone's faith in Mormonism?

2. Suppose plural marriage is something that God truly wanted Christians to practice. Even so, how does Joseph Smith's example go beyond the norms of plural marriage? Should the LDS religion be judged on the founder's personal bad behavior?

3. Some Mormons have insisted that Smith's boasting is no different from what Paul claimed for himself in 2 Corinthians 11. If a Mormon used this argument to explain Smith's boasting, how would you respond?

Final Thought

According to President Joseph Fielding Smith, "Mormonism, as it is called, must stand or fall on the story of Joseph Smith. He was either a prophet of God, divinely called, properly appointed and commissioned, or he was one of the biggest frauds this world has ever seen. There is no middle ground."[55] When we look at Smith's life, we see that there is plenty that ought not to be emulated. While we're not claiming that he needed to be perfect in order to be a prophet of God, at the same time there was blatant adultery, lying, and boastfulness involved in this man's life, with no evidence that repentance ever took place. Is this the man whose approval everyone will need in order to enter God's presence? No, we'd rather focus our attention on Jesus Christ and not someone who, if followed, will lead his followers away from the true God of the Bible.

Notes

1. *Teachings of Presidents of the Church: George Albert Smith*, 34.
2. *Teachings of Presidents of the Church: Harold B. Lee*, 71. For a similar testimony, see *True to the Faith*, 90.
3. Mormons meet twice a month in church to study two chapters of the current manual. Three manuals were larger and required two years of study; in 2010–2011, the manual *Gospel Principles* was the topic.
4. *Teachings of Presidents of the Church: Brigham Young*, 345.
5. *Teachings of Presidents of the Church: Joseph F. Smith*, 18.
6. *Teachings of Presidents of the Church: Heber J. Grant*, 16.
7. *Teachings of Presidents of the Church: George Albert Smith*, 27.
8. *Ensign* (December 2005): 2.

9. *Church History in the Fulness of Times Student Manual*, 284.

10. *Ensign* (February 2013): 39.

11. D. Michael Quinn, *The Mormon Hierarchy: Origins of Power* (Salt Lake City: Signature Books, 1994), 261–62.

12. *Teachings of Presidents of the Church: Spencer W. Kimball*, 230; ellipses in original.

13. For example, go to the Voice of the Martyrs website located at www.persecution.com.

14. Quinn, *The Mormon Hierarchy*, 91.

15. Stephen C. LeSueur, *The 1838 Mormon War in Missouri* (Columbia, MO: University of Missouri Press, 1987), 3.

16. James B. Allen and Glen M. Leonard, *The Story of the Latter-day Saints* (Salt Lake City: Deseret Book Co., 1976), 83. Allen and Leonard wrote, "Impressed by the Mormon image of group solidarity, some old settlers expressed fears that as a group the Mormons were determined to take over all of their lands and business," 82.

17. Joseph Fielding Smith, ed., *Teachings of the Prophet Joseph Smith*, 302. The United States never met Smith's demands and continued as a nation, despite his threat. Let it be said at this point that the authors of this work heartily condemn the persecutions faced by early Latter-day Saints. Physical violence is no way to settle differences, especially those of a religious nature. When scriptural debate fails to sway an individual toward the Christian position, the believer has no retreat but that of prayer. It should be understood that while Christians should reason from the Scriptures with unbelievers, it is ultimately God who draws people to Himself. There is no such thing as strong-arming a person into God's kingdom.

18. *Doctrine and Covenants Student Manual*, 315.

19. Richard Van Wagoner, *Sidney Rigdon: A Portrait of Religious Excess* (Salt Lake City: Signature Books, 1994), 290–91. *The New World Dictionary* defines *pedantic* as laying "unnecessary stress on minor or trivial points of learning, displaying a scholarship lacking in judgment or sense of proportion. A narrow-minded teacher who insists on exact adherence to a set of arbitrary rules."

20. *Church History in the Fulness of Times Student Manual*, 256.

21. Recorded September 28, 2010. See Eric Johnson, "A fiery 2010 fireside in Stockholm, Sweden," Mormonism Research Ministry, http://www.mrm.org/fiery-fireside.

22. In the fall of 2014, the church did publish a Gospel Topics essay that discusses Smith's polygamy. However, many Latter-day Saints do not know about these articles printed on the official LDS website, and they're not easy to find unless one knows where to look. For more, see http://www.mrm.org/gospel-topics-polygamy.

23. Compton, *In Sacred Loneliness*, 11. The church admitted in October 2014 that "careful estimates put the number [of Smith's wives] between 30 and 40." https://www.lds.org/topics/plural-marriage-in-kirtland-and-nauvoo, accessed January 9, 2015.

24. Ibid., 15, 16. For a list of Smith's wives and more information, see "Joseph Smith and Polygamy," Mormonism Research Ministry, www.mrm.org/joseph-smith-and-polygamy.

25. Ibid., 12, 14; italics in original. The church acknowledged in October 2014 that plural marriages for "time" performed in the nineteenth century included "the possibility of sexual relations." https://www.lds.org/topics/plural-marriage-in-kirtland-and-nauvoo, accessed January 9, 2015.

26. Ibid., 15.

27. Newell and Avery, *Mormon Enigma: Emma Hale Smith*, 98. Most of Smith's wives remained quiet about their relationship with the Mormon prophet, and Newell and Avery add that these women "refused either to confirm or deny whether they had given birth to his children," 99.

28. "Plural Marriage and Families in Early Utah," The Church of Jesus Christ of Latter-Day

Saints, accessed May 29, 2014, https://www.lds.org/topics/plural-marriage-and-families
-in-early-utah?lang=eng.

29. Van Wagoner, *Sidney Rigdon*, 295–96.

30. Ibid., 293–94.

31. Newell and Avery, *Mormon Enigma: Emma Hale Smith*, 152.

32. Ibid., 98.

33. Ibid., 134.

34. Ibid., 143; ellipses in original.

35. Ibid., 145, 158.

36. For instance, see George D. Smith, *Nauvoo Polygamy* (Salt Lake City: Signature Books, 2011), xiii.

36. *Ensign* (November 1999): 64.

37. *Old Testament Gospel Doctrine Teacher's Manual* (Salt Lake City: The Church of Jesus Christ of Latter-day Saints, 2001), 53; bold in original.

38. *Selections from Answers to Gospel Questions*, 338.

39. As listed on page 63 of the October 1994 *Ensign*, these were God the Father (*Joseph Smith—History*, 1:17); Jesus Christ (D&C 110:2–10); Moroni (*Joseph Smith—History*, 1:30–49, 59); John the Baptist (D&C 13:1; *History of the Church*, 1:39–40); Peter, James, John (D&C 27; *History of the Church*, 1:40–42); Moses (D&C 110:11); Elias (D&C 110:12); Elijah (D&C 110:13–16); Adam (Michael); Noah (Gabriel); Raphael; various angels (D&C 128:21); Lehi, Nephi (Watt, ed., *Journal of Discourses*, 16:266); Mormon (Watt, ed., *Journal of Discourses*, 17:374).

40. *Ensign* (May 2013): 46.

41. Brigham Young, *Journal of Discourses*, ed. Watt, 14:203.

42. *History of the Church*, 6:78. The footnote to this passage says that Smith's ending comment was "reverently said," and "not in the blasphemous sense attributed to him by some anti-Mormon writers; namely, that God was subordinate to him—his right hand man." This was obviously written well after the fact of this statement, so we're curious how the editor (who wasn't there) knew that it was "reverently said." The Mormon founder was assassinated less than a year after the three occasions on which these quotes were given.

43. Ibid., 319–20.

44. Ibid., 408–9.

45. Philip E. Hughes, *The New International Commentary on the New Testament: The Second Epistle to the Corinthians* (Grand Rapids: Wm. B. Eerdmans Publishing Co., 1962), 397.

46. *Doctrine and Covenants Student Manual*, 334; bold in original.

47. Brigham Young, *Journal of Discourses*, ed. Watt, 4:271.

48. Ibid., 7:289. This quotation from Young was reprinted in the 1984 *"Search These Commandments" Melchizedek Priesthood Personal Study Guide* as well as in the article "Joseph Smith among the Prophets" printed in the June 1994 issue of *Ensign* magazine.

49. George Q. Cannon, *Gospel Truth* (Salt Lake City: Deseret Book Co., 1987), 199.

50. Joseph Fielding Smith, *Doctrines of Salvation*, 1:189–90.

51. Andrew Jenson, January 16, 1891, in *Collected Discourses*, ed. Stuy, 2:149–50.

52. Brigham Young, *Journal of Discourses*, ed. Watt, 8:176–77. Young went on to say in the same sermon that those who refuse to acknowledge that Joseph Smith was sent of God will "never have visions of eternity opened to them." Such people, he said, are "unbelievers."

53. For more information on this topic, see chapter 35, "Why do you have difficulty accepting Joseph Smith as a true prophet of God?" and chapter 36, "Why would Joseph Smith be willing to die as a martyr if he didn't believe God spoke to him?" in *Answering Mormons' Questions*.

54. *Doctrines of Salvation*, 1:188.

18 | The Church and Its Leadership

A prophet does not become a spiritual leader by studying books about religion, nor does he become one by attending a theological seminary. . . . One becomes a prophet or a religious leader by actual spiritual contacts. The true spiritual expert thus gets his diploma directly from God.

President Harold B. Lee [1]

MORMONESE:

Ensign: A monthly church magazine that includes First Presidency messages and, twice a year, general conference addresses.

Liahona: A monthly church magazine published in up to forty-seven languages each month.

President Gordon B. Hinckley once told a reporter that this is "not a reformist church but a restored church."[2] Mormonism's leaders believe that their organization, which was founded by Joseph Smith in 1830, has God's complete authority, unlike any other institution on the face of the earth. A teacher's manual instructed,

Testify that although other churches teach some truths and do many good things, The Church of Jesus Christ of Latter-day Saints is the only *true* church on the earth because it is the only church that has the complete gospel of Jesus Christ and the priesthood authority to perform ordinances in the name of Jesus Christ. It is Jesus' Church. It has his name and his law, and it is led by his appointed representatives. Express your gratitude to Joseph Smith, the prophet through whom the Lord restored the true Church.[3]

These leaders claim that "the Church today teaches the same principles and performs the same ordinances as were performed in the days of Jesus."[4] They have made it clear that "through the Restoration, the priesthood was returned to the earth. Those who hold this priesthood today have the authority to perform ordinances such as baptism. They also have the authority to direct the Lord's kingdom on earth."[5] President Joseph F. Smith was adamant that only the church founded by his uncle (Joseph Smith) had divine authority:

> The Church of Jesus Christ of Latter-day Saints is no partisan Church. It is not a sect. It is *The Church of Jesus Christ of Latter-day Saints*. It is the only one today existing in the world that can and does legitimately bear the name of Jesus Christ and his divine authority. I make this declaration in all simplicity and honesty before you and before all the world, bitter as the truth may seem to those who are opposed and who have no reason for that opposition.[6]

President Joseph Fielding Smith even claimed that the Protestant church was guided by Satan's cunning plan:

An aerial view of Temple Square in downtown Salt Lake City, including the Mormon Tabernacle and temple.

While some sectarian churches have introduced a system of tithing, and perhaps there have come modifications in some instances of former long established doctrines, this does not prove that the Protestant world is coming any nearer to the fundamental principles of the gospel. Satan is just as cunning today as he ever was, and he may cause some peoples to modify former teachings, but you may be assured that he has no intention of having them accept any of the fundamental teachings of The Church of Jesus Christ of Latter-day Saints. You may be sure he never permits one church or people to have very much of revealed truth. He may have scattered some teachings in order to maintain his deceptions, but he is not leading anyone to the restored gospel.[7]

President Spencer W. Kimball taught:

This set of laws and ordinances is known as the gospel of Jesus Christ, and it is the *only* plan which will exalt mankind. The Church of Jesus Christ of Latter-day Saints is the sole repository of this priceless program in its fulness, which is made available to those who accept it. The Lord restored his kingdom in these days, with all its gifts and powers and blessings. Any church that you know of may possibly be able to take you for a long ride, and bring you some degree of peace and happiness and blessing, and they can carry you to the veil and there they drop you. The Church of Jesus Christ picks you up on this side of the veil and, if you live its commandments, carries you right through the veil as though it weren't there and on through the eternities to exaltation.[8]

Because they believe their church is true, the leaders say complete sacrifice ought to be made for the institution:

The Apostle Paul wrote that we should become living sacrifices, holy and acceptable unto God (see Romans 12:1). If we are to be a living sacrifice, we must be willing to give everything we have for The Church of Jesus Christ of Latter-day Saints—to build the kingdom of God on the earth and labor to bring forth Zion.[9]

A Church with Authoritative Leaders

From the very beginning, Mormonism's leaders have been the figureheads of the LDS Church. What they say goes. As President Joseph Fielding Smith explained,

The Latter-day Saints should put their trust in their leaders, and follow the teachings of the authorities of the Church, for they speak unto them with the voice of prophecy and inspiration. The Lord has declared in the very first section in the Doctrine and Covenants, that whether he speaks by his own voice or through the voice of his servants, it is the same [see D&C 1:38]. Therefore, we are under just as great responsibility and obligation to hearken unto the voice of the one who stands at the head to teach the people, or to listen unto the voice of the elders of Israel, as they carry among the people the message of truth, as we are [if] the Lord should send from his presence an angel or should come himself to declare these things unto us.[10]

In a general conference talk in 2010, Seventy Kevin R. Duncan said,

Brothers and sisters, like the Saints of 1848, we can choose to follow the prophet, or we can look to the arm of flesh. May we have the wisdom to trust in and follow the counsel of the living prophets and apostles. I am a witness of their goodness. I testify that they are called of God. I also testify that there is no safer way to approach life, find answers to our problems, gain peace and happiness in this world, and protect our very salvation than by obeying their words.[11]

Mormons are told specifically to keep their eyes on their top leader, the president (also known as the prophet), whose presidency was "foreordained in the premortal life."[12] An experience at a Utah high school seminary (a church building located near the public school where academic classes on LDS scripture are offered to Mormon students) illustrates this point. The classroom teacher of thirty students drew two stick men on the white board and explained how the figure on the right symbolized humanity while the figure on the left stood for God the Father. Then he drew a tall wall separating the two, saying it represented the isolation suffered by all humans who, by themselves, do not have access to God. Because of mankind's rebellion, he said, the wall prohibits God from communicating with humans. Then the teacher drew a third stick figure that stood on top of the wall. Arrows were drawn going up and down on both sides to show how it is possible in the twenty-first century to have communication take place between God and people. It was all dependent on the middle man on the wall. According to a Christian worldview, this could be a symbol of Jesus Himself! As it says in 1 Timothy 2:5, "there is one God, and one mediator between God and men, the man Christ Jesus." But who did the

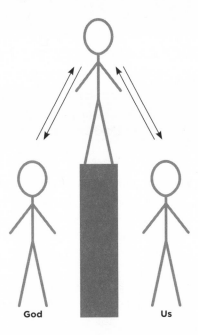

teacher claim the man on the wall represented? He said that this figure symbolized the latter-day Mormon prophets, beginning with Joseph Smith and embodied today in the current LDS prophet. Jesus's name was never even mentioned.

This interpretation appears to be in line with the thoughts of LDS presidents, as quoted in the *Teachings of Presidents of the Church* series:

- Joseph F. Smith: "Honor and praise be unto [the President of the Church], that instrument in the hands of God of establishing order in the midst of uncertainty, and certain rules by which we know our bearings."[13]

- George Albert Smith: "We have had misguided souls in the Church who have, in their ignorance, opposed the advice of [the President of the Church], not sensing the fact that they were opposing the Lord and they have fallen into darkness and sorrow, and unless they repent they will not find a place in the celestial kingdom. Let us remember that the President of this Church has been officially designated as the pilot of the Church here in mortality to represent the Master of heaven and earth."[14]

- Joseph Fielding Smith: "The President of the Church holds the keys over all the Church. . . . In him is concentrated the power of the Priesthood. He holds all the keys of every nature, pertaining to the dispensation of the Fulness of Times. All the keys of former dispensations which have been revealed, are vested in him."[15]
- Harold B. Lee: "The Mormon people are told to look to the President of the Church for your instructions. If ever there is a conflict, you keep your eyes on the President if you want to walk in the light."[16]

Consider these additional quotes from church resources:

- "We can learn about Jesus by listening to the words of the living prophets. The Lord has told us to 'give heed' to the words and commandments of His prophets and to receive those words as if they are from the Lord Himself (see D&C 21:4–5). The President of The Church of Jesus Christ of Latter-day Saints is the mouthpiece of God on the earth. Through his sermons and printed messages he reveals God's directions for us today."[17]
- "Like the prophets of old, prophets today testify of Jesus Christ and teach His gospel. They make known God's will and true character. They speak boldly and clearly, denouncing sin and warning of its consequences. At times, they may be inspired to prophesy of future events for our benefit. . . . Your greatest safety lies in following the word of the Lord given through His prophets, particularly the current President of the Church. The Lord warns that those who ignore the words of the living prophets will fall (see D&C 1:14–16)."[18]
- "We may never have a General Authority visit our home, but we can receive similar blessings if we accept the General Authorities by following their inspired counsel in our homes."[19]

The Prophet and LDS Doctrine

It is important to understand how Mormon doctrine comes to the membership. BYU professor Robert L. Millet explained:

> To determine whether something is part of the doctrine of the Church, we have asked ourselves and one other [sic]: Is it in the four standard works? Is

it in official declarations or proclamations? Is it taught in general conference or other official gatherings by general authorities or general officers of the Church today? Is it in the current general handbooks or approved curriculum of the Church? If it meets one or more of these criteria, we have felt safe in drawing upon it.[20]

Let's take a look at each:

Standard Works

The four written standard works are the Bible (King James Version), the Book of Mormon, the Doctrine and Covenants, and the Pearl of Great Price.[21]

Official Declarations or Proclamations

There are two "official declarations," which are included at the end of the Doctrine and Covenants. Official Declaration-1, dated October 6, 1890, agreed to "submit" to the anti-polygamy laws of the United States. Official Declaration-2, dated September 30, 1978, referred to a June 8, 1978

The outside of the Mormon Tabernacle, which for many years is where the LDS general conferences were held and where the Mormon Tabernacle Choir performed.

letter from the First Presidency allowing "all worthy male members of the Church" to receive "the priesthood without regard for race or color." There have been a total of five proclamations:

- January 15, 1841, in Navuoo, Illinois, "to the Saints Scattered Abroad," giving instructions about how the church was gathered at Nauvoo, Illinois.

- April 6 and October 22, 1845, in Nauvoo, Illinois. This invited people to join the Mormon Church and prepare for Christ's second coming. President Spencer W. Kimball quoted from this proclamation on October 3, 1975 in general conference.

- October 21, 1865, explaining how authorized doctrine can only be announced by the First Presidency.

- April 6, 1980, the 150th anniversary of the church, providing a history of the church and a summary of its beliefs.

- September 23, 1995, "The Family: A Proclamation to the World" was read by President Gordon B. Hinckley in a message to the General Relief Society. Among other things, this proclamation declared how marriage was "between a man and a woman" and that families "are ordained of God."

There have been no declarations or proclamations since 1995.[22]

General Conferences and Authorized Handbooks

One of the main ways that the Latter-day Saints can learn from their leaders is at the biannual general conference. As the January 2011 *Ensign* reported,

God continues to reveal truths to living prophets through the inspiration of the Holy Ghost. These truths are considered scripture (see D&C 68:4). They come to us primarily through general conference, held the first weekend in April and October, when members throughout the world hear addresses from our prophet and other Church leaders.[23]

A student manual states:

The Words of the Prophets Delivered through the Spirit during General Conference Are Latter-day Scripture. Scripture is the mind and will of God

310

revealed through His servants (see D&C 68:4). The apostle Peter declared, "Prophecy came not in old time by the will of man: but holy men of God spake as they were moved by the Holy Ghost" (2 Peter 1:21). Such scripture has been written and preserved in the standard works as priceless gems of eternal truth. However, the standard works are not the only source of scripture. Elder James E. Talmage (1862–1933) of the Quorum of the Twelve Apostles identified the connection between the standard works and the words of living prophets: "The Standard Works of the Church constitute the written authority of the Church in doctrine. Nevertheless, the Church holds itself in readiness to receive additional light and knowledge 'pertaining to the Kingdom of God' through divine revelation. We believe that God is as willing today as He ever has been to reveal His mind and will to man, and that He does so through His appointed servants—prophets, seers, and revelators—invested through ordination with the authority of the Holy Priesthood. **We rely therefore on the teachings of the living oracles of God as of equal validity with the doctrines of the written word**" (*Articles of Faith* [1968], 7; emphasis added).[24]

To be sure, the talks at the general conferences are not to be ignored. Dieter F. Uchtdorf, a member of the First Presidency, wrote,

> Occasionally I ask myself, "Did I listen to the words given by the men and women who spoke at the most recent general conference of the Church? Have I read and reread their words? Have I pondered them and applied them to my life? Or have I just enjoyed the fine talks and neglected to apply their inspired messages in my personal life?"[25]

The May and November issues of the *Ensign* and *Liahona* magazines are extremely important resources because they include all of the talks given the previous month at the conference. Saying they contained "the marching orders for each six months," President Ezra Taft Benson taught, "For the next six months, your conference edition of the *Ensign* should stand next to your standard works and be referred to frequently."[26]

President Howard W. Hunter said,

> Our modern-day prophets have encouraged us to make the reading of the conference editions of our Church magazines an important and regular part of our personal study. Thus, **general conference becomes, in a sense, a supplement to or an extension of the Doctrine and Covenants.** In addition

to the conference issues of the Church magazines, the First Presidency writes monthly articles that contain inspired counsel for our welfare.[27]

References in church magazines about how the conference talks are "approved curriculum" are commonplace. For instance:

> Pray that the Holy Spirit will be with you as you study and teach the talk(s). You may at times be tempted to set aside the conference talks and prepare the lesson using other materials. But the conference talks are the approved curriculum. Your assignment is to help others learn and live the gospel as taught in the most recent general conference of the Church.[28]

One student manual gives specific instructions on how this can be done:

> As you identify scriptural interpretations or clarifications, it can be helpful to write the reference of the conference address in the margin next to the scripture that is taught or clarified. Following are some examples:
> - Next to Revelation 22:18 you could write the citation: Elder Jeffrey R. Holland, *Ensign* (May 2008): 91–94. In this talk, Elder Holland referred to Revelation 22:18 and discussed the importance of continuing revelation.
> - Next to Psalm 24:3–4 you could write: Elder David A. Bednar, *Ensign* (November 2007): 80–83. Elder Bednar discussed what it means to have clean hands and a pure heart.
> - Next to Nehemiah 6 you could write: President Dieter F. Uchtdorf, *Ensign* (May 2009): 59–62. President Uchtdorf discussed Nehemiah rebuilding the walls surrounding Jerusalem and the idea that "we are doing a great work and cannot come down."[29]

Mormons are instructed that the words of the living prophet have more importance than the standard works:

> Show students a Bible and ask: What books of scripture do we have in the Church that other religions do not? (The Book of Mormon, the Doctrine and Covenants, the Pearl of Great Price.) Show students these other scriptures, and then stack them on top of the Bible. Ask: Do we have any other scripture in the Church? Read Doctrine and Covenants 68:2–4 to find the answer to this question. Stack some conference issues of the *Ensign* on top of the scriptures. Share the following statements. President Ezra Taft Benson, then President of the Quorum of the Twelve, said: "God's revelations to Adam did not instruct Noah how to build the ark. Noah needed his own revelation.

Therefore, the most important prophet, so far as you and I are concerned, is the one living in our day and age to whom the Lord is currently revealing His will for us. Therefore, the most important reading we can do is any of the words of the prophet contained each week in the [*Church News*] and any words of the prophet contained each month in our Church magazines" ("Fourteen Fundamentals in Following the Prophet," in *1980 Devotional Speeches of the Year* [1981], 27).[30]

Joseph Fielding McConkie, son of the apostle Bruce R. McConkie, answered the question "How do we distinguish the doctrine of the Church from that which is not doctrine?" He said that "*good doctrine will always sustain the idea that the living prophet, not scripture or any other document, is the constitution of the Church.*"[31]

Over and over again, the message is that the teachings of the leadership must take precedence over anything else because these men will never guide the Mormon people wrong. Wilford Woodruff is quoted in three different church resources, saying:

> The Lord will never permit me or any other man who stands as President of this Church to lead you astray. It is not in the programme. It is not in the mind of God. If I were to attempt that, the Lord would remove me out of my place (*Teachings of Presidents of the Church: Wilford Woodruff* [2004], 199).[32]

Joseph Fielding Smith agreed with such a teaching, saying, "I think there is one thing which we should have exceedingly clear in our minds. Neither the President of the Church, nor the First Presidency, nor the united voice of the First Presidency and the Twelve will ever lead the Saints astray or send forth counsel to the world that is contrary to the mind and will of the Lord."[33] The idea was reinforced in a manual written to the women of the church:

> The prophet who leads the Church will never lead us astray. He tells us things that pertain to our lives now. The prophet gives us instruction from the Lord at general conference, which is held twice each year. He also gives us the Lord's counsel to us at other conferences held throughout the world. Many of the prophet's addresses are printed in the Church magazines. In addition to the President of the Church, other men are sustained as prophets, seers, and revelators. These are the prophet's counselors and the Quorum of the Twelve. These Brethren also receive revelation, bring us the will of the Lord, bear witness of the divinity of Christ, teach the plan of salvation, and perform ordinances.[34]

The Mormon people are told they can trust these men as delivering the truth because

if [the President of the Church] should become unfaithful, God would remove him out of his place. I testify in the name of Israel's God that He will not suffer the head of the Church, him whom He has chosen to stand at the head, to transgress His Laws and apostatize; the moment he should take a course that would in time lead to it, God would take him away. Why? Because to suffer a wicked man to occupy that position, would be to allow, as it were, the fountain to become corrupted, which is something He will never permit.[35]

What about when a current prophet's teachings disagree with a former prophet? In a speech given on February 26, 1980, called "14 Fundamentals in Following the Prophets," Ezra Taft Benson, then an apostle, made a number of points about the prophet, including the idea that he would never mislead the church, that he does not need to say "Thus saith the Lord" for something to be authoritative, and that he speaks for the Lord in everything. He also made it a point to say that the living prophet is more important than a dead prophet. For those who might think that this teaching no longer applies because it is said by a man who is now dead, the speech was dusted off in 2010 and quoted at length by two general authorities, showing how Benson's ideas are still valid.[36]

This authority apparently even extends to the ability for a general authority to add or subtract facts related to the Bible. For example, referring to the Gospel account in John 19, the February 2010 edition of *Ensign* reports:

John's testimony does not record how Jesus was bound, but Elder Bruce R. McConkie of the Quorum of the Twelve Apostles (1915–85) provided a powerful insight when he said that Jesus was then "led away with a rope around his neck, as a common criminal." This detail is not found in the Gospel accounts and must therefore be ascribed to the prophetic understanding of one sustained as a prophet, seer, and revelator.[37]

With absolutely no historical or ancient manuscript support, some Mormon people are willing to grant divine inspiration to something that is no more than mere speculation. Yet for those who may even entertain the idea that their leaders are wrong, Mormons are firmly instructed that "they should never criticize priesthood leaders or say unkind things about them. Criticizing our leaders endangers our own salvation."[38]

Paul took a position opposite to that held by the leaders of Mormonism. He invited his followers in Galatians 1:8–9 to closely scrutinize his teachings: "But though we, or an angel from heaven, preach any other gospel . . . let him be accursed." He made it clear that even he was not above criticism. When he saw an inconsistency in Peter's behavior among the Gentiles, Paul saw no problem in confronting Peter "to the face" about the matter (Gal. 2:11). This is especially significant since Peter's seniority far surpassed that of Paul.

Discussion Questions

1. In the opening quote, Gordon B. Hinckley said that this is "not a reformist church but a restored church." What did he mean? How would you respond to such a claim?

2. If you were given a quote from a living human being (such as an LDS leader) and the words of the Bible, and the two quotes conflicted, which source do you think is more worthy of your trust? How would you explain your decision to a Latter-day Saint?

3. What are some of the problems when the newer revelations of LDS prophets and apostles abrogate or cancel out revelations from deceased general authorities?

Final Thought

A Christian who hopes to share the faith with Latter-day Saints must understand the influence these leaders have. In effect, the unwavering trust many Mormons have in their leaders and their teachings may take precedence even over their trust in the Word of God! If they feel that their leaders can never lead them astray, a blind faith can be the result. While this attitude might be frustrating to the Christian who wants to share truth with LDS friends and relatives, we must understand this mind-set in order to prayerfully share the truth in a loving and kind way.

Notes

1. *Teachings of Presidents of the Church: Harold B. Lee,* 73; ellipses in original.
2. Don Lattin, Sunday Interview, *San Francisco Chronicle,* April 13, 1997.

3. *Preparing for Exaltation Teacher's Manual*, 99; italics in original.

4. *Gospel Principles*, 98.

5. Ibid., 97.

6. *Teachings of Presidents of the Church: Joseph F. Smith*, 396; italics in original.

7. *Selections from Answers to Gospel Questions*, 293.

8. *Teachings of Presidents of the Church: Spencer W. Kimball*, 5; italics in original.

9. *Gospel Principles*, 151.

10. *Teachings of Presidents of the Church: Joseph Fielding Smith*, 145; brackets in original.

11. *Ensign* (November 2010): 36.

12. *Teachings of the Living Prophets Teacher Manual: Religion 333* (Salt Lake City: The Church of Jesus Christ of Latter-day Saints, 2010), 13.

13. *Teachings of Presidents of the Church: Joseph F. Smith*, 222.

14. *Teachings of Presidents of the Church: George Albert Smith*, 116; brackets in original.

15. *Teachings of Presidents of the Church: Joseph Fielding Smith*, 157; ellipses in original.

16. *Teachings of Presidents of the Church: Harold B. Lee*, 85.

17. *The Latter-day Saint Woman: Basic Manual for Women, Part B* (Salt Lake City: The Church of Jesus Christ of Latter-day Saints, 2000), 6.

18. *True to the Faith*, 129–30.

19. *Duties and Blessings of the Priesthood, Basic Manual for Priesthood Holders, Part A* (Salt Lake City: The Church of Jesus Christ of Latter-day Saints, 2000), 83.

20. Millet et al., *LDS Beliefs*, xi.

21. See chapters 7, 8, and 9 for more information on Mormonism's standard works.

22. Robert J. Matthews, "Proclamations of the First Presidency and the Quorum of the Twelve Apostles," *Encyclopedia of Mormonism*, accessed May 29, 2014, http://eom.byu.edu/index.php/Proclamations_of_the_First_Presidency_and_the_Quorum_of_the_Twelve_Apostles.

23. *Ensign* (January 2011): 15.

24. *Teachings of the Living Prophets Student Manual: Religion 333* (Salt Lake City: The Church of Jesus Christ of Latter-day Saints, 2010), 72; bold in original.

25. *Ensign* (June 2013): 4.

26. *Ensign* (April 2012): 8; and *Teachings of the Living Prophets Student Manual*, 23.

27. *The Teachings of Howard W. Hunter*, ed. Clyde J. Williams [1997], 212; emphasis added, quoted in *Teachings of the Living Prophets Student Manual*, 73; bold in original.

28. *Ensign* (May 2013): 133. For other examples, see quotes from President Thomas S. Monson in *Ensign* (May 2010): 113; (November 2012): 110; (April 2013): 8; and (May 2013): 113.

29. *Teachings of the Living Prophets Student Manual*, 87; italics in original.

30. *Doctrine and Covenants and Church History Seminary Teacher Resource Manual*, 117.

31. McConkie, *Answers*, 214; italics in original.

32. *Teachings of Presidents of the Church: Wilford Woodruff*, 199, *Gospel Principles*, 41, and *Teachings of the Living Prophets Student Manual*, 20.

33. *Teachings of Presidents of the Church: Joseph Fielding Smith*, 159.

34. *The Latter-day Saint Woman, Part B*, 99.

35. *Teachings of Presidents of the Church: Joseph F. Smith*, 227; brackets in original.

36. In *Ensign* (November 2010), see Seventy Claudio R. M. Costa, "Obedience to the Prophets," 11–13, and Seventy Kevin R. Duncan, "Our Very Survival," 34–36. The speech is also found in *Teachings of the Living Prophets Student Manual*, 22–27.

37. *Ensign* (February 2010): 52.

38. *The Latter-day Saint Woman, Part B*, 106.

Appendix

15 Common Logical Fallacies Explained

When dialoguing with those who have different views, it is important to utilize sound reasoning skills. Sometimes, though, people resort to unfair tactics, which we call logical fallacies. These are errors in reasoning that do not lead to the proper conclusion. Listed are fifteen of the most common fallacies we encounter in our ministry:

Ad hominem: Criticizing a person making the argument rather than the argument itself. Ex: "Because John is a former Mormon, an apostate from the LDS Church, his argument against the Book of Abraham cannot be considered valid."

Analysis: Labeling someone ("apostate") is meant to introduce a negative bias and should be avoided.

Appeal to pity: Attempting to sway the audience by using emotional tactics to gain sympathy. Ex: "Since Mormons have been persecuted throughout the years, this faith must be true or otherwise these people wouldn't have been attacked."

Analysis: It is true that some Mormons have been persecuted over the past two centuries. However, even if it's true that Mormons have been unduly persecuted, this does not validate Mormonism's truth claims. If so, would the Mormon consider biblical Christianity to be true merely because Christians around the world are persecuted on a daily basis for *their* faith?

Appeal to the people: Insisting that your position is true because other people agree with it. Ex: "The Church of Jesus Christ of Latter-Day Saints has millions of members. Do you really think that many people can be wrong?"

Analysis: Just because many people (even a majority) share the same position is not a guarantee that the view they share is correct.

Bandwagon: Believing a view is correct because of its popularity. Ex: "Since Mormonism is one of the fastest growing religions, there must be some truth to it."

Analysis: Even if it were true that Mormonism is "one of the fastest growing religions," this does not necessarily mean it's true. Spiritual truth is not determined by popularity or growth in numbers.

Begging the question (circular reasoning): An argument that assumes what it is trying to prove. Ex: "I prayed about the Book of Mormon, and its truthfulness was confirmed to me (i.e., burning in the bosom). This feeling I have can be trusted and I know that the Book of Mormon must be true because this is what Moroni 10:4 said would happen."

Analysis: Because personal feelings can be and often are biased, they are not usually a good way to determine truth.

"Either or" fallacy/false dilemma: Claiming that "either" proposition A or B is true when a third option is possible. Ex: "If the Mormon Church isn't true, nothing is."

Analysis: This statement sometimes used by faithful Latter-day Saints ignores the possibility of other options. If Mormonism isn't true, something else must be (and even if there is no God at all, that means atheism is true).

Equivocation: Using the same word with different meanings. Ex: "All the gods of the people are idols (Ps. 96:5). Therefore, the creator of all other reality (God) must be an idol."

Analysis: False gods, not the true God as defined in the Bible, are referenced in Psalm 96.

Faulty appeal to authority: Basing an argument on the opinion of a person or group. Ex: "I know for a fact that the Bible cannot be trusted. My bishop is a doctor and he said so."

Analysis: This person's bishop may be knowledgeable in his particular field of expertise, but it does not necessarily mean he is an expert when it comes to the accuracy of the Bible.

Genetic fallacy: Rejecting an idea based on its origin rather than on its merit. Ex: "I found this video critical of Mormonism on a website that is not sponsored by the church, so it must be wrong."

Analysis: Rather than disparaging the source of the information, the argument itself should be the focal point of the disagreement.

Loaded question: Asking a question that is meant to introduce prejudice by making an unjustified assumption. Ex: "Since you are an 'anti-Mormon,' have you stopped persecuting Mormons for the day?"

Analysis: This is just as unfair as asking, "Have you stopped beating your wife?" There are no possible answers that could be given without implying guilt. For example, a person who answers the above question affirmatively is guilty of persecuting Mormons. A negative response means the person is willing to continue persecuting Mormons.

Personal incredulity: Because something is difficult to understand, it must be untrue. Ex: "The doctrine of the Trinity is complicated and can't be comprehended. This proves it can't be true."

Analysis: Trying to harmonize all the verses in the Bible that speak about God certainly involves in-depth study. Just because an explanation of something is not simple does not make the premise false. There are many mysteries in Mormonism that also can't be understood, including determining the reality of an infinite regression of the gods (determining just who the first God is).

Red herring: Diverting the topic at hand by introducing another topic. Ex: After having a Christian share about salvation by grace through faith outside the grounds of Temple Square, a Mormon responds, "Do you share your faith at Muslim mosques or Buddhist temples? If not, why don't you go to those places instead of targeting Latter-day Saints?"

Analysis: Getting off topic is a diversionary tactic meant to sideline the conversation. A possible reply is, "I'd be more than happy to talk about that issue, but could we first finish our conversation on salvation by grace through faith?"

Special pleading: Having standards that apply to others, but not oneself, without applying justification for the exemption. Ex: "Yes, Doctrine and Covenants 1:31 does say the Lord will not look upon sin with the least degree of allowance, but Heavenly Father loves me, so I'm sure I will be eligible for exaltation."

Analysis: Even though LDS scripture insists that no sin will be acceptable to God, those using this argument feel that they are somehow exempt from any penalty for their sin.

Straw man: Making a particular position look weak by misrepresenting the argument. Ex: According to *History of the Church* 6:476, Joseph Smith said the following: "Many men say there is one God; the Father, the Son and the Holy Ghost are only one God! I say that is a strange God anyhow—three in one, and one in three! It is a curious organization. . . . All are to be crammed into one God, according to sectarianism. It would make the biggest God in all the world. He would be a wonderfully big God—he would be a giant or a monster."

Analysis: Smith gives an inaccurate analysis of what the Trinity teaches, making it easy to dismiss a God as described here. This version is certainly not an argument anyone would want to believe or defend.

Tu quoque: An attempt to ignore a criticism by pointing out an inconsistency or hypocrisy on the part of the critic. Ex: "Yes, it is true that several of our past leaders made remarks that certainly sound racist. But have you never exhibited behavior that might make you appear to be prejudiced or bigoted? Besides, many people during that time period had similar views."

Analysis: From the Latin, tu quoque means "you too." It has sometimes been called the "two wrongs don't make a right" fallacy. Instead of explaining the racist comments made by past LDS leaders, it avoids the criticism by pointing out the possible hypocrisy of the one asking the question.

Bibliography

Allen, James B., and Glen M. Leonard. *The Story of the Latter-day Saints*. Salt Lake City: Deseret Book Co., 1976.

Beasley-Murray, G. R. *Baptism in the New Testament*. Grand Rapids: Eerdmans, 1962.

Beckwith, Francis, Carl Moser, and Paul Owen, eds. *The New Mormon Challenge: Responding to the Latest Defenses of a Fast Growing Movement*. Grand Rapids: Zondervan, 2002.

Bennett, Bob. *Leap of Faith*. Salt Lake City: Deseret Book Co., 2009.

Benson, Ezra Taft. *The Teachings of Ezra Taft Benson*. Salt Lake City: Bookcraft, 1988.

Book of Mormon Seminary Student Study Guide. Salt Lake City: The Church of Jesus Christ of Latter-day Saints, 1999.

Book of Mormon Student Manual: Religion 121–122. Salt Lake City: The Church of Jesus Christ of Latter-day Saints, 2009.

Bromiley, G.W., ed. *The International Standard Bible Encyclopedia*. 4 vols. Grand Rapids: Eerdmans, 1979.

Brown, Harold O. J. *Heresies: The Image of Christ in the Mirror of Heresy and Orthodoxy from the Apostles to the Present*. Grand Rapids: Baker, 1984.

Bruce, F. F. *Paul: Apostle of the Heart Set Free*. Grand Rapids: Eerdmans, 1977.

Bushman, Richard Lyman. *Joseph Smith: Rough Stone Rolling*. New York: Alfred A. Knopf, 2005.

BYU Studies. Provo, UT: Brigham Young University.

Cannon, George Q. *Gospel Truth*. Salt Lake City: Deseret Book Co., 1987.

Church Handbook of Instructions, Book I: Stake Presidencies and Bishoprics. Salt Lake City: The Church of Jesus Christ of Latter-day Saints, 1998.

Church History in the Fulness of Times Student Manual: Religion 341–343. Salt Lake City: The Church of Jesus Christ of Latter-day Saints, 2003.

Church News. Select issues from the weekly LDS newspaper, published by Deseret News, Salt Lake City.

Clark, George Edward. *Why I Believe.* Salt Lake City: Publisher's Press, 1989.

Clark, James R., ed. *Messages of the First Presidency of The Church of Jesus Christ of Latter-day Saints* (1833-1951). 6 vols. Salt Lake City: Bookcraft, 1975.

Compton, Todd. *In Sacred Loneliness: The Plural Wives of Joseph Smith.* Salt Lake City: Signature Books, 1997.

Conference Reports of the Church of Jesus Christ of Latter-day Saints. Salt Lake City: The Church of Jesus Christ of Latter-day Saints, 1889–1970 (139 total conference reports).

Deseret News. Select articles from the newspaper, published daily in Salt Lake City, Utah.

Dialogue: A Journal of Mormon Thought. Select issues from the quarterly journal published by the Dialogue Foundation in Salt Lake City.

Doctrine and Covenants and Church History Gospel Doctrine Teacher's Manual. Salt Lake City: Intellectual Reserve Inc., 2003.

Doctrine and Covenants and Church History Seminary Student Study Guide. Salt Lake City: The Church of Jesus Christ of Latter-day Saints, 2001.

Doctrine and Covenants and Church History Seminary Teacher Resource Manual. Salt Lake City: The Church of Jesus Christ of Latter-day Saints, 2001.

Doctrine and Covenants Student Manual: Religion 324–325. Salt Lake City: The Church of Jesus Christ of Latter-day Saints, 2001.

Doctrines of the Gospel Student Manual: Religion 430–431. Salt Lake City: The Church of Jesus Christ of Latter-day Saints, 2004.

Durham, Reed C., Jr. *Is There No Help for the Widow's Son?* Nauvoo, IL: Martin Publishing, 1980.

Duties and Blessings of the Priesthood: Basic Manual for Priesthood Holders. Salt Lake City: The Church of Jesus Christ of Latter-day Saints, 2000.

Edersheim, Alfred. *The Temple: Its Ministry and Services.* Peabody, MA: Hendrickson Publishers, 1994.

Endowed from on High: Temple Preparation Seminary Teacher's Manual. Salt Lake City: The Church of Jesus Christ of Latter-day Saints, 2003.

Ensign. Select issues from the magazine, published monthly by the LDS Church since 1971. Salt Lake City: The Church of Jesus Christ of Latter-day Saints.

Family Home Evening Manual. Salt Lake City: The Church of Jesus Christ of Latter-day Saints, 1972.

Grant, Heber J. *Gospel Standards.* Comp. G. Homer Durham. Salt Lake City: Improvement Era, 1943.

The Gospel and the Productive Life Student Manual: Religion 150. Salt Lake City: The Church of Jesus Christ of Latter-day Saints, 2004.

Gospel Fundamentals. Salt Lake City: The Church of Jesus Christ of Latter-day Saints, 2002.

Gospel Principles. Salt Lake City: The Church of Jesus Christ of Latter-day Saints, 2009.

Handbook 2: Administering the Church 2010. Salt Lake City: The Church of Jesus Christ of Latter-day Saints, 2010.

Harrell, Charles R. *"This Is My Doctrine": The Development of Mormon Theology.* Draper, UT: Greg Kofford Books, 2011.

Heinerman, Joseph. *Temple Manifestations.* Salt Lake City: Magazine Printing and Publishing, 1974.

Hinckley, Gordon B. *Teachings of Gordon B. Hinckley.* Salt Lake City: Deseret Book, 1997.

History of the Church of Jesus Christ of Latter-day Saints. 7 vols. Introduction and notes by B. H. Roberts. Salt Lake City: Deseret Book Co., 1973.

Holland, Jeffrey R. *Christ and the New Covenant.* Salt Lake City: Deseret Book Co., 2003.

Hughes, Philip E. *The New International Commentary on the New Testament: The Second Epistle to the Corinthians.* Grand Rapids: Wm. B. Eerdmans Publishing Co., 1962.

Hunter, Milton R. *The Gospel through the Ages.* Salt Lake City: Stevens and Wallis, 1945.

———. *Pearl of Great Price Commentary.* Salt Lake City: Stevens and Wallis, 1948.

The Improvement Era. Salt Lake City: The Church of Jesus Christ of Latter-day Saints (published 1897–1970 when it became the *Ensign*).

Introduction to Family History Student Manual: Religion 261. Salt Lake City: The Church of Jesus Christ of Latter-day Saints, 2012.

Jenson, Andrew. *Church Chronology.* Salt Lake City: Deseret News, 1899.

Kelly, J.N.D. *Early Christian Doctrines.* New York: HarperSanFrancisco, 1978.

Kimball, Spencer W. *Faith Precedes the Miracle.* Salt Lake City: Deseret Book Co., 1978.

———. *The Miracle of Forgiveness.* Salt Lake City: Bookcraft, 1969.

———. *The Teachings of Spencer W. Kimball: Twelfth President of the Church of Jesus Christ of Latter-day Saints.* Comp. Edward L. Kimball. Salt Lake City: Bookcraft, 1992.

Kirkham, Francis W. *A New Witness for Christ in America*. 2 vols. Salt Lake City: Bookcraft, 1982.

Larson, Charles M. *By His Own Hand upon Papyrus*. Grand Rapids: Institute for Religious Research, 1992.

The Latter-day Saint Woman: Basic Manual for Women. Salt Lake City: The Church of Jesus Christ of Latter-day Saints, 2000.

Lee, Rex E. *What Do Mormons Believe?* Salt Lake City: Deseret Book Co., 1992.

LeSueur, Stephen C. *The 1838 Mormon War in Missouri*. Columbia, MO: University of Missouri Press, 1987.

The Life and Teachings of Jesus and His Apostles Course Manual: Religion 211–212. Salt Lake City: The Church of Jesus Christ of Latter-day Saints, 1979.

The Life and Teachings of Jesus and His Apostles Instructor's Manual: Religion 211–212. Salt Lake City: The Church of Jesus Christ of Latter-day Saints, 1978.

Ludlow, Daniel H., ed. *Encyclopedia of Mormonism*. 4 vols. New York: Macmillan, 1992.

Lund, John Lewis. *The Church and the Negro: A Discussion of Mormons, Negroes and the Priesthood*. Paramount Publishers, 1967.

McConkie, Bruce R. *Doctrinal New Testament Commentary*. Salt Lake City: Bookcraft, 1966.

———. *Doctrinal New Testament Commentary: The Gospels*. Vol. 1. Salt Lake City: Bookcraft, 1966.

———. *Mormon Doctrine*. 2nd ed. Salt Lake City: Bookcraft, 1966.

———. *The Mortal Messiah*. Salt Lake City: Deseret Book Co., 1982.

———. *A New Witness for the Articles of Faith*. Salt Lake City: Deseret Book Co., 1985.

McConkie, Joseph Fielding. *Answers: Straightforward Answers to Tough Gospel Questions*. Salt Lake City: Deseret Book Co., 1998.

McConkie, Joseph Fielding, and Robert L. Millet. *Doctrinal Commentary on the Book of Mormon*. Vol. 1. Salt Lake City: Bookcraft, 1987.

McKay, David O. *Gospel Ideals*. Comp. G. Homer Durham. Salt Lake City: Improvement Era, 1953.

McKeever, Bill. *In Their Own Words: A Collection of Mormon Quotations*. Kearney, NE: Morris Publishing, 2010.

McKeever, Bill, and Eric Johnson. *Answering Mormons' Questions: Ready Responses for Inquiring Latter-day Saints*. Grand Rapids: Kregel, 2013.

Millennial Star. An official LDS publication that was published in the British Isles from 1840–1970 and later became the *Ensign*.

Millet, Robert L. *A Different Jesus: The Christ of the Latter-day Saints*. Grand Rapids: Eerdmans, 2005.

Millet, Robert L., Camille Fronk Olson, Andrew C. Skinner, and Brent L. Top. *LDS Beliefs: A Doctrinal Reference.* Salt Lake City; Deseret Book Co., 2011.

Missionary Preparation Student Manual: Religion 130. Salt Lake City: The Church of Jesus Christ of Latter-day Saints, 2005.

Morris, Leon. *The Atonement: Its Meaning and Significance.* Downers Grove, IL.: InterVarsity Press, 1983.

New Era. Select issues from the magazine, published weekly by the *Deseret News.*

Newell, Linda King and Valeen Tippetts Avery. *Mormon Enigma: Emma Hale Smith,* 2nd ed. Urbana: University of Illinois Press, 1994.

Old Testament Gospel Doctrine Teacher's Manual. Salt Lake City: The Church of Jesus Christ of Latter-day Saints, 2001.

Old Testament Seminary Teacher Resource Manual. Salt Lake City: The Church of Jesus Christ of Latter-day Saints, 2003.

Old Testament Student Manual: Genesis–2 Samuel: Religion 301. Salt Lake City: The Church of Jesus Christ of Latter-day Saints, 2003.

Old Testament Student Manual: 1 Kings–Malachi: Religion 302. Salt Lake City: The Church of Jesus Christ of Latter-day Saints, 2003.

The Pearl of Great Price Student Manual: Religion 327. Salt Lake City: The Church of Jesus Christ of Latter-day Saints, 2000.

The Pearl of Great Price Teacher Manual: Religion 327. Salt Lake City: The Church of Jesus Christ of Latter-day Saints, 2000.

Petersen, LaMar. *Hearts Made Glad: The Charges of Intemperance against Joseph Smith the Mormon Prophet.* Salt Lake City: LaMar Petersen, 1975.

Pratt, Orson. *Divine Authenticity of the Book of Mormon.* From a series of pamphlets. Liverpool, England: n.p., 1851.

———. *The Seer.* Photo reprint of newspapers published January 1853 through August 1854. Republished in 1990 by Eborn Books (Salt Lake City).

Preach My Gospel: A Guide to Missionary Service. Salt Lake City: The Church of Jesus Christ of Latter-day Saints, 2004.

Preparing for Exaltation Teacher's Manual. Salt Lake City: The Church of Jesus Christ of Latter-day Saints, 1998.

Quinn, D. Michael. *Early Mormonism and the Magic World View.* Salt Lake City: Signature Books, 1987.

———. *The Mormon Hierarchy: Origins of Power.* Salt Lake City: Signature Books, 1994.

———. *The New Mormon History: Revisionist Essays on the Past.* Salt Lake City: Signature Book, 1992.

Richards, LeGrand. *A Marvelous Work and a Wonder.* Salt Lake City: Deseret Book Co., 1976.

Ridges, David J. *Mormon Beliefs and Doctrines Made Easier*. Springville, UT: CFI, 2007.

Roberts, B.H. *New Witnesses for God*. 3 vols. Salt Lake City: Deseret Book Co., 1950.

Roberts, B. H., comp. *Comprehensive History of the Church of Jesus Christ of Latter-day Saints*. 6 vols. 1930. Reprint, Orem, UT: Sonos Publishing, 1991.

Robinson, Stephen E. *Believing Christ*. Salt Lake City: Deseret Book Co., 1992.

Ross, Bob L. *Acts 2:38 and Baptismal Remission*. Pasadena, TX: Pilgrim Publications, 1987.

Salt Lake Tribune. Select articles from the newspaper, published daily in Salt Lake City, Utah.

Search These Commandments: Melchizedek Priesthood Personal Study Guide. Salt Lake City: The Church of Jesus Christ of Latter-day Saints, 1984.

Selections from Answers to Gospel Questions: A Course of Study for the Melchizedek Priesthood Quorums 1972–73. Salt Lake City: The First Presidency of The Church of Jesus Christ of Latter-day Saints, 1972.

Shields, Steven L. *Divergent Paths of the Restoration*. Los Angeles: Restoration Research, 1990.

Smith, George D. *Nauvoo Polygamy*. Salt Lake City: Signature Books, 2011.

Smith, Joseph. *The Book of Mormon*. Salt Lake City: The Church of Jesus Christ of Latter-day Saints, 1830 and 1981 editions.

———. *The Doctrine and Covenants of the Church of Jesus Christ of Latter-day Saints*. Salt Lake City: The Church of Jesus Christ of Latter-day Saints, 1981.

———. *Joseph Smith's "New Translation" of the Bible*. Independence, MO: Herald Publishing House, 1970.

———. *The Pearl of Great Price*. Salt Lake City: The Church of Jesus Christ of Latter-day Saints, 1981.

Smith, Joseph Fielding. *Answers to Gospel Questions*. 4 vols. Salt Lake City: Deseret Book Co., 1957–63.

———. *Church History and Modern Revelation*. Salt Lake City: Deseret News Press, 1949.

———. *Doctrines of Salvation: Sermons and Writings of Joseph Fielding Smith*. 3 vols. Ed. Bruce R. McConkie. Salt Lake City: Bookcraft, 1954–56.

———. *Gospel Doctrine*. Comp. John A. Widtsoe. Salt Lake City: Deseret Book Co., 1919.

———, ed. *Teachings of the Prophet Joseph Smith*. Salt Lake City: Deseret Book Co., 1938.

———. *The Way to Perfection*. Salt Lake City: Deseret Book Co., 1975.

Stewart, John. *Joseph Smith, the Mormon Prophet*. Salt Lake City: Hawkes Publishing, 1966.

———. *Mormonism and the Negro*. Orem, UT: Bookmark, 1960.

Stuy, Brian H., ed. *Collected Discourses.* 5 vols. Burbank, CA, and Woodland Hills, UT: B.H.S. Publishing, 1987–92.

Sunstone. Select issues. Salt Lake City: Sunstone Foundation.

A Sure Foundation: Answers to Difficult Gospel Questions. (Several authors.) Salt Lake City: Deseret Book Co., 1988.

Talmage, James E. *The Articles of Faith.* Salt Lake City: Deseret Book Co., 1987.

———. *Jesus the Christ.* Salt Lake City: Deseret Book Co., 1981.

———. *The Vitality of Mormonism.* Boston: Gorham Press, 1919.

Tanner, Jerald, and Sandra Tanner. *Evolution of the Temple Ceremony 1842–1990.* Salt Lake City: Utah Lighthouse Ministry, 1990.

———. *Mormonism—Shadow or Reality?* Salt Lake City: Utah Lighthouse Ministry, 1982.

Teachings of Presidents of the Church: Brigham Young. Salt Lake City: The Church of Jesus Christ of Latter-day Saints, 1997.

Teachings of Presidents of the Church: Ezra Taft Benson. Salt Lake City: The Church of Jesus Christ of Latter-Day Saints, 2014.

Teachings of Presidents of the Church: George Albert Smith. Salt Lake City: The Church of Jesus Christ of Latter-day Saints, 2011.

Teachings of Presidents of the Church: Harold B. Lee. Salt Lake City: The Church of Jesus Christ of Latter-day Saints, 2000.

Teachings of Presidents of the Church: Heber J. Grant. Salt Lake City: The Church of Jesus Christ of Latter-day Saints, 2002.

Teachings of Presidents of the Church: John Taylor. Salt Lake City: The Church of Jesus Christ of Latter-day Saints, 2001.

Teachings of Presidents of the Church: Joseph F. Smith. Salt Lake City: The Church of Jesus Christ of Latter-day Saints, 1998.

Teachings of Presidents of the Church: Joseph Fielding Smith. Salt Lake City: The Church of Jesus Christ of Latter-day Saints, 2013.

Teachings of Presidents of the Church: Joseph Smith. Salt Lake City: The Church of Jesus Christ of Latter-day Saints, 2007.

Teachings of Presidents of the Church: Lorenzo Snow. Salt Lake City: The Church of Jesus Christ of Latter-day Saints, 2012.

Teachings of Presidents of the Church: Spencer W. Kimball. Salt Lake City: The Church of Jesus Christ of Latter-day Saints, 2006.

Teachings of Presidents of the Church: Wilford Woodruff. Salt Lake City: The Church of Jesus Christ of Latter-day Saints, 2004.

Teachings of the Living Prophets Student Manual: Religion 333. Salt Lake City: The Church of Jesus Christ of Latter-day Saints, 2010.

Teachings of the Living Prophets Teacher Manual: Religion 333. Salt Lake City: The Church of Jesus Christ of Latter-day Saints, 2010.

Times and Seasons. A six-volume series that contains copies of the LDS newspaper printed between November 1839 and February 1846.

True to the Faith: A Gospel Reference. Salt Lake City: The Church of Jesus Christ of Latter-day Saints, 2004.

Tozer, A. W. *The Knowledge of the Holy.* New York: HarperOne, 1961.

Van Wagoner, Richard S. *Mormon Polygamy: A History.* Salt Lake City: Signature Books, 1989.

———. *Sidney Rigdon: A Portrait of Religious Excess.* Salt Lake City: Signature Books, 1994.

Vogel, Dan, ed. *Early Mormon Documents.* Salt Lake City: Signature Books, 1999.

Watt, George D., ed. *Journal of Discourses.* 26 vols. Liverpool, England: F. D. Richards, 1854–86.

White, James. *The Forgotten Trinity: Recovering the Heart of Christian Belief.* Minneapolis: Bethany House, 1998.

Whitmer, David. *An Address to All Believers in the Book of Mormon.* Richmond, MO: David Whitmer, 1887.

Whitmer, David. *An Address to All Believers in Christ.* Richmond, MO: David Whitmer, 1887.

Widtsoe, John A. *Evidences and Reconciliations.* Comp. G. Homer Durham. 3 vols. 1943–51. Reprint (3 vols. in 1), Salt Lake City: Bookcraft, 1960.

———. *A Rational Theology as Taught by the Church of Jesus Christ of Latter-day Saints.* 7th ed. Salt Lake City: Deseret Book Co., 1965.

Woodruff, Wilford. *The Discourses of Wilford Woodruff.* Comp. G. Homer Durham. Salt Lake City: Bookcraft, 1946.

Young, Brigham. *Discourses of Brigham Young.* Comp. John A. Widtsoe. Salt Lake City: Deseret Book Co., 1978.

Index of Scriptural References

101 Topics Index

People Index

335